Cycling Fast

Contents

Preface

If you're reading this first sentence of *Cycling Fast*, congratulations—you've just taken an important step in improving your racing ability!

Across all ages and categories, bicycle racing is one of the fastest-growing sports. Masters racers (those over 30 years of age) and racers in their 20s are the true impetus behind the growth of the sport.

If You Race Bicycles, Or Want to Race Bicycles, This Book Is for You

Cycling Fast is for racers in men's categories 5, 4, 3, and 2 and women's categories 4, 3, and 2. If you are a beginning racer, this book will give you the edge on the competition and enable you to prepare for racing intelligently and confidently. If you are an experienced racer looking to sharpen your edge, this book will help you fill the gaps in your racing knowledge and get a jump on your competition.

Through a systematic review of all racing aspects—equipment, nutrition, strategy, and tactics—this book will help you attain your start or improve your season in bicycle racing. Each chapter provides information that is easy to read, easy to understand, and even easier to apply. You will be amazed at how changing only a few things in how you train, how you race, or how you prepare to race will improve your performance dramatically.

In addition to the common topics of nutrition and physical training, this book tackles ideas such as mental training for racing, goal setting, skills training, and choosing the right team. As a bonus, keep an eye out for special sidebars and boxes throughout *Cycling Fast*, which feature true-life stories from seasoned professionals.

What You'll Find Inside

Chapter 1 lays the foundation you'll need in order to find teams that suit your needs and tells you what is expected of you when you join a team. This chapter encourages beginning racers to think as a team and to enter the sport of cycling with the team in mind.

Chapter 2 covers racing equipment and general bike fit to ensure you have the proper gear and the correct position for racing.

Chapter 3 covers the USA Cycling category system, procedures for entering races, and the types of races that exist.

Chapter 4 details the physical aspects of race training as well as workouts for improving fitness. Practice makes perfect, but this chapter will teach you that *perfect* practice makes perfect.

Chapter 5 gives you information on handling yourself in the pack, whether you're a new or a seasoned racer. You will learn to control your bike with simple drills, control other racers with proper positioning, and prepare for the more intense portions of races—sprints, hill climbs, and fast corners.

Chapter 6 is a precise overview of race strategy and tactics, which you can execute with a team or even as a solo racer without team support. In addition to in-depth information on analyzing courses for improving performance, you will find tips that are illustrated for clarity and easy to execute in the rolling chess match of racing.

Chapter 7 provides the tools for mentally preparing yourself before the race, during the race, and after the race. The physical part of race training is the easy part; the difficult part is clearing your mind and focusing on goals before and during a race.

Chapter 8 covers some basic nutrition strategies for race training. You can race well only if properly fueled during training and racing and, more important, during recovery.

Chapter 9 covers what to do in the off-season to prepare for the next season.

Chapter 10 explains the theory behind a five-year training outlook. Goal setting is also covered in chapter 10 and is the keystone to successful racing in the long term.

Thanks for choosing *Cycling Fast*—your first big step toward more effective racing in the upcoming season and beyond.

Acknowledgments

I would like to thank the following people:

Connie and Robert Panzera for constant encouragement. Jim Skelley for sharing stories from the road, always providing a place to which I could return, and putting me on my first fast pair of wheels. Bob Kaplan for never-ending guidance in cycling and life, a good ear for bouncing off ideas, and friendship. Gero McGuffin and Arnie Baker for guidance in all matters great and small and highly prized recommendations. Nathan Heidt for a sharp eye for photography and design and consistently being there for a laugh. Peggy McCloskey and Bobby Carter for unquestioning support without any pause for remuneration, delicious baked goods, and belief in my ideas. Jeff Clark for good nature and never-flagging interest to help take my cycling endeavors to the next level. Joe Herriges for excellent on-the-spot mechanical support, a venue for training ventures, a trusty support van, and a place to get away from it all. Bill Holland for keeping me grounded as my business grows and placing me on one of the best bikes being built today. Neil Shirley for guidance, good humor, and interest in being a part of my cycling endeavors. Cody Stevenson for hard work, great ideas, timely execution of projects, and good humor. Janel Holcomb and Chad Holcomb for always listening and pushing my boundaries in training, all the while smiling. Dez Wilder for endless energy and exuberance in all cycling projects, plus having a sharp mind for business. Jacobo Melcer for guidance in all aspects of business great and small and being an inspiration for fitness at any age. Sherri Wilkins for support and understanding. Cyclo-Vets for believing in me as a young coach and always providing a forum in which to sharpen my coaching skills.

Special thanks to Tom Heine, acquisitions editor, for a phone call that opened many doors of opportunity. To Anne Hall, developmental editor, for an easygoing manner when deadlines became tight and for keeping me on task. To copyeditor Patrick Connolly for ensuring a tidy manuscript. And thanks to John Husk, Luis Zamudio, and Jose Blanco for providing good technique for the photo shoot.

Chapter 1

GETTING STARTED

There's a feeling that you can only get from racing and finishing—the feeling of pushing yourself beyond what you're capable of doing in training. It's about achieving the ultimate physical accomplishment— and you can't feel that on the sidelines.

—Ned Overend, Mountain Bike and U.S. Bicycling Hall of Famer

When we watch the sport of cycling, the coverage usually focuses on the endeavors of the individual: the inspiring escape of a solo rider toward the mountaintop finish, the daring maneuver of the sprinter as he powers past his competitors in the last 500 meters of a race, or the fear-inducing descent of a rider trying to gap his competitors in a bid for the finishing line. However, the team endeavors that go into making those stunning moments possible are often overlooked. For success in this sport, a cyclist needs to have team support on the road, coach support in the lead-up to the race, mechanical support throughout the year, and familial support to make chasing a dream possible.

Competitive cycling is an exciting undertaking that can also be very social—a cyclist will train with coaches, travel to events with teammates, and race against known rivals. The first chapter of *Cycling Fast* will help you find the support you need in order to properly prepare for racing. For many, this support will not be on a professional level, but rather on a personal level. Finding the teams and coaches that fit your style will help put you in the right frame of mind and on the right training path for racing. Topics covered in this chapter include finding the right club or team, finding a personal or team coach, understanding the organization of entry-level racing, and acquiring a racing license.

Finding the Right Club or Team

One misconception that many beginning racers bring to the sport is that cycling is a sport for the individual. Beginning racers often think that they are capable of winning all types of races under all types of race conditions without being a member of a team. This naïveté may be part of what initially

Group rides can provide racelike elements, like this simulated sprint to the finish.

drives the individual to the sport of cycling; however, an early foundation in the team aspect of the sport is essential to overall cycling success. Although many beginning racers choose to go it alone and ride "unattached," the benefits of belonging to a team far outweigh the freedom one may feel on his own.

Many cyclists who are interested in racing start out by participating in a competitive group ride in their local community. These rides include situations that simulate those that occur in a race. Competitive group rides are truly the heart and soul of cycling, and they provide experiences that endear many people to the sport. An example is a weekend group ride that includes some racelike elements: sprints for town signs, races to the top of well-known local climbs, or hard-tempo areas where riders may be dropped. The participants in these local rides often include both racers and nonracers, providing a competitive atmosphere and a gateway experience for those who want to start racing. For some, this weekly group ride may be their "racing" experience. Others will take this experience and make the immediate leap into the world of organized bicycle racing.

The Value of Finding the Right Team

When you are first starting out in cycling, finding the right team can be incredibly valuable. Cycling teams can provide

- camaraderie,
- opportunities to help teammates win,
- opportunities to help you win,
- training partners,
- insight into local racing and training, and
- race support.

Fred "Pop" Kugler, coach of several national champions and founder of the Tour of Somerville, said that the most important aspect of being on a team is the ability to train with similar-minded and similar-bodied individuals. According to Pop, riding with a team provides the following benefits:

- A support network in case of on-the-road emergencies
- A network of individuals by whom you can gauge your progress
- A controlled forum where pack-riding skills are learned
- A controlled forum in which to test your limits and then regain group contact to test them again

As an amateur racer—whether or not you have had experience in other competitive sports—you will not know all the nuances of bicycle racing. A team may be your greatest source of guidance and help as you get your feet wet.

How *Not* to Find a Team

Many beginning racers align themselves with the teams that they ride with on their local group ride. You will likely find it easy to connect with other participants in the group ride. You may even hang around after the group ride and receive riding and training tips on the fly. This may not be the best approach for entering racing or finding the right club or team. The camaraderie and comfort may trump constructive thoughts about your own skills, abilities, goals, or desires.

Participants in weekend group rides sometimes have very little interest in organized racing. Many will focus on only a few local races a year, and these races may not involve the execution of team plans before or during the race. When looking for a team, the beginning cyclist may be best served by focusing on teams that *act like a team*—as opposed to a team that only wears the same jerseys.

Fellow cyclists who perform like a team—that is, a group of cyclists who train together, show up to race with a team plan, and support each other in races throughout the season—may help the beginning cyclist improve overall.

How to Locate Clubs or Teams

In most areas, locating a team or club is easy, especially with the increasing interest in the sport of cycling worldwide. Resources that can help you locate a club or team include local bike shops, the Internet, and the USA Cycling Web site. Local bike shops usually fully sponsor their own teams, or they may partially sponsor other teams. The local bike shop is also a good social network for finding rides, learning about equipment, or simply making friends. Most teams and clubs now have Web pages advertising their membership fees (usually less than US$50, but team or club clothing often costs extra), training rides, and races sponsored. A quick Internet search on your geographic location along with keywords such as *cycling*, *teams*, and *clubs* should yield Web page results for the teams or clubs in your area. The USA Cycling Web site lists all teams that are in current good standing (usually with links to the team Web site), categorized by geographic location.

The terms *team* and *club* are often used interchangeably. This is because many clubs, which are made up of both racing and nonracing cyclists, have a team of licensed racers attached to them. The club is usually the unofficial gateway to the team for those interested in racing. The club often supports the team via sponsorship or increased benefits for team members from regular club sponsors. Normally, teams are registered with an official racing body such as USA Cycling, while clubs may have no affiliation with any local, regional, or national associations.

Know Yourself to Find Your Team

Many teams appear similar, but the focus, vibe, and general conduct of each team may be widely varied. Teams are often started by an individual or a small group of individuals; these teams may continue to focus on the principles of the original founder or founders. In this way, teams have personalities. You should try to find a team environment that matches your own cycling personality.

To find out your cycling personality, you need to ask yourself what you expect from competitive cycling. The 10 questions in the sidebar may help you identify your cycling personality. This will help you better understand the type of team that will enable you to function at your best.

Identifying Your Cycling Personality

Consider the following 10 questions to help discover your cycling personality and the best type of team for you:

1. Do you want to work toward yearly, monthly, and weekly racing goals?
2. Are you willing to work for others at races?
3. Are you only looking for camaraderie at races?
4. Are you only looking to meet others with a similar competitive spirit?
5. Are you interested in joining a team solely to obtain free or discounted gear?
6. Are you looking for a social outlet in which you can burn off some stress?
7. Are you interested in various bicycle racing disciplines (i.e., road, track, cyclo-cross, mountain biking)?
8. How much time are you willing to invest in the team?
9. Do you expect your teammates to be focused on local, regional, or national racing?
10. How much structured team training do you seek?

Many types of teams are covered in the subsequent sections. Most of these teams display a combination of the general team traits reflected in the 10 questions.

Types of Teams

As stated earlier, many clubs or teams focus on the principles of the original founder or founders. It is impossible to classify all club or team types, or place any club or team in a specific category. It is possible to provide general categories into which clubs and teams fall. Knowing and recognizing these general categories will help your team or club selection.

Club-Oriented Teams In general, the club-oriented team may provide an outlet for social networking, race camaraderie, and training instruction. Club-oriented teams usually focus on what benefits the club, as opposed to what benefits the racing individual or a group of racing individuals. One advantage of this type of team is that it provides a large base of riders who may be involved in varied disciplines of racing (i.e., road, track, cyclocross, and mountain). Plus, the club-oriented team may have a variety of group rides and structured group training available to the beginning cyclist. Club-oriented teams usually have clinics on general racing skills—pacelining, pacing, race-day warm-up, and so on. Large club-oriented teams may even hold intraclub races.

Many club-oriented teams are structured around the social aspects of group riding and racing. These teams are usually not focused on entering races and planning a race season based on individual racers' capabilities. In addition, this team may shy away from developing sponsorships or race-specific reimbursements. It may also avoid providing monetary remunerations to its racing members (for race fees, travel, lodging, and board). As mentioned, this type of team may hold the idea of "what's best for the club" over "what's best for the individual racer."

As a member of a club-oriented team, you may find one of your teammates at any given local race. Although you may not have a team plan, you can usually count on team camaraderie before, during, and after races. Club-oriented team members sometimes race for smaller teams and only opt to train with the larger club. In many instances, club-oriented team members will ride exclusively in intraclub races, without venturing into interclub competition.

Club-oriented teams are a good choice for those who are new to competitive cycling or new to competition in general. If you want to enter only a few events each year, this may be a good option. Very little race-related time commitments are placed on team participants. Conversely, a club may require volunteer hours in the form of social events or help in putting on intraclub or interclub races.

These clubs can be very large and may have a few hundred or even a few thousand members.

Race-Oriented Teams On a race-oriented team, members will focus their time and training on goals that are determined by the team's seasonal racing calendar. Race-oriented teams usually select a few local and regional races, and team members train with the goal of being at their peak for these events. These teams are usually very competitive on the local group ride and local racing circuit.

The race-oriented team develops camaraderie based on the drive of competition. Team members are usually not required to commit much personal time for social activities; however, they are expected to spend a large amount of time in training to prepare for races.

Race-oriented teams usually offer little structured race training, but they do provide information via a team coach or a mentor. Coaches may be hired, or they may volunteer their time. Mentors are usually seasoned team members who are willing to invest personal time in developing new members. A race-oriented team is often led by someone who has the vision to develop a team and to plan a race schedule.

Race-oriented teams are becoming more prevalent and are filling the gap left by club systems. These teams may be small; they may have fewer than 20 members. Some race-oriented teams will ride with larger clubs to round out their social network.

Club Subteams In major population centers, some clubs may have a system of subteams. Essentially, you can be a club member only or a club member who races for a subteam. Larger clubs often hold intraclub races where subteams challenge each other and practice against each other to improve their racing for interclub events.

Clubs that offer subteams are becoming more popular as the sport of cycling grows. In this system, members are usually asked to volunteer at the intraclub races. Subteams may also be expected to find their own sponsorship and to pay increased dues to the overall club.

Club subteams may be a good option for beginning racers because these clubs provide a general arena in which to experience racing. Initially, you may be able to observe how the subteams race. Many subteams perform very well in interclub races on a regional level. With the support of the overall club, the subteam may not have to administer club operations and can therefore focus on sponsorship, rider development, and racing.

It may be easy for a subteam to begin within a larger club, so the beginning racer needs to be careful. Beginners should heed the words of Peter Ward, a former national-level rider with a storied past in Britain. Peter states that there is a tendency for small teams to persuade too many inexperienced riders to join in order to build a roster. He adds that these small teams may not be equipped to look after their new recruits.

The Alternative: Riding for a Club, Racing for a Team The luxury of having a large selection of teams to choose from is not always available. A good option may be to join a club and race for a separate team. This is allowed in most jurisdictions, but some clubs frown on this method. Check with the club before choosing this route.

The Other Alternative: Riding Unattached Although this alternative is not recommended, some riders choose to ride unattached. You are not required to be on a team to race in the United States. As unattached riders move up in racing category to more advanced fields, they usually see the benefits in finding a team. Starting out early with a team that will help you grow is the recommended route for the beginning cyclist. Riding unattached may mean missing out on opportunities early.

What You Can Do for Your Team

As you are looking for the right team, you should keep in mind that teams are also looking for the right type of members. Focusing on your personal racing desires is important; however, you must also be sure to support your team with time, energy, and possibly monetary funds.

A team is only as strong as its individual members. When joining a team, you may forfeit some of your training time to assist other team members. You may forfeit your chances to win races so that other team members can win. In addition, you may need to have an active voice in the team administration. Participation is key, and it comes on many levels—from providing car pooling to race sites to assuming the role of sponsorship coordinator. The more you invest in the team, and the more you encourage your teammates to invest in the team, the better the outcome for all members in racing and training.

Teams that do well in races are often the teams that grow outside of the actual race. In other words, teams that are active in their communities (e.g., hosting races and setting up structured group rides) usually fare better in racing and training.

Finding the Right Coach

A beginning racer will usually benefit from finding a qualified coach. Having a coach is not necessary for racing, but the investment may prove invaluable. Coaches can lessen the time spent on trial-and-error methods, explain racing nuances and forms of cycling etiquette, and provide succinct training protocols. Coaches may be a source of guidance to help manage your time and abilities for better performance. The time and energy needed to undo poor training and racing habits will far outweigh the costs of attaining good coaching from the start.

Cycling coaches can provide the following:

- Training plans
- Constructive criticism
- Motivation

- Skills orientation
- Race selection
- Support
- Identification of strengths and weaknesses
- Time management

A Pro's Experience

Neil Shirley (Kelly Benefit Strategies Pro Cycling Team)

Neil Shirley has raced bicycles for over 15 years. He has spent 8 years as a professional, racing nationally and internationally in numerous grueling and competitive events. His specialty is climbing and stage racing, so he knows the value of having a cohesive team to help achieve race goals.

Throughout his career, Neil has had his fair share of teams and team changes. He says, "Shopping around for a team is just like anything—the more experience you have, the better decisions you can generally make." Still, Neil indicates that in order to get that experience, you will have to pay your dues a time or two along the way.

Neil started out as a mountain biker and was looking to make the transition to a professional team in road racing. This is not an easy jump, and pro contracts for road racing are limited and very competitive. Initially, Neil had an opportunity fall into his lap. A new pro team was starting up in San Diego, California, where he was living at the time, and the team was looking for strong, young riders who could be signed for "cheap." Neil explained, "That sounded great! At least *cheap* meant that you get paid something, right? That would be better than anything I got from racing mountain bikes!" After one meeting with the owner of the team's title sponsor, Neil was hooked. The deal sounded very promising, with talk of grandeur and prosperity. The reality set in soon enough when the budget that the sponsoring company had promised was cut. Paychecks were late from the beginning. And things never got better. By midseason, Neil and his teammates were pretty much on their own.

The adversity of this situation provided the groundwork for some strong bonds between Neil and his teammates. Neil acquired good friends through the poor team experience. He says, "I learned a lot that season, mostly about not trusting talk of grandeur, abundant promises, and impossible deliverables." He also says, "Although I value the great friends I made through that initial team experience, now I am a lot more discerning when talking with teams and their directors."

What Can You Learn?

Although Neil's experience is on a professional level, his message is applicable to all amateur cyclists who are seeking a team (or even a coach): Watch out for empty promises, situations dominated by only one individual, and unattainable goals. It's true that friendships can be found in these situations, but the main goal is to find a team or coach who can deliver on your racing expectations.

How to Locate Coaches

Finding a coach has become easy because of the increase in cycling world-wide, along with the availability of many good coaching services through the Internet. Resources that can help you locate a coach include club- or teammates, the Internet, the USA Cycling Web site, and race listing Web sites. Many of your club- or teammates may currently have a coach or may have been coached in the past. These teammates will likely have good insight into local coaches or even remote coaches (those who provide coaching from outside your local riding area). You can also perform an Internet search using your geographic location along with the keywords *cycling* and *coaching*. The USA Cycling Web site lists all cycling coaches sanctioned by the organization's coaching program; the coaches are listed by geographic location and the coaching level attained within the program. Race-listing Web sites usually list local coaches who are affiliated with regional teams as well.

Coaches usually charge by the month, and they may include a startup fee. Each coach's prices will vary based on expertise, location, coaching plan chosen, and what the market will bear. However, you can expect to pay a few hundred dollars a month for full coaching.

Know Your Style to Find Your Coach

Various coaching styles exist. The two main types are team-oriented and individual-oriented coaches. With team-oriented coaches, you may expect less individual attention. However, team-oriented coaches provide benefits such as true insight into your team role, group or team training, and a commitment to the team aspect of the sport.

To help discover which type of coach is a good match for you, review the 10 questions in the sidebar on the next page. These questions may help you find a compatible coach.

Team-Oriented Versus Individual-Oriented Coaches

A cyclist's first experience with a racing coach is commonly with a team-oriented coach. This may be a hired coach (hired by individuals or the team) or may be a team member who serves as a mentor for beginning racers. A benefit of aligning yourself with a highly structured racing team is that coaching is usually free, included in your team fee, or offered at discounted rates. You can expect a lot of initial attention from this type of coach. As you become more experienced, you may receive less attention, because this coach will focus on newer team members.

The team-oriented coach will be in tune with the team goals. This coach usually targets your training (and the training of the group) around specific races. You can expect to learn mainly in a group setting, which can be beneficial for a beginning racer. The group setting allows you to discover where your strengths and weaknesses lie relative to others.

finding a Compatible Coach

Consider the following 10 questions when searching for a coach:

1. Are you looking for a coach to ensure the completion of workouts?
2. Are you self-motivated?
3. Are you willing to research cycling beyond what you learn from coaching instruction?
4. Are you technically oriented or someone who works more on "feel"?
5. How much attention do you need from a coach?
6. What do you expect from a coach?
7. What do you expect from yourself?
8. Are you flexible?
9. Do you have confidence in the ability of others to guide you?
10. Are you willing to cede control of training and planning to a coach?

The team-oriented coach may use similar tactics for teaching individuals, regardless of the individual's personal limitations or talents. This type of coach may be a good sounding board, because he or she is usually available when your team trains or races.

Being more free to work outside a group setting, individual-oriented coaches have many styles, strengths, and resources. When working with an individual-oriented coach, you should expect all the benefits of the team-oriented coach. However, more emphasis will be placed on individual attention, specifically tailored training programs, and individually tailored race schedules.

The following coaching styles apply to team-oriented coaches and individual-oriented coaches.

Task-Driven Coaches This type of coach may ensure that you follow training plans—to the letter. Little flexibility may be worked into this coach's plans, because you are expected to agree to a plan and stick with it.

The task-driven coach may be a good choice if any of the following apply to you:

- You want to be told what races to attend, what workouts to do, and when to do them.
- You are motivated to race but not motivated to train.
- You are time-crunched by other commitments in your daily life, and you need someone to help manage your time and put you back on track when necessary.

What the task-driven coaches may lack in flexibility, they can make up for by keeping you on target year-round.

Technology-Driven Coaches A technology-driven coach will perform scientific breakdowns of your workouts to determine modifications for your next workout. Your performance for this coach may be measured in numbers. Expect a lot of workout modifications, which will include individual attention to detail. You may be expected to manage your own time and to commit some off-the-bike time to training analysis.

The technology-driven coach may be a good choice if you are

- on top of the latest technology that is used to get the most out of a workout,
- prepared to spend the funds to obtain the equipment needed for specific training protocols, and
- flexible enough to adapt to an evolving workout regimen.

This coach may be suitable for a beginning bicycle racer who has an elite athletic background or who has a firm understanding of workout frameworks.

Methods Coaches The methods coach may have tried many training and racing methods—and as a result of those experiences, the coach knows what works. This coach may not be open to change or to the use of newer methods. You can expect tough workouts, but they'll work.

The methods coach may be a good choice if any of the following apply to you:

- You are embarking on racing with little or no previous training experience in any sport.
- You are in need of individual attention based on proven structured training plans.
- You are a believer in the coach's previous experience.
- You are confident that the coach's approach is effective and best.

Listeners The listener is a coach who focuses more on sport psychology. Many beginning racers have the work ethic and physical capacity to undertake bicycle racing, but their weakness lies in their inability to achieve the proper state of mind for athletic competition.

This coach will prepare you mentally for the rigors of training and racing. The coach may be a guiding voice to help you through the psychological stress produced by bicycle training and racing. This coach realizes that the real trick of racing lies in teaching the athlete to deal with these mental ups and downs during racing and training. The coach may discuss prerace jitters, postrace emotions, and the general highs and lows in cycling. This type of coach will provide guidance when you need it most and will help you tap your inner best so you can achieve your athletic potential.

The tactical coach is often hands-on during race day.

The listener may be a good choice if any of the following apply to you:

● You need to talk through training and racing.

● You lack confidence in your ability.

● You are prone to plateaus in athletics.

● You are returning to competitive sports after a long break.

Tacticians Bicycle racing has often been referred to as a rolling chess match. The tactical coach may help you master strategies and tactics to get you to the podium or to other desired race goals (i.e., *primes*, *king of the mountains*, and so on). This coach may be very hands-on during your weekly group ride or local training race—shepherding you to the appropriate locations within the pack, guiding you on when to expend energy and attack, and supervising you when you become too eager.

This coach is a welcome addition to any team-coaching environment. A tactician should also not be discounted on an individual level. This type of coach will teach you to race and train smarter, not harder.

The tactician may be a good choice if any of the following apply to you:

● You need guidance on racing strategy and tactics.

● You are working with a team toward specific event goals.

● You have proven to be an all-around rider with no specific event strengths.

The Right Coach for You

Coaches, whether individual oriented or team oriented, encompass many of the coaching traits listed in the previous sections. The degree to which they exhibit certain traits varies. As Arnie Baker, MD—national champion, U.S. record holder, and coach of world-class cyclists—says, "You will read about different methods and different coaching philosophies, but there may be no one right way." The information in the previous sections is intended to eliminate confusion about coaching styles and philosophies so that you can make an educated decision when choosing a coach.

Coaching Resources

All coaches should have connections with specialists who can answer questions or offer services beyond the coach's realm of knowledge. This enables the coach to refer athletes to these specialists or resources when necessary. A coach's list of core resources should include sport doctors, physical rehabilitators, nutritionists, psychologists, mechanics, and bicycle parts suppliers. Ensure that your coach has a cadre of these individuals who can be called on when needed.

Coaching Plans

A coach must be committed to an athlete, but the athlete must also be committed to the coach. No coach can be effective if the athlete does not listen and follow instructions. Coaches should be respected for their opinions even in the light of poor results or drops in fitness. A good coach will develop yearly plans (or even five-year plans) to see you through the ups and downs of fitness. Athletes should do their part to reach goals. This means following instructions, completing workouts, communicating with the coach (e.g., when you need to change plans because of changes in available time), honestly assessing race results, and investing in your development through cycling research.

If a coach is not meeting your expectations, you may consider searching for another coach. This may be unrelated to race results—for example, if the coach is not adequately modifying training plans to suit your available time, if the coach is forcing you to race or train in uncomfortable situations, or if the coach is incorrectly evaluating changes in fitness. Another problem is when a coach is regularly unavailable or is not available to ride with you locally. Traveling down the wrong road just to keep traveling is usually not a good idea. If the path that the coach is laying out before you is not working to your satisfaction, it may be time to change.

Understanding the Organization of Racing

Racing, as sanctioned by governing bodies, involves rules and standards for race promotion, along with racer expectations. Many governing bodies employ a rank system whereby individuals are placed in categories (e.g., category 3 means expert) so that racers will be competing with others at the same level of racing. In age-graded races, the racers usually select a category based on their age—for example, any racer who is 35 years of age or older can choose to race in the 35-plus category. In other instances, usually in track or cyclocross events, a racer may have the option to select a category (e.g., A, B, or C), but a chief referee will automatically upgrade any racer who is able to "run away" with each race.

Racing Categories

Common categories are found in most governing bodies, although the actual names used for the categories may vary. These categories include beginner, intermediate, expert, semiprofessional, and professional. In USA Cycling, beginners are category 5, intermediates are category 4, experts are category 3, and semiprofessionals are category 2 and category 1. Professionals are those who have received a contract from a professional team, allowing them to procure a professional license.

As you move up in category, you will face fewer competitors but stiffer competition. Think of it as climbing a pyramid: At the base, there are many beginners climbing up the pyramid. As the pyramid becomes smaller, there are fewer places for you to place your feet and hands. As the pyramid becomes higher and you tire, your competition may be able to find spots for their feet and hands more quickly. This equates to cycling: As you move up in category, be prepared for increases in competition, which will be reflected in race speed, length of races, race conditions, and competitor dedication.

Beginner All racers start as beginners, whether or not they have the talent to become a paid professional. In this category, you will get your feet wet, learn the craft of race preparation and training, and learn the rudimentary aspects of racing itself. Advancement from this category is usually based on the number of races entered as opposed to merit. Beginners are not usually beginning cyclists in the traditional sense, but rather beginning racing cyclists. Beginners usually have a road bike, have participated in either official or unofficial group rides, and have ridden with racers outside of official racing settings.

Intermediate Most racers can achieve the intermediate category if they enter enough beginner races. In this category, racers begin learning the art of what works and what does not work during races (individually and for a team). Advancement to this level usually means an increase in focused commitment. The racer starts to develop good (or bad) racing and training habits. Many racers in this category have aligned themselves with teams, although team tactics usually do not play a big part in overall race outcomes. Many intermediate racers also employ a coach, as these racers realize that movement from this category may require knowledge beyond a self-coached, try-and-fail method of training and racing.

Expert To achieve the expert category, racers have usually raced for 3 years. For some, it may take 5 years. The expert category starts to separate dedicated racers from weekend warriors. For many racers, this is the highest category that they will achieve in their racing experience. In many instances, masters racers (i.e., racers aged 30 years and above) will need to achieve this category in order to qualify for racing in state, provincial, national, or world events.

In this category, team dynamics become more prevalent; a team will often be working for one talented individual who has the potential to move to the semipro category. Racers in the expert category have devoted most of their free time, outside of family and work obligations, to the craft and sport of cycling.

The disparity among racers in this category is usually minimal. Individuals with true talent move through quickly, while others make expert racing their focus for the duration of their racing experience.

Semiprofessional To achieve the semipro category, racers have usually raced for 5 to 8 years. Semipros are not under contract and do not receive a salary for their efforts, but they have the opportunity to race with pros in local and some regional races. This category may be the first rung in the ladder of a professional racing career. Many masters-level racers can achieve the semipro category if they have talent and a sincere, passionate dedication to the sport and craft of cycling.

The semipro category is mostly dominated by younger individuals on their way to the pro ranks, but the category also contains masters. The disparities among racers in this category are usually great—dedicated individuals who are talented dominate the ranks, while those who have lost a bit of their competitive fire flounder under the pressures of the time commitment to training and racing. Teams control this level regionally, but there is some room for individual heroics in local training races.

Racers who achieve this level have shown talent and a singular dedication; however, they realize that leaving this category or keeping up may be nearly impossible if they are not destined for the professional ranks.

Professional Professionals are individuals who receive a contract to race for a salary. These men and women represent the cream of the sporting crop, and they may be talented above and beyond the normal person in any endurance sport. Their talent is usually noticeable even at a young age (i.e., teens), and they only become stronger and more dedicated as the years pass. By entering a contract with a professional team, professional racers are able to enter high-level invitation-only races to which their team receives an invite. In addition, these athletes may be picked by their national cycling federation to represent their country in Olympic games.

As an amateur racer, you may come across these individuals when they are starting out in the lower ranks, or even on local club rides. You should find inspiration for your own goals in these individuals, especially if you have the talent.

Worldwide Professional Although this is not an actual category, worldwide professionals represent the best racers in the world. Racers who compete at this level are the top professionals from their respective countries. They come from the professional ranks of countries worldwide to race in cycling's premiere stage-race events such as the Tour de France, the Giro d'Italia, and the Vuelta a España, as well as one-day classic monuments such as the Tour of Flanders (Ronde van Vlaanderen), Paris-Roubaix, and Milan-San Remo. These racers' abilities are a confluence of specific physical talent, intense work ethic, and mental perseverance.

Age-Based Racing Categories

All sanctioning bodies have age-graded categories for the masters-level racer. Masters-level racing starts at age 30 in the United States and is broken into 5-year intervals. Local and regional races usually set a minimum age for a category (e.g., 35-plus or 45-plus). National and world events set upper and lower limits (e.g., 35 to 39, 40 to 44, and so on).

All sanctioning bodies also have age-graded categories for the junior-level racer. Junior-level racing can start as early as 10 years of age, so the first category may be age 10-11 with 2-year increments up to age 18. The next age-graded category is under 23 (or U23), which covers racers aged 19 to 22.

Officially, elite racers (or seniors) are normally considered to be in the category for ages 23 to 29, although masters-level racers (30 years of age or greater) can also compete in elite events in their achieved category.

© Human Kinetics

Cyclists eagerly await the sound of the starting gun.

Racing Around the World

Amateur bicycle racers not only race on a national level, but also on an international level. Amateurs, especially masters-level amateurs (i.e., those 30 years of age or older), commonly race in world amateur events. Also, many amateurs who live close to international borders will cross the border to compete in events; these events may be as close to the racer's home as regional events in the racer's own country.

Although you may not always need to know the sanctioning systems for foreign races, you do need to understand that various systems exist. This will allow you to understand the level of racing and competition that you will be facing at an international event. If you choose to compete internationally, this information may be invaluable.

Union Cycliste Internationale The Union Cycliste Internationale (UCI) is the worldwide governing body for bicycle racing. All national sanctioning bodies defer to the rules and regulations set forth by the UCI for the conduct of bicycle racing within their respective countries. The UCI also works with the International Olympic Committee (IOC) to administer choosing cyclists from national sanctioning bodies for the Olympic Games, in addition to administering most international-level professional racing.

Amateurs may encounter UCI events, and racers who compete in a professional-level category may receive points in an international system for ranking riders. UCI-administered races mainly occur in Europe, but they can be found worldwide with an ever-growing global list.

United States The main sanctioning body in the United States is USA Cycling. Overseeing the majority of race sanctioning in the United States, USA Cycling is connected with regional subsidiaries that provide assistance to local race promoters. USA Cycling is the only cycling body in the United States that is recognized by the IOC; therefore, USA Cycling chooses which cyclists compete at the Summer Games.

In the United States, all categories of racers are required to purchase either a one-day license for the event (i.e., category 5 or citizens) or an annual license. Through a system of race completion and points, racers can navigate their way into more advanced categories based on race placings and race difficulty.

Other racing bodies do exist in the United States, including the American Bicycle Racing Association. These other sanctioning bodies provide similar services to race promoters as USA Cycling (i.e., insurance, race sanctioning, referees, ranking systems), but they are not recognized by the IOC. In most cases, USA Cycling recognizes points obtained in races sponsored by other sanctioning bodies. Table 1.1 shows the categories in the USA Cycling system and the points needed to move up in category.

TABLE 1.1

Moving Through the USA Cycling Category System

Categories	Points needed for upgrade request*	Automatic upgrade**
5 to 4	Experience in 10 mass-start races	Local associations may also establish policies where upgrade credit is given for taking a sanctioned rider education clinic.
4 to 3	20 points in any 12-month period; or experience in 25 races with a minimum of 10 top-ten finishes with fields of 30+ riders; or 20 pack finishes with fields of 50+ riders	Cyclists who acquire 30 points in 12 months receive an automatic upgrade.
3 to 2	25 points in any 12-month period	Cyclists who acquire 40 points in 12 months receive an automatic upgrade.
2 to 1	30 points in any 12-month period	Cyclists who acquire 50 points in 12 months receive an automatic upgrade.

Note: USA Cycling may add additional requirements for upgrading at its governing discretion. Any such changes shall be made available on the USA Cycling Web site.

*Points are acquired through race placing. Points are distributed on a sliding scale based on the length or distance of the event, along with the number of competitors entered in the event. Please refer to USA Cycling's official Web site for up-to-date category upgrade information and points distribution schemes.

**An automatic upgrade is a forced upgrade to a more advanced cycling category. USA Cycling reserves the right to enforce this in the case of a cyclist "sandbagging"—remaining in a less competitive category to garner higher race placings more easily.

Australia The main sanctioning body in Australia is the Australian Cycling Federation, also known as Cycling Australia (CA). CA is the Australian cycling affiliate of the UCI, as well as the country's cycling liaison with the IOC.

CA cyclists reaching masters age (30 years or greater) may elect to have an elite license (for elite-level racing) or a masters license (for masters-level racing). A CA cyclist may compete in an event of a different age category (an older category in the case of juniors and a younger category in the case of masters), provided the events are approved by CA or a constituent association.

CA racers are required to purchase an annual license.

Britain The main sanctioning body in Britain is British Cycling (BC). BC is the British cycling affiliate of the UCI. BC is also the country's cycling liaison with the IOC.

A racing license from BC is normally required to enter competitive cycling events in the United Kingdom. A racing license is free to racers under 16 years of age and is good for an entire year. The license gives full access to ability categories, participation in national and international events, upgrading, national rankings, and National Points Series competition.

To race in interclub competition in Britain, BC racers are required to ride for a club. Most clubs require a minimum of 2 years of time trialing in intraclub races before granting a racing license for interclub events. Through a system of racing starts and points, racers can navigate their way into more advanced categories based on race placings and race difficulty.

Mexico The main sanctioning body for racing in Mexico is the Mexican Cycling Federation (MCF). The MCF is part of the Comité Olímpico Mexicano (Mexican Olympic Committee). A local branch of the MCF exists in each town where cycling activities take place.

The MCF recognizes various age categories. Youth are organized into 2-year age groups from 7 to 14 years. Juniors are organized into two 2-year age groups: 15 to 16 and 17 to 18.

The U23 racers are organized into three categories: 3rd, 2nd, and 1st. A racer starts in the 3rd category and then accumulates points to upgrade to the next category. Once a racer reaches the 1st category, the racer is entitled to obtain a UCI license; this license enables the cyclist to race in international races. Juniors are also able to obtain a UCI license if they are planning to race abroad.

Clubs in Mexico are privately organized, and they register with the MCF in their local town. The branch of the MCF in each town has its own organization with a local president and delegates.

For masters racing, the MCF recognizes the categories shown in the sidebar.

MASTERS

Age	Categories
30-34	Primera
35-39	Segunda
40-44	Tercera
45-49	Especial
50-54	Super especial
55-59	Platino
60 and up	Diamante

Canada The main sanctioning body in Canada is the Canadian Cycling Association (CCA). CCA is the Canadian cycling affiliate of the UCI, as well as the country's cycling liaison with the IOC.

Athletes aged 30 years or older must decide whether they will compete in the elite or master category for the season. Age groupings for road categories mirror those of USA Cycling, including juniors, U23, elite, and masters. However, a ranking system of 1 through 4 is used within the elite and masters categories.

An athlete may only belong to one team. The rider's license will show the name of the team or club. A rider cannot change teams or clubs during the season unless the team or club disbands. A club is a team affiliated with the provincial or national federation. Clubs are composed of licensed riders who do not belong to a team registered with the UCI.

Obtaining a Racing License

The various national governing bodies provide trained referees and judges, as well as insurance and permit procedures to allow promoters to legally promote races with sound jurisdiction. Beginning racers need to know which governing body is sanctioning events in which they enter and what fees and licensures are necessary to take part in these events.

In most instances, a beginning racer can go to the governing body's Web site to procure a license, register for a race, or find out contacts for local teams and clubs. The governing body will often offer one-day licenses, usually available on the day of the race, that enable racers to enter the beginner category if they pay a nominal fee. The license provides racers with the right to race and usually includes event-only insurance. In all cases, if a racer wants to advance in the categories and move into more competitive fields, the racer will need to purchase a governing body's annual racing license to begin to accrue points toward advancement.

The license usually depicts the licensee's name, license number, category number, and contact information. Review the sidebar for Web sites containing important cycling information from various national governing bodies.

National Governing Bodies for Cycling

For each of the listed countries, you'll find information on racing at the following Web sites:

United States: www.usacycling.org
Australia: www.cycling.org.au
Britain: new.britishcycling.org.uk
Canada: www.canadian-cycling.com
France: www.ffc.fr
Italy: www.federciclismo.it
Mexico: www.fmc.com.mx

Chapter 2

GEARING UP

Of all the sports, cycling is the one that requires the most perfect match of man and machine. The more perfect the match, the more perfect the result.

—Paul Cornish, first U.S. cross-country record holder

The bicycle is an amazing vehicle—and the rider's body serves as the engine. A bicycle is the most energy-efficient form of travel that humans have invented. This efficiency has inspired the sport of bicycle racing.

Racing bicycles—taking that amazing invention and fine-tuning it to achieve maximum speeds and distances—requires the proper gear, from clothing to a proper frame, right down to the tires. Proper equipment will be critical to your success and enjoyment in racing and training. Having equipment that properly fits your requirements will enable you to maneuver deftly in a pack, to achieve and sustain high speeds, and to maintain comfort for many miles of training and racing.

This chapter will help you select the right gear for racing and training. Many choices are available for all types of gear, but the general overview in this chapter will get you out and racing in no time. The chapter covers how to equip yourself for racing and provides information on finding a frame, wheels and tires, and pedal and cleat systems. You will also learn about achieving the perfect fit in clothing and other important equipment.

Equipping Yourself to Race

At first glance, cycling appears to be an expensive sport, especially when you start shopping around for a racing bicycle frame. True, the initial investment can be a bit harrowing for some, but keep in mind that most equipment will last you for many years and through many miles. Being a careful consumer—that is, reading product reviews before purchasing, starting a dialogue with the employees at your local racing bicycle shop, and heeding the information in this chapter—should help you obtain the proper equipment for numerous hours of racing and training.

If you'll be riding in cooler temperatures, you might consider equipping yourself with arm warmers.

This is an important time to build a relationship with your local racing bike shop, or if necessary, a regional racing bike shop where you feel comfortable. The shop will be a place for you to do the following:

- Try out equipment
- Get adjustments on purchased equipment
- Learn about what equipment might help improve your racing or training

The bike shop will also be a resource to help you find teammates, training companions, and information on local training routes.

UCI Rules

According to UCI racing rules, which are the rules to which sanctioning bodies defer, a racing frame must have a triangular shape formed by the *downtube*, *top tube*, and *seat tube*. The frame must also have a triangular shape between the seat tube, *chainstays*, and *seat stays*. Both front and rear wheels must be the same size—standard wheels are 700c or approximately 27 inches in diameter; some frames under 52 centimeters will have wheels that are 650c or approximately 26 inches in diameter. Of course, certain rules apply such as having rubber-compound tires, a seat, handlebar tape, bar end plugs, and brakes.

Different rules apply to different racing events. For example, in mass-start events for road racing, a frame can have no extraneous attachments—bike racks, lights, pumps, gear bags, or aerobars. A road racing bike must have two operable brakes—one for the front and one for the rear—and the bike must be able to *freewheel* (be able to coast), because no *fixed gears* are allowed.

This book is concerned mainly with road racing, but you should also note the rules for other forms of racing that you may encounter. For track racing, brakes are *not* allowed; only fixed-gear bikes (i.e., no coasting) are allowed on velodromes. For time trialing, a complex set of rules apply and are forever being modified as racers and manufacturers push the limits of aerodynamics through rider position. The most important item to note is that time trials allow the use of aerobars, and in some instances, fixed-gear bikes are allowed as long as they have a front brake. General setup and equipment for time trialing are covered in chapter 3.

Never get caught at the start line with the wrong equipment. Always review the rules and regulations of the race's sanctioning body before taking the start.

Frames

The first piece of gear that any aspiring racer needs to obtain is a proper racing bicycle frame. Numerous brands are on the market today—they are designed with a variety of styles (e.g., compact, standard, or aerodynamic) and are built with numerous materials (e.g., carbon fiber, titanium, or aluminum). The most important thing is to find a race-specific frame that fits you properly.

If you are purchasing a custom-built frame—meaning the manufacturer will take your measurements, ask about your proposed use of the bike, and build the bike specifically for your body and intended use—then the fit will be determined on assembly. For most cyclists, their first racing frame will be a standard frame (not custom built), meaning right from the bike store rack. A bike store representative should be able to determine a couple of frames that fit you reasonably well based on your body type.

Frame Size

In the past, riders determined proper frame size by simply standing over the frame to see if their crotch was approximately two inches above the *top tube* (the tube that runs from the front-top of the bike to seat post junction). Unfortunately, this old technique no longer applies. Because of the quest for aerodynamics, lightness, stiffness, and style, many bike frames no longer have a traditional horizontal top tube. In addition, new frame designs make previous formulas for selecting a frame based on a *seat tube* length (the tube that runs from the *bottom bracket* of the bike to the seat post junction) virtually extinct. Seat posts on new frames are much longer—and thus more adjustable—than on traditional bikes. As a result, more generally sized frames fit a larger range of rider heights.

Instead, we must rely on *virtual top tube lengths* to determine what frame size fits a rider. Regardless of the actual length of the top tube, virtual top tube length is determined by measuring an imaginary line (parallel to the ground) from the top of the *headtube* to the spot where the seat tube would be located if it was a standard design.

The majority of bike manufacturers sell their frames based on a virtual or actual top tube length. The length is measured in centimeters and is usually available in 2-centimeter increments (e.g., 50, 52, 54, 56 centimeters).

Many formulas can be used to determine your general frame size based on a virtual or actual top tube length. A simple formula that will give you a general idea of your frame size involves measuring your inseam, converting the measurement to centimeters, and multiplying it by 0.71. For example, someone with a 30-inch inseam would multiply 30 inches by 2.54 to convert the measurement to centimeters. The result would be rounded to 76 centimeters. The person would then multiply this product by 0.71, and the result would be 54 centimeters. Therefore, a person with a 30-inch inseam would generally look for a frame with a 54-centimeter virtual top tube.

You may also find frames measured as small, medium, or large. There is no standard for these "beverage-size" specifications, so check individual manufacturer specifications for the virtual top length when making your decision.

Frame Angles and Wheel Base

The largest force that a racer must overcome is wind resistance, or drag. Racing frames have steeper headtube angles and seat tube angles to place the rider in a more aggressive position—over the pedals—and to allow a more aerodynamic form. Although this position may seem uncomfortable at first, over time the racer will find that it provides the best combination of power and comfort.

Most headtube angles on racing bikes are between 72.5 and 74 degrees depending on the manufacturer and the size of the frame. This angle may be compared with those on more relaxed touring frames, which may have a head angle below 72 degrees, bringing the handlebars closer and placing the rider in a more upright position.

Most seat tube angles on racing bikes are between 72 and 74 degrees depending on the manufacturer and the size of the frame. Many touring frames have comparable seat tube angles, so the difference in position is solely based on the headtube angle and the height of the headtube—a higher headtube means higher handlebars, placing the rider in a more upright position. Some touring frames have a seat tube angle below 70 degrees, which places the rider in a very relaxed position. In contrast, time trial frames normally have seat tube angles at 77 to 79 degrees. Time trial bikes use these steeper angles to get riders even farther forward, allowing them to be "on top" of the pedals while allowing them to lower their bodies farther by flattening the back. This will be discussed in more detail in chapter 3.

Wheel base refers to the distance measured in a straight line between the dropout (the slot where the axle of the wheel attaches) of the front wheel and the dropout of the rear wheel. In the past, steel frames required a very short wheel base. This shortened wheel base provided for smaller, stiffer frames that handled more responsively—think of it as the comparison between the long body of a cruising Cadillac versus the short body of a Porsche. Recently, with the advent of stiffer materials, the necessity for the shortened wheel base has been diminished. This has resulted in stiffer racing bikes without sacrificing comfort or responsiveness. Most race frames have a wheel base between 97 and 101 centimeters, but again, you may find touring bikes with similar wheel bases.

The simple fact is that you need to acquire a racing bike, preferably a modern variety made from modern materials. Retrofitting a touring bike to make your position more racelike may never work as well as purchasing a bike designed for competition. The good news is that many manufacturers provide race-specific geometry frames at low prices—the only difference being that higher-priced versions come stocked with higher-end *components* and are usually much lighter.

When you are looking for a frame, industry jargon can be overwhelming. Here are a few terms that may assist you when purchasing a frame (also see figure 2.1):

- Top tube length—The distance between the top of the headtube and the top of the seat tube.
- Virtual top tube length—A measurement of an imaginary line (parallel to the ground) from the top of the headtube to the spot where the top of the seat tube would be located if the seat tube was as tall as the headtube. Most bike manufacturers provide this measurement in frame specifications.

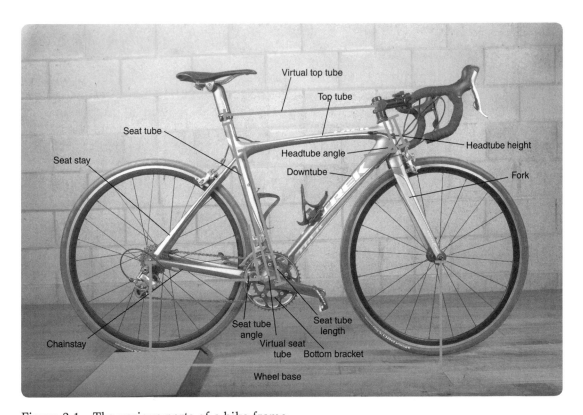

Figure 2.1 The various parts of a bike frame.

● Seat tube length—Normally measured as the distance from the center of the bottom bracket to the top of the seat tube. The measurement may also be from the center of the bottom bracket to the center point of the intersection of the top tube and seat tube.

● Virtual seat tube length—Normally measured as the distance from the center of the bottom bracket to an imaginary point extending from the end of the seat tube to where the top tube would cross if it ran parallel to the ground.

● Seat tube angle—The angle (measured to the rear of the seat tube) between the seat tube and an imaginary line running parallel to the ground and through the bottom bracket.

● Headtube height—The length of the headtube.

● Headtube angle—The angle (measured to the rear of the headtube) between the headtube and an imaginary line running parallel to the ground.

● Wheel base—The distance measured in a straight line between the *dropout* (the slot where the axle of the wheel attaches) of the front wheel and the dropout of the rear wheel.

● Bottom bracket—The intersection of the seat tube and the *downtube* (tube that runs from the headtube to the bottom of the seat tube); the connection point for the crank.

Frame Materials

Bicycle racing frames (and even components) are developed from various materials. Carbon is commonly the choice of manufacturers because of its lightness and stiffness and because it can be easily shaped into various designs. Other materials have evolved from their earlier predecessors, but the most important factor in your choice of materials comes down to whether *you feel* that the frame is comfortable and responsive.

Bike shops usually allow test drives of bikes—a quick spin within the local vicinity of the shop—if you leave a driver's license and credit card. Some larger bike shops may even offer a "demo test drive." Many shops have demo bikes that are not for sale. Cyclists are allowed to take a demo bike on an extended ride under their normal riding conditions or normal riding routes. Both types of test drives are a good way to see if you like the feel and responsiveness of a particular frame material.

Carbon Fiber Carbon fiber is the material used in fighter jets and race cars, and it has slowly taken over the high-end bicycle racing industry. The main advantage for manufacturers is that this material can be developed to their specifications, rather than being tied to the intrinsic natural properties of metals. Carbon fiber can also be shaped more easily (by layering and molding) compared to some metals. Carbon fiber provides the benefit of usually being flexible vertically (meaning a smoother ride) while being stiff laterally (meaning more power transfer as you crank down on the pedals).

Titanium Titanium is also used in high-end aeronautics. Titanium was an extremely popular frame material before the increasing availability of carbon fiber frames, and titanium still holds a nice share of the higher-end bicycle market. New and improved methods of shaping the material have helped titanium frames maintain their place as one of the lightest and stiffest frames that still provide a comfortable ride. Titanium is repairable and has the added bonus of being rustproof. Newer technologies have allowed titanium frames to have carbon integrated into their tubing, thereby providing benefits of both materials (durability, smooth ride, and lateral stiffness).

Aluminum Most entry-level to mid-range racing frames are developed from aluminum. The vast availability of the material, along with long-proven welding and shaping methods, has set aluminum up as the most affordably priced frame material on the market. Aluminum frames are rustproof and lightweight, and they are the most rigid frames on the market. To mitigate the rougher ride produced by aluminum frames, larger tubing is used, as well as various-shaped *chainstays* and *seat stays* in combination with carbon fiber *forks*. Because of its stiffness, aluminum is an excellent frame material for fast races on smooth surfaces, such as *criteriums* and *track racing*.

Steel The old adage is "steel is real," and the owners of steel bikes will tell you that it's the only way to go. However, steel is rarely used as the choice of material for contemporary racing frames. Rolling up on a steel bike might get you some respect at your local coffee shop, but this type of bike may be a heavy anchor to your racing ability on the course. Improved steels and the use of more modern alloying techniques (involving chrome-moly boron and vanadium) have helped improve the stiffness of the material and reduce the weight. Steel has long held the distinction of providing the smoothest ride, and if damage occurs, it can be easily repaired. Steel does have the propensity to rust if not cleaned and maintained regularly.

A great advantage of steel is its wide availability and ease of shaping. Thus, if you need to have a custom-built bike because standard frames do not fit your body well, steel can be a great, inexpensive alternative. Keep in mind that it's better to be on a bike that fits you than on a bike made of the latest, fashionable materials.

Wheels

As a beginning racer, you may not be too concerned about wheels at first; you will likely use whatever wheels come with your racing frame. However, as you become more involved in racing and training, you will see the benefit of having a dependable pair of wheels for training along with specific sets of race wheels for various events (i.e., criteriums, road races, time trials).

A multitude of wheel manufacturers are developing wheels made from varied materials and containing various spoke counts. In the past, a larger spoke count (32 or 36) was usually recommended for heavier riders, while lighter riders could get away with lower spoke counts (24 or 28). With improvements in materials, better lacing systems for spokes, and better hub and rim designs, almost any wheel can now be ridden by any rider of any weight.

For training, a rider needs to have a dependable wheel. Usually, dependable wheels have common manufacturing styles for spokes (i.e., J-bend, nonaero, outward nipple seating); these wheels are normally manufactured from aluminum, and they use standard alloy bearings. Many carbon fiber wheels have begun to infiltrate the wheel market, and these wheels are also dependable. However, carbon fiber wheels are often priced more aggressively, and they usually need special brake pads if the braking surface is also carbon (instead of aluminum). Dependable wheels should be easily repairable and should maintain their *true* (i.e., rolling straightness) with little tweaking. They should also be able to withstand many miles without microcracks forming around the spoke nipples on the rim. Your local bike dealer or wheel builder should be able to recommend a good pair of wheels. Many racers use the wheels that come with their frame as their training set, and they buy another set designed for race day.

For racing, a couple pairs of wheels may be necessary. For road racing and events that require climbing, you should choose the lightest pair of wheels that will withstand the rigors of racing and your weight. The weight of the wheel should be researched, because two wheels of the same weight will accelerate and roll differently. Wheels with lighter rims will accelerate more quickly than those with heavier rims. The more the mass of the wheel is closer to the axle (i.e., the hub), the better. Most truly lightweight wheels are made from carbon fiber.

For flat races or criteriums, the most important aspect of the wheel is aerodynamics. As mentioned earlier, the largest force that a cyclist must overcome is drag due to wind resistance. A deep-dish or aero rim will reduce drag through the use of the same principles as plane wing aerodynamics. Aero rims have a deeper vertical profile, reducing turbulent air flow over the surface of the rim and creating lift to pull the bike along. Most manufacturers of deep-dish rims recommend a depth that is three or four times the width of the rim to achieve true aerodynamic benefits. Deeper rims are not always better, because crosswinds will make them difficult to handle, especially on descents. Be sure to speak with your local bike shop or the manufacturer about your intended use of the wheel before making a purchase.

For flat or rolling time trials, a deep-dish front wheel and a deep-dish or disc rear wheel are your best bets. More information on this topic is provided in chapter 3.

For all types of race wheels, performance can be enhanced with aero spokes (flattened to reduce drag), lighter spokes, and lower spoke counts. These features will reduce the weight of the wheel and reduce air turbulence, thus reducing drag. Also, in recent years, the use of ceramic bearings has become more prevalent for racing wheels (along with many training wheels and other rotating bicycle components, such as bottom brackets and jockey pulleys). Ceramic bearings can be manufactured to have increased hardness and roundness as compared to their alloy counterparts; thus, they roll more smoothly.

Tires

Beginning racers need to understand the basics of bike tires. Different manufacturing processes make it somewhat difficult to provide hard-and-fast rules regarding what makes a great training or race tire. You should try many tire brands until you find one that suits your purpose and *feels* right.

The majority of racers will use 700 × 23c tires—700 indicating a standard bicycle wheel diameter (approx. 27 inches) and the 23 indicating the diagonal measurement of the tire in millimeters. Some racers use 700 × 20c tires for their race wheels because these tires are lighter. Racers sometimes use 700 × 25c tires during harsh-weather months; these tires can be run using lower pressures, thereby providing a more cushy ride and possibly better traction in poor road conditions. Beginning racers should use the standard 700 × 23c tires for both racing and training.

Threads per inch (TPI) of cloth is a rating system for tires. Thinner, more flexible tires will have a higher TPI number (usually over 100 and up to 350 TPI). Tires with a high TPI count may have lower rolling resistance and may be lighter. The drawback is that they may get damaged (i.e., cut) more easily by road hazards. Using silica compounds on tread at lower TPI counts may provide the same effects as a high TPI count.

The tread is the rubber part of the tire that makes contact with the ground. The tread area of a tire is usually made of a harder rubber to resist wear, while the sidewall rubber is more flexible to provide comfort and traction. Manufacturers vary the tread patterns, tread covering, and tread hardness on various areas of the tire to provide the best contact patch with the road in different cycling situations. In addition, manufacturers mix different additives with the rubber to modify traction and wear characteristics. The softer the rubber, the more rapid the wear, but possibly the better the traction. Dual-compound tires are very common today; these tires have hard rubber in the center (for improved wear and lessened rolling resistance) and softer rubber on the sides of the tread (for improved traction when leaning and cornering the bike).

Clincher, Tubular, or Tubeless?

Clinchers are the predominant type of tire (and rim) used in amateur cycling and training. Clincher rims have a bead for holding a clincher tire, and an inner tube is placed within the tire. Almost all complete bikes are sold with clincher wheels. Tubular tires have two edges of the tire sewn together around an inner tube; these tires are glued on rims that contain no beads. Gluing a tubular tire on a rim is a skill. Tubulars were previously more common in racing, but the ease of use of the clincher tire and rim has slowly decreased the use of tubulars in amateur racing. As you become more advanced in racing, you may find that tubulars are a good option for your race wheels but not for your training wheels.

Pros of Tubulars

● Tubular systems (tire and wheel) are normally lighter.

● Tubulars have a reduced chance of a pinch flat (i.e., inner tube getting pinched against the rim).

● Tubulars provide better traction because lower tire pressures can be run.

● Tubulars provide better comfort because lower tire pressures can be run.

● Tubulars provide increased safety because the tire usually does not roll off the rim if a sudden flat occurs.

Cons of Tubulars

● Tubulars are more expensive.

● The rider needs to carry a complete tubular spare (as opposed to just an inner tube) on training rides.

● Hastily replaced tubulars on the road are not seated well because the glue has not bonded (you must roll home slowly and carefully).

● Tubulars may have a higher rolling resistance compared with newer tube and tire pairings for clinchers

● An improperly glued tubular may roll off the rim.

Another newer option may be tubeless tires that are fit to specially designed tubeless rims. Without a tube either inserted in the tire (like clinchers) or sewn into the tire (like tubulars), tubeless tires provide the benefits of both. A sealant needs to be injected into the tubeless tire when mounting in order to ensure that small cuts seal quickly when on the road. If you do get a flat that the sealant cannot repair, tubeless tires have the advantage of being able to accept a tube to get you home.

Tires that have smooth tread provide the best traction. Many beginning riders find this counterintuitive because athletic shoes and car tires always have grooved or knobby tread patterns. The grooved or knobby tread patterns are placed on these items because of their larger surface area. Tread patterns are necessary if walking or driving on loose surfaces or surfaces that are covered in water. Track shoes (i.e., running flats) and race car tires are always smooth, because this provides the most traction on surfaces that are known to be smooth and mostly water free. Bicycle tires find better traction—even on mildly wet or mildly loose surfaces—because they are so narrow that they cut through debris or water to the pavement. This is known as having a small footprint.

For wetter months of the year—which may include rainstorms or snowmelt (and a lot of loose debris being washed into the road)—you can look for road tires designed for such conditions. Manufacturers also use varying tread patterns to provide a pushing effect off an unstable surface to allow the tire surface to make contact with the road surface. In most instances, you will notice that the tread pattern is only on the side of the tread; this is because the pushing action is only necessary when leaning or cornering.

The beginning racer should find the tire that provides the best value based on lightness, TPI count, and the smoothness of the tread.

Pedal and Cleat Systems

Many cyclists choose a pedal and cleat system by simply buying the brand that their local bike shop carries when they buy their bike. This is a perfectly logical way of choosing a system, because you will have the service of the bike shop in the event of mechanical failure, along with the availability of parts, such as cleats. Reasons for trying different cleat systems include availability, price, style, and weight. The most important thing for a starting racer is that the cleat system fits properly without causing overuse injury—and that the system is designed for the rigors of racing.

Pedal and cleat systems are extremely adjustable. A rider can usually set

- the release tension (the force needed to cause the cleat to disengage from the pedal),
- the release angle (how many lateral degrees a cleat must be twisted to disengage), and
- the float (how many lateral degrees the cleat will move while engaged).

The cleat itself can be attached to the shoe at varying lateral angles, along with a forward or back position on the shoe bottom.

Fitting shoes, pedal, and cleats will be covered in a later section. Note that some riders who have knee problems have stated that a system with more float helped solve those problems. From my own personal experience, I have found that a nonfloat system helped with my knee problems, so obviously different systems work for different people. You can attempt to set your cleats up with a general bike fit, but the best strategy for an aspiring racer is to use trial and error in choosing brands and to tweak the general fit, with an eventual move to a fit by a professional coach.

Achieving the Perfect Fit

People are attracted to cycling for many reasons—such as fitness, travel, or competition—but the most important reason is usually that the person has fun doing it. For most cyclists, this means being comfortable on a bike for a long ride in the country or the mountains, or for a local group ride and then a roll back home. When changing from a more recreational cycling stance to a competitive cycling stance, you will most likely need a change in fit. You still want cycling to fill the most important priority—fun—but you also want to take advantage of on-the-bike position, which will help you succeed in races. A proper fit is of the utmost importance in competitive cycling. A proper fit allows the transmission of maximum energy to the pedals, places the rider in the most aerodynamic position (without sacrificing comfort for long events), and allows total control of the bicycle in close quarters with other racers.

Achieving the perfect fit takes time and patience. As mentioned earlier, a good start is to speak with professionals at your local bike shop. Many bike shops now have fit kits available; these kits include tools and knowledge for properly fitting a racer on the bike. If a fit kit is not available, you can use the information in this book as a solid start.

Keep in mind that bike fitting is a process that may take a fair amount of tweaking and possibly some changing of components, such as handlebars, pedal and cleat systems, stems, and saddles. Also understand that as you develop more race-specific skills and as your body transforms because of physical training, your fit may morph as well.

In reality, there is no *perfect* fit. Racers usually settle on a position that provides them with the most power, the best aerodynamic advantage, and enough comfort to train and race consistently. Like other racers, you may find yourself becoming slightly obsessed with your position. You may even find yourself stressing out if you replace equipment or if your equipment slips even a millimeter. If this is the case, you are in good company. Greats such as Eddy Merckx were famous for their dedication to the perfect position. Eddy, as seen in archival footage in the film *La Course en Tête*, was so obsessed that he would change his saddle height in the middle of a race, depending on how he felt. Amazingly, he changed his saddle height by acquiring a wrench from his team car, standing on his pedals, and adjusting his seat height while rolling along in a breakaway! Although Eddy's back problems may have contributed to his desire to change his saddle height, he was still dedicated to the perfect fit. This level of dedication is not recommended, and it may not be safe or beneficial. However, you may want to follow a practice used by 7-time Tour de France winner, Lance Armstrong. Lance carries around a carpenter's level and tape measure to ensure that his saddle tilt and height are exactly where he wants them. Rumor is that Lance was shown the leveling trick by none other than Eddy Merckx.

Make sure you write down all measurements and subsequent changes when setting your bike position. You should record this information in your training diary. You will find this invaluable as you purchase new equipment and physically develop in the sport. More information on keeping a training diary is provided in chapter 9.

Saddle Height

To find your approximate saddle height, stand on a hard floor with your feet about 15 centimeters apart and with a book pulled up firmly between your legs. Measure, in centimeters, from the floor to the top of the book. Multiply this measurement by 0.90 to find your minimum saddle height, and multiply the measurement by 0.94 to attain your maximum saddle height. This product represents the distance from the center of the bottom bracket to the crown of the saddle. The crown of the saddle is the area directly above and in a straight line from the seat post. As an example, someone with an inseam of 77.5 centimeters would multiply this measurement by both 0.90 and 0.94. This person would have a minimum saddle height of 70 centimeters and a maximum saddle height of 73 centimeters.

To avoid injury, always make saddle adjustments modestly—move the saddle only millimeters on each adjustment, and go on at least one ride before adjusting again. If you find yourself overwhelmed by the height—even while riding at the minimum recommended height—build up to it slowly over months. With more experience, you will find that you want your saddle to be higher for maximum power output. As a general rule, if your hips are rocking excessively (i.e., you are moving your buttocks back and forth over the saddle), or if you are reaching for the pedals with your feet, then the saddle is too high. Also, if you experience pain in the back of your knee, this may indicate that your saddle is set too high. Conversely, if you experience pain in the front of your knee, or if your knees are sticking out when you pedal, this may indicate that the saddle is set too low.

Arnie Baker has a simple analogy for why a higher saddle may be beneficial. He asks this question: Is it easier to step up on a box if your knee is raised closer to your chest (i.e., the knee is closer to a 90-degree angle) or if the knee is farther away (i.e., the knee is straighter)? The answer is farther away, because your quadriceps muscles are at a greater mechanical advantage, allowing for more power at lower aerobic cost. This can be applied to saddle height and pedaling position—the farther your knee is away from your chest (i.e., the higher the saddle), the more easily you can push down on the pedals.

As an additional note, racers exhibit different pedaling styles. In general, beginning racers pedal flat-footed at first and then begin to take a more toe-pointed approach as they become more experienced. There is no correct way, but the change may be due to more experienced riders letting

Determining Saddle Height

Thought leaders in the industry each have their own measurement styles for determining the proper saddle height. Your best bet is sticking with the method recommended by your local bike shop and readjusting over numerous test rides.

Arnie Baker, MD, national champion, professional coach, and medical doctor

Arnie recommends a 25-degree bend in the knee when the rider is seated on the saddle with shoes clipped in and with the pedal at the six o'clock position (the pedal on the side of the leg being measured). Another way to look at it is when seated and clipped in, with the pedal in the six o'clock position, the angle between your lower and upper legs should be 155 degrees (see figure 2.2). Arnie has set this parameter as a good compromise between performance and injury prevention.

Figure 2.2 Rider with pedal in six o'clock position.

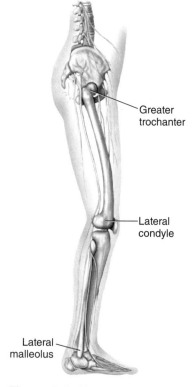

Figure 2.3 Use these three points to measure an angle of 20 to 25 degrees.

Andy Pruitt, physician's assistant and certified athletic trainer

Andy's recommendations are similar to Arnie's, but he uses the entire leg to set the measurement (not just the knee). Using three landmarks on the leg (see figure 2.3)—the greater trochanter (the bony portion you can feel through the skin on the hip), the lateral condyle (the bump on the outside of the knee), and the lateral malleolus (the bump on the outside of the ankle)—measure an angle of 20 to 25 degrees.

Greg LeMond, three-time Tour de France champion

Greg recommends multiplying your inseam length in centimeters (measured in stocking feet from the floor to the top of a book placed between the legs) by 0.883. The product should equal the distance from the center of the bottom bracket to the crown of the seat.

the foot float over the top of the stroke or allowing the foot to naturally pull the pedal through the upstroke.

Saddles

As a bicycle racer, you will be spending many hours in your saddle as you train and race. Saddle comfort and fit are of the utmost importance. Many cycling careers have been derailed by discomfort and chafing caused by an improperly fit saddle. An improperly fit saddle may make riding uncomfortable or could even cause persistent sores.

Many beginning racers use the saddle that comes with their racing bike as a default. If you find the saddle comfortable, stick with it. If not, a good starting point is choosing a saddle in which your ischial tuberosities (i.e., your sit bones) are firmly planted on the seating wings toward the back of the saddle.

If you experience numbness, tingling, or persistent discomfort, you need to change saddles immediately. A multitude of saddle designs are available that employ different curvatures, widths, and cutouts. When looking for a saddle, take advantage of a common bicycle shop policy known as "ride, try, and return." This will allow you to try different saddles until you find one that is comfortable.

Saddle Tilt Set your saddle to a level position or slightly elevated at the front. To determine saddle tilt, use a carpenter's level placed on top of the saddle in line with level ground. Setting the saddle level or pointing it slightly upward keeps the rider securely placed in the "cockpit" of the bike. This allows the rider to have more control of the bike (through steering and leaning via the lower body). It also relieves pressure on your arms and hands, because you will not have to continually push to hold yourself in the saddle. Women sometimes prefer to have the saddle tilted slightly downward to relieve pressure on their crotch. Some men may slightly lower the nose of their saddles, especially for time trialing, but this angle could lead to urologic or neuropathic problems.

Saddle Fore-Aft Position Setting the fore-aft position of the saddle is best done on a stationary trainer. Pedal for five minutes and then stop with the right crank arm parallel to the ground (i.e., three o'clock position). Have a friend or professional drop a plumb line from the front of the knee toward the pedal. Generally, the plumb line should fall about a centimeter behind the pedal spindle (see figure 2.4). Cyclists who ride shorter distances at higher cadences using larger gears (i.e., criterium riders or time trialists) may want to have the plumb line bisect the pedal spindle. To move the saddle fore and aft, loosen the screws attaching the seat to the seat post, and slide the saddle along its rails.

Setting the fore-aft position of the saddle may take several rides after the initial fitting. If you move the saddle forward, be mindful that you are effectively lowering the saddle height, while moving it backward means

Figure 2.4 Rider with crank arm in the three o'clock position. Notice the plumb line falling just behind the pedal spindle.

you are effectively raising the saddle height. As a general rule, the U.S. Olympic Committee (USOC) suggests that for each centimeter the saddle is moved forward, the saddle height should be raised 0.5 centimeter.

Stem Length

Choose a stem length that feels comfortable, allows for the most aerodynamic benefit, and can be maintained through racing and training without causing constant discomfort during and after rides. To find the initial fit, the rider should be seated on the bike with arms bent comfortably (i.e., somewhere between a 110- and 130-degree angle between the upper and lower arm); the hands are in the drops, and the head is looking forward. A friend or professional should drop a plumb line from the top of the rider's nose, and the bob should bisect the stem at the headtube. Another common approach is assuming the same position and checking to see if the handlebar blocks the view of the front axle. If this fit is not being achieved, change out your stem. If you need to purchase a stem shorter than 80 millimeters or longer than 140 millimeters, you may need a different frame or a custom-built frame.

Height Difference Between Saddle and Handlebar

Smaller riders may prefer the handlebar to be 1 to 2 inches (2.5 to 5 cm) below the top of the saddle. Taller riders may prefer as much as 5 inches

(12.5 cm) difference. Numbness, aching wrists, a sore lower back, or excessive tightness in the hamstrings after a few trial runs may indicate the need for a smaller difference (i.e., higher handlebars). Cyclists who ride short events (i.e., criteriums or track) or events requiring maximum aerodynamics (i.e., time trials) will prefer a greater distance between the saddle and handlebar; 4 to 5 inches (10 to 12.5 cm).

Handlebar Width

The width of the handlebars should be the same as the width of the shoulders. The width of the shoulders can be determined by measuring across the front of the body from the ends of the acromion processes (i.e., the outermost point of the spine of the shoulder blade—see figure 2.5) then adding 2 cm for handlebars that measure center to center or adding 4 cm to handlebars that measure outside to outside. For example, if the shoulder measurement is 42 cm, you would want a 44 cm handlebar, which is measured center to center. Measure in centimeters because that is the industry standard. Unfortunately, the way that handlebars are measured is not standardized (similar to frames)—some brands measure center to center and some from outside to outside. A quick way to approximate handlebar width is to hook an unmounted pair of handlebars over the rear of your shoulders across your back. If the acromion processes fall directly under the start of the drops, the bars will most likely be a good fit.

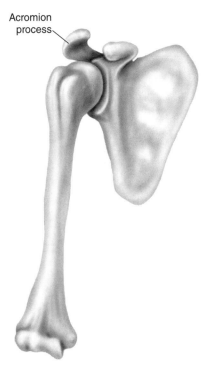

Acromion process

Figure 2.5 Feel for the bump above the shoulder blade for the acromion process.

You can also perform a simple on-the-road check. When seated on the bike with your arms bent and your hands in the drops, your upper and lower arms should be in alignment without putting pressure on your upper chest or causing your shoulders to roll in excessively. If you feel pressure on your upper chest, your handlebars may be too narrow. This can cause discomfort, and in the worst-case scenario, it can impede proper breathing. If your lower arms or elbows are angled outward to hold the bars, your handlebars may be too wide, which causes unnecessary aerodynamic drag.

Handlebar Tilt and Brake Hood Tilt

The proper setting as initially set by most bike shops is usually with the tips of the brake levers in line with the lower part of the handlebar (see figure 2.6). This can be set or checked by placing a straightedge under-

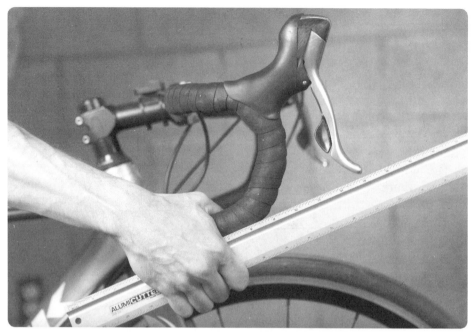

Figure 2.6 Tips of brake levers in line with lower part of handlebars.

neath the lower part of the drop and ensuring that the tip of the brake lever touches the straightedge.

You should note, however, that you will often find that the handlebars are not tilted enough (i.e., not rotated enough in their stem mount). The usual setting for handlebar tilt is with an imaginary line drawn from the bar end to the middle point of the seat tube as measured from top to bottom. A better position for many is rotating the bars even farther so an imaginary line can be drawn from the bar ends to the rear dropout. Because many road cyclists ride for extended periods with the hands on the hoods, this tilt position allows for a more relaxed upper body position. It may also make climbing more powerful by opening the hip angle. The compromise may be in reaching the brake levers when you are in the drops.

If reaching the brake levers is an issue, as is sometimes the case for women or riders with smaller reaches, other handlebar shapes and options may be considered. Handlebars with shallower drops—thereby putting the brake levers closer to the drops—may be a good choice. Check with your local bike shop to see what handlebar shapes may work for you. Using an adjustable-reach brake lever, or a shim designed by the brake lever manufacturer, may be necessary to permanently place the brake lever closer to the handlebar without compromising braking power or safety.

A Pro's Experience

Lance Armstrong (Seven-Time Tour de France Champion)

As mentioned earlier, like other greats of cycling, Lance Armstrong was extremely particular about changes to his bike fit. After overcoming cancer and winning five Tours de France, in 2003, he and his world-renowned coach, Chris Carmichael, couldn't explain a persistent pain in Lance's left shoulder while he was training. "At first we thought the cancer had returned; then we looked at his position on the bike," Carmichael said.

Armstrong had recently acquired a new bike that had a handlebar width of 40 centimeters. The handlebars of his previous bike measured 42 centimeters across. Armstrong switched the handlebars and, almost immediately, felt the pain start to recede.

A simple change of only 2 centimeters was causing Armstrong to suffer from an overuse injury. The narrow handlebars were impinging muscles, joints, and possibly nerves, causing Armstrong to feel pain. A well-thought-out analysis of his pain and possible triggers indicated that a switch to a handlebar with a larger width would solve the problem almost instantaneously.

What Can You Learn?

Problems with on-the-bike pain or discomfort are usually not as readily solvable as Armstrong's situation. Note that bike fit is extremely important—in Armstrong's case, down to the centimeter. You should be properly fitted on your race bike, attempting to reach a good balance between performance and comfort. Be cautious when trying out new equipment, and only make slight adjustments in fit as necessary.

Shoes, Pedals, and Cleats

Most shoes are compatible with all major cleat systems. Like running shoes, cycling shoes come in many shapes, which are usually manufacturer specific. Some cycling shoes have low heels, some have wide toe boxes, and some have narrow insteps. Although the choice of foot bed should be self-determined based on personal comfort level, the beginning cyclist is best served by finding the lightest shoe with an extremely stiff sole. An extremely stiff sole is necessary to transmit as much force as possible to the pedals (instead of having force absorbed by a flexible, "walking type" shoe).

Most brands have a wide selection of systems. Make sure that you purchase race-specific pedal and cleat systems. Race systems are set apart from other models; these systems are usually lighter and contain better bearings and springs with the highest adjustable release tension.

Finding the proper cleat placement is a process that occurs over numerous rides (and possibly numerous brands). A misaligned cleat can cause knee problems. To start, attach your bike to a stationary trainer. Attach

Measuring Components

Bicycle components are measured in different ways. No industry standard exists, just the whim and will of the bike manufacturers. Here are a couple of ways that manufacturers measure parts.

Center to center: Measurement is taken from the center of the bar or tube on one side to the center of the bar or tube on the other measured side.

Outside to outside: Measurement is taken from the outside of the end of the bar or tube to the outside of the bar or tube on the other measured side.

the cleats to the bottom of the shoe with the cleat centered laterally (i.e., side to side) on the mounting plate of the sole; the cleat should be center aligned with where the ball of your foot will be in the shoe. Mount the bike on the stationary trainer. Start by attempting to pedal with your feet in a natural walking gait—if you walk with your toes out a bit, then pedal with your toes out a bit. While attempting to pedal with your feet in a natural gait, note which way you would have to move the cleats to achieve this. Dismount and move the cleats. Repeat the process until you reach a cleat attachment with your feet closest to your natural walking gait and with your knees going up and down in alignment.

Your foot should not rub the crank or frame while pedaling. In addition, you should not feel as though your foot is being forced into a position—such as a position where your heel is being pressed against the inside or outside of the heel bed, causing pain or discomfort. If pressure exists in the sides of the heel, this means that your feet are not centered in the heel bed. Move your cleats, keeping your initial settings in mind, to relieve the pressure. If the pressure continues, try new shoes, look into custom foot beds, or obtain a professional bike fit.

In most cases, the knees should not stick out nor rub the top tube. Keeping the knees from doing this will usually help you achieve optimum power output. You may find that your saddle is too low, causing you to push your knees out in an attempt to lengthen your leg. If you are changing cleat systems, you may find that the *stack height* is lower (stack height is the height of the cleat along with its connection to the pedal), causing you to reach for your pedals. If your knees are out, raise the saddle slightly. If you are reaching for the pedals, lower the saddle slightly.

After you have set your cleats and fastened them securely to your cycling shoes, you may need to check your saddle fore-aft position one more time before heading out for a test ride. In mounting the cleat, you may have moved your knee forward or backward. Go for a short, low-intensity ride. If you feel tugging or pulling at your knees, adjust the cleats as follows:

- If pain or tension is felt on the inside of the knee, first try moving the cleat slightly—only millimeters—toward the inside of the shoe when turned over.
- If pain or tension is felt on the outside of the knee, first try moving the cleat slightly—only millimeters—toward the outside of the shoe when turned over.

If you feel as though you are being forced to "ankle" through your pedal stroke—meaning there is excess up-and-down movement of the heels or toes through the pedal stroke—you may need to slide your cleat farther down the shoe (in the direction of the heel).

If you use custom-made orthotics (or even store-bought inserts) in your walking shoes, you will most likely need them in your cycling shoes as well. If you've had numerous professional bike fits but you still have continued knee issues, pains in your lower leg, or a pedaling stroke with knees sticking out, you may need custom foot beds.

Once the cleats are fitted, ensure that they are set with a comfortable float—self-select and see if you are more comfortable with a lot of float (greater than 9 degrees), minimal float (about 4 degrees), or no float (0 degrees). If using spring release tension systems, ensure that your cleats are set with a relatively high release tension—easy enough for you to unclip, but difficult enough that you can't accidentally unclip in a jump or sprint. A cleat unclipping because of the tremendous pressures caused by a jump or sprint can have disastrous consequences for you and your racing comrades, such as a high-speed crash or a severe swerve (which may cause a high-speed crash).

Clothing

At a minimum, racers are required to wear a short-sleeved jersey, shorts, shoes, and an approved helmet. No sleeveless jerseys are allowed in competition. Wearing the jersey of a team not shown on your racing license is not allowed. If riding unattached, you should ensure that your jersey and shorts do not display another team's logo or sponsors. Most racers prefer the comfort of bib shorts (instead of regular shorts) for racing and training, because bib shorts do not constrict the waist and they allow for belly breathing. This form of breathing is recommended as opposed to pulling air high into your chest. With belly breathing, you relax your upper body and voluntarily pull down your diaphragm by expanding your belly, thereby taking full air capacity into your lungs. (Additional information on the psychological benefits of belly breathing can be found in chapter 7.) Bib shorts are also less likely to catch on the nose of the saddle when you are moving from a stopped or standing position to a sitting position. Socks, gloves, and sunglasses are optional, but they are a good idea. Socks prevent blistering of the feet and lessen your chance of getting athlete's foot (compared to riding sockless). Gloves absorb road shock through the handlebar. They also allow for a more secure grip on the handlebar when sweating, provide a place to wipe your lip or brow under heavy exercise, and protect your hands from *road rash* in the event of a crash. Sunglasses protect your eyes from insects, the sun, and flying road debris kicked up by other cyclists and cars. In addition, sunglasses add some protection for your eyes in the event of a crash.

Helmets

Helmets are approved either by ANSI (American National Standards Institute) or by the Snell Memorial Foundation. Riders should always wear a helmet when training and racing, whether or not this is required by country or state law. There is no excuse for not wearing a helmet. The Bicycle Helmet Safety Institute has compiled statistics from highway and safety transportation agencies in the United States and Canada. These statistics indicate that a very high percentage of the brain injuries suffered by cyclists can be prevented by a helmet (estimated at anywhere from 45 to 88 percent).

Clothes for Training

Depending on the climate in the area where you race or train, you may need some additional items of clothing. In cold weather, you may need the following: long-fingered gloves or lobster mitts; tights; wind jacket or sub-zero jacket; arm, knee, or leg warmers; head, chin, and neck covering; shoe covers or booties; wool socks; heavy base layers; cycling cap worn under the helmet to keep the head warm.

Basic Equipment List for Training and Racing

Here are the basics of what you need to get started in competitive cycling, along with the approximate cost of each item:

Bike: US$1,000 to US$6,000

Helmet: US$80 to US$200

Shoes: US$80 to US$250

Pedals and cleats: US$50 to US$300

Jersey, shorts, and socks: US$100 to US$250

Sunglasses: US$40 to US$200

In warm weather, you might want to have the following items: sleeveless jersey (for training only); light, wicking base layer; cycling cap worn under the helmet to shade the eyes from glare; lightweight socks; fingerless gloves. In wet weather, any of the items listed previously for cold weather can be useful. In addition, you may need the following: cycling cap to keep rain off of eyeglasses; rain jacket; rain pants; water-resistant shoe coverings; fender for your rear tire (this is not clothing but is very useful for keeping clothes somewhat dry); clear eyeglasses.

Other Important Equipment

All cyclists should wear eye covering when racing and training. On sunny days, sunglasses will allow you to see obstacles in the road. On rainy days, clear eyeglasses will keep debris out of your eyes. On cold days, eyeglasses will help prevent your eyes from watering. Choose an eyeglass system made from synthetic, shatterproof materials—preferably a system that comes with multiple lenses for varying light conditions. Many brands provide inserts (which are barely noticeable) for people who need corrective lenses. The unfortunate reality of cycling is that we are often sharing the road with faster moving traffic. The traffic can kick tiny bits of debris into the air, and this debris may hit you—therefore, it is best to cover your eyes at all times. Plus, in the case of an accident, your eyeglasses may help protect your eyes.

A stationary trainer—one in which you mount the rear wheel of your racing or training bike—is a necessary piece of equipment for a proper race warm-up, especially for short, intense events such as time trials or criteriums. Stationary trainers are not expensive and will make a difference in your results. For people who live in wintry climates, the stationary trainer will be a necessary tool for completing indoor workouts during the off-season.

All cyclists should carry a reliable pump and a seat bag on all training rides. Riders are not allowed to have these items attached to their bike during a race. Many cyclists choose to carry CO_2 cartridges and an inflator because these items are lighter and they allow the cyclist to fill tires more quickly with less work. However, a good hand pump may be a better option because it is more reliable, plus reusable. Many models are available today that are both light and reliable; these models can pump your tires up to maximum pressure. In your seat bag, you should carry a couple of spare tubes, tire levers, and a mini *multitool*. Getting stranded without these essential items or having to borrow them from a ride comrade will not do the trick. You should learn how to use these items so you can be self-reliant—the more intense and specific your training becomes, the more you may train on your own. The multitool should contain standard Allen wrench sizes (4, 5, 6, and 8 millimeter), a spoke wrench, and a screwdriver. Some well-built mini multitools even contain a chain repairing tool.

Chapter 3

CHOOSING YOUR RACE

There's a sound of being in the middle of the pack. There's a big sort of rush.

—Alison Sydor, silver medalist in mountain bike, 1996 Summer Olympics

ompetition is the heart and soul of cycling, whether it's beating out a friend at a town-line sprint or dropping riding companions on the local gut-wrenching hill. Friendly competition can be very exciting, but the true excitement lies in entering organized events. Races are the place to bring together all your work from training on the bike and to size yourself up against the local competition—especially riders whom you normally do not ride with.

Bicycle racing offers something for everyone, including road races, circuit races, criteriums, and time trials. If you choose to invest in other bicycles, you can also partake in track (on a velodrome) and cyclocross. All events have their particular pleasures—and pains. This chapter is dedicated to fleshing out the finer details of each event so you are able to choose which event matches your desires and style. In this chapter, each type of racing is explained, and information is provided on the process of entering and competing in your first race.

Road Races

Road racing is what most people think of when they picture bicycle racing— rolling through beautiful countryside, flying through towns of screaming fans, climbing sharp narrow hills, and descending in packs at unimaginable speeds. This is the keystone of competitive road cycling. With the increasing number of worldwide road racing events (as promoted by the UCI), road racing has become the most common type of cycling seen on television and the Internet.

Simply put, road racing is a bicycle race on the road. On the professional circuit, the road race is considered a point-to-point event, where you start in one town and end in another town. In some professional road races, the

© Human Kinetics

Road racing can take you as far or as near as you like. Some amateur races stay within the same town, while others start in one city and end in another.

start and finish are in the same town, with various circuits along the way. Amateur road racing contains similar elements to professional road racing, except the start and finish are most likely in the same town, and circuits of 10 to 30 miles (16 to 48 km) are used.

The following items usually define a road race:

- The race is a point-to-point event.
- A neutral rollout is used, meaning no official racing begins until the race leaves a starting area or town.
- If circuits exist, they are large (usually over 10 miles).
- The route normally includes hills or a technical set of turns to make the race challenging.
- The race may include a hilltop finish.
- The race route is through multiple towns.
- The race usually contains intermediate sprint contests for king of the mountain points.
- The race normally has a feed zone.
- Depending on category and age group, the race usually covers a distance of 30 to 110 miles (48 to 177 km).
- A race caravan containing referees and wheel support is located in front of and to the rear of the *peloton* (the main body of cyclists in a race).
- Event completion is dependent on a specified distance to a finish line.

Who Is Suited for Road Races

Road races suit the all-around racer—one who can climb, drive (or, *power*) a breakaway, sprint at the finish, and take advantage of team tactics. Successful road riders train a variety of physical disciplines—sprinting, climbing, tempo efforts—in order to be a jack-of-all-trades so they can adapt to race situations. In addition to being an all-around racer, road racers usually have a particular strength, such as a powerful sprint. If you want to enter road races, climbing should be a part of your weekly program. Hills are unavoidable on the open roads.

Through practice and gut instinct, road racers get a feel for good areas to attack in races—hills, technical corners, and windy areas—and they learn to use them to their advantage. An *attack* is an attempt by a racer or group of racers to leave the peloton behind. Racers need to participate in racelike group rides in order to prepare for this type of event.

A road racer should master bike-handling skills, because road races encompass daring descents, pack riding on narrow roads, and quick corners. Road racers must develop confidence in their abilities. In road races, it is usually not the strongest riders who win, but the riders who (a) are most confident under pressure, (b) can bluff their competition into thinking they are stronger, and (c) can convince themselves to endure while the other riders give in to mental, physical, and psychological fatigue.

Most road races last longer than 90 minutes; therefore, these races are long enough to warrant eating during the event. Energy replenishment is as essential as turning over the pedals. Learning how to eat and drink on the bike under duress will be essential to completing road races and having enough energy to push for the win. More information on fueling before, during, and after an event is provided in chapter 8.

A road racer needs to analyze the course before racing. This analysis should include doing the following:

- Studying the turns and their locations
- Studying the hills, including their distance and grade
- Examining the finish line to mark off where to start the sprint
- Determining wind direction on each section of the course to note where to hide in the *draft*
- Noting the location of the feed zone
- Noting where the road narrows, widens, or contains obstructions in order to determine where to launch or watch for attacks

Racers should also check the roster before the race to see if they know any of the registered competitors and to identify which teams and how many members are registered. Riding the course (preferably simulating race pace) before race day is essential. When analyzing a course, you should bring some team members along if possible. This is helpful because it provides multiple perspectives and makes prerunning certain sections at race pace more realistic.

Road races are best approached with a team plan, although racing solo may be your only option when starting out. The team should discuss who will cover attacks early in the race, who will cover attacks late in the race, who will be the lead-out in a sprint, and who will be protected until the hills really start or until the final sprint. A *protected* racer is a teammate for whom all other teammates work. For example, a sprinter may be a protected racer who sits in the draft while his teammates chase down breaks and set up a sprint with a *lead-out*. A climber can be a protected rider who remains in the draft until the race-defining hill. On the hill, the protected racer's teammates may increase the tempo until other teams drop off or are weakened by the effort—the protected climber can then attack.

What to Expect at a Road Race

Road races usually start at a pace that is slower than a normal race pace. Most of the competitors understand that it is nearly impossible to cover the entire distance at race pace. Once the first real environmental or geographic feature is encountered—such as a windy section, a hill, or a technical corner—the racing will begin in earnest. Racers will attempt to use the geographic feature as a launch pad for an attack. Riding near the front (in the top 20 riders) is essential in order to watch for attacks at important geographic locations.

After the first attacks go off, you can expect chasing by other riders and teams to bring the attacks back. Once the attacks are brought back, expect counterattacks. In a road race, vigilance for these cat-and-mouse games is important. In many instances, especially where there is extreme wind or difficult hills, a break will slip away, or the field will split. Be prepared to *bridge gaps* (i.e., close gaps between riders) when this occurs.

If the race does not contain many defining features, you should be prepared for a *bunch sprint*. A bunch sprint is when a large group of riders—many with a chance of winning—make a dash for the finish line. Bunch sprints can be dangerous yet exhilarating. Many racers who are at their physical limits of exhaustion are attempting to win simultaneously. If a race comes down to a bunch sprint, your position—that is, where you are in the pack when the sprint starts—will help determine your chances of being the overall winner. You cannot win a sprint from the back; therefore, to have a chance at victory, you need to be near the front when the sprint begins. Although you should be near the front, you also want to be out of the wind (i.e., you should be in the top five, but not first in line). More information on sprinting is provided in chapter 6. Knowing the finishing straight will assist you in attaining victory.

Where to Find Road Races

Road races are usually found away from major metropolitan areas. At the amateur level, the logistics of closing and temporarily blocking roads prohibits these types of races from going through major population centers. With the increasing use of automobiles, fewer and fewer road races are becoming available to amateur racers. The opposite is true for professional road races, because the increasing interest in the sport of cycling is prompting new events to crop up every year. Outside many major metropolitan areas, there are still enough open roads to conduct amateur road races. Many rural towns welcome the business of the racers.

Circuits

Circuit racing is a happy medium between road racing and a criterium. A circuit race provides many of the thrills and challenges of a road race, but within a more manageable geographical area. Many urban parks hold circuit races in the early-morning hours before the park fills with other recreationalists. Other circuits are held for short distances on lightly traveled roads.

Circuits are approximately 5 miles (8 km) each lap. In addition, each lap contains a race-defining geographic feature, such as a hill or a technical turn. A circuit race is advantageous for promoters because they usually do not have to close roads, provide wheel support, or disrupt multiple

Racers lined out in a circuit race during a fast section of competition. The faster the race speed, the more lined out the race becomes.

communities. This type of race is advantageous for spectators because they can stay in one spot and see the peloton multiple times. For racers, one of the advantages is that many circuit races are run multiple times over the same season, providing a testing ground for racing tactics and strategies.

Circuit races are defined by the following:

- The race usually includes laps of 5 miles or less.
- The race usually takes place on an auto-free road.
- Primes (pronounced "preems"), or lap prizes, are awarded on announced laps.
- Recurring races occur on the same circuit within the same season.
- Depending on category and age group, the race will cover a distance of 25 to 50 miles (40.2 to 80.5 km).
- Each lap usually has a defining geographical feature, such as a hill.
- The race usually does not include wheel support.
- The race usually does not include a feed zone.
- Race completion (finish line) is based on a number of laps.

Who Is Suited for Circuits

Road races normally suit one type of rider—for example, a road race on a flat and windy course will be good for sprinters, and a road race on a very hilly course will be good for climbers. Circuit races, because of their short laps, usually provide opportunities for all types of racers. It is not uncommon for the same circuit race to finish in a bunch sprint one week and then finish in a breakaway the next week.

Because the laps are repeated, this type of race provides a fruitful playing ground for racers to attempt different attacks and tactics. You can learn from your successes and failures each lap and thus improve your ability as a racer, even within the same race. Circuit races are a good place to begin for the beginning racer; you can preview the course easily, often repeat the same course multiple times in the same season, and actually learn and analyze the course each consecutive lap. For a more seasoned racer, the circuit race can be a training ground for practicing strategies and tactics that will be used in future road races on larger courses.

What to Expect at a Circuit Race

Circuit races are unpredictable. Many early-season circuit races are around 30 miles (48 km) long, allowing for a faster pace from the outset with more constant attacking. Circuit races that occur later in the season may be more like road races, because the length is longer and races are more likely to have breakaways because racers are tired from a long season.

Be prepared to race hard because the race action starts early. Some racers and teams will be using the circuit as a training race to help them build form. These races will also include racers who have studied the circuit intently and are looking to win or dominate the race.

Preparation for Circuit Races

An all-around training program can be used to prepare for circuit racing. The program does not need to include a large emphasis on climbing, although climbing skills may be necessary for shorter, power climbs on the course. Examining the circuit before the race is important. In many instances, this is easy to do because the race takes place on your actual training ground (e.g., races in urban parks). You also need to be familiar with the finish straight and the major geographical features on each lap. In addition, you should spend some time focusing on sprinting and pack skills. This will be beneficial because the roads for circuits are usually narrow, and pack position will be important as you run into the finish. Be prepared to carry enough water and food to maintain you through the whole race. Feed zones are not permitted in races under 50 miles.

Criteriums

The excitement of criteriums lies in their speed, the roar of a constant crowd, the fast corners, and the even faster sprint finishes. Because fewer roads are available for road races or circuits, criteriums have stepped in to fill the gap.

Criteriums are run on short courses that cover a few city blocks. For race promoters, the advantages of criteriums include a limited need for road closures (and permits), larger fields of racers (because races are held close to metropolitan centers), and the ability to service any part of the course quickly. The shortness of races allows racers to register for multiple events throughout the day. For example, a 35-year-old male racer can race in his category event, his age event, and sometimes a combined age and category event in one day.

Criteriums are usually defined by the following:

- The races are held on flat, fast courses.
- The distance per lap is less than 1 mile (1.6 km).

- The course includes tight, fast corners.
- The races have fast sprint finishes.
- The race involves close-quarter racing that requires good bike-handling skills.
- Large cash purses and prizes are awarded.
- Multiple prime laps are included.
- Race completion is determined based on time (e.g., 50 minutes); a bell signals the last lap once the allotted time is reached.

Who Is Suited for Criteriums

Criteriums are good races for powerful or explosive riders who can either drive the pace into the wind or *sit in* (i.e., sit in the draft of other riders, saving energy) and explode from the bunch in a sprint. Bike-handling skills are important so that a rider can hold position in a fast pack that is rushing around multiple corners. In criteriums, getting into a rhythm and flow is of utmost importance, because it will allow you to stay in the pack without wasting unneeded energy.

What to Expect at a Criterium

Criteriums are fast from the gun, and they involve nonstop attacking. Expect to make contact with other racers, bumping shoulder to shoulder or hip to hip. The pace will surge and abate with each attack and each corner. Teams can play a big part in a criterium by launching attacks and then controlling the pack by slowing it down through the use of *blocking*. See chapter 6 for more information on blocking and other race strategies and tactics.

Most criteriums come down to sprint finishes, but a carefully timed attack or a breakaway can sometimes stay away. Breakaways normally succeed in criteriums only if they are far enough ahead and around so many corners that they are out of sight. The old saying "Out of sight, out of mind" rings true in criteriums. Once a breakaway is out of sight, the pack loses interest and fights for the remaining places in a bunch sprint.

Preparation for Criteriums

Training for criteriums requires very little work on climbs. Intense group workouts are appropriate. These workouts should include large amounts of work at a high heart rate and with high power output. Racers should also perform interval workouts on their own to ensure that they can withstand the rigors of the surging nature of criteriums. The training plan needs to include work on sprinting and jumping skills. Sprinting is crucial to winning the race or attaining primes, and jumping helps the racer move with the pack out of corners. Sprints are maximal efforts in which high cadences and maximum power are generated for defined finishes—that is, either a race finish or a mid-race sprint. Jumps are short, high-cadence efforts (not at maximal effort) that require leg speed to close gaps or move up in pack position quickly.

You should show up to a criterium start line with a few hard efforts in your legs. As a colleague once said, "I show up to the starting line of a criterium dripping with sweat." In other words, racers need to perform a warm-up involving a race-type effort right before the start. This is necessary because once the gun goes off, it will be full gas. You should bring a stationary trainer to criteriums so you can perform an intense hour-long warm-up. Using a trainer guarantees that you will have a place to warm up, and it is a way to control your warm-up efforts. The trainer will also be used to cool down after the race effort.

Chapter 4 will cover the nuances of warming up and cooling down in more depth. The shorter the event, the more intense and longer the warm-up needs to be. Short, hard events such as criteriums require the racer to be prepared for hard efforts from the start. A hard, long warm-up will "open up the legs and lungs." This allows blood to flow properly to all parts of the leg muscles and heart, adjusts hormone levels, alerts metabolic pathways, and awakens psychological receptors, thereby preparing the body for the hard effort to come. Table 3.1 features an example of a criterium warm-up routine.

Time Trials

The time trial is also known as "the race of truth" because there is no hiding, no drafting, and no tactical advantages; it's just the racer against the clock. Time trialing is a special discipline that many racers bypass, but the ones who choose to embrace it usually become obsessed with it. Bob Kaplan, a talented national-level masters racer, says the following: "All great road racers are also great time trialists."

The effort put into training, equipment choices, and course selection usually pays off in improved performances in time trials. With time trialing, especially on similar courses over similar distances, racers can truly see if they are improving with faster times, faster speeds, or higher sustained wattages.

Time trials usually encompass the following:

- The courses cover fixed distances such as 7 miles, 10 miles, 20 kilometers, or 40 kilometers.
- The courses used are minimally technical (usually).
- The courses are on smooth roads.
- The courses are exposed to wind.

TABLE 3.1

Criterium Warm-Up (One Hour)

Time (min)	Gear	rpm	Instruction	Heart rate	Comment
0:00-29:00	39 × 27	60-70	Spin easy	Below 75% of MHR	Loosen up the legs. Get comfortable in the trainer. Grab water.
30:00	53 × 19	50-60	Push big gear	Below 80% of MHR	Get all those muscle fibers activated.
31:00	53 × 17	50-60	Increase one gear		
32:00	53 × 15	50-60	Increase one gear		
33:00	39 × 27	60-70	Rest	Below 75% of MHR	Let the legs recover.
34:00			Rest		
35:00			Rest		
36:00	39 × 27	90	Spin-up: increase rpm each minute	N/A	Don't look at HR.
37:00		95			
38:00		100			
39:00		105			
40:00		110			
41:00		115			
42:00		120			
43:00			Rest		
44:00			Rest		
45:00	53 × 19	90-100	2-min interval	80% of MHR	Build up through the interval to the target HR.
46:00					
47:00			Rest		
48:00			Rest		
49:00	53 × 17	90-100	2-min interval	85% of MHR	Build up through the interval to the target HR.
50:00					
51:00			Rest		
52:00			Rest		
53:00	53 × 15	90-100	2-min interval	90%+ of MHR	Build up through the interval to the target HR.
54:00					
55:00	53 × 19	90-150	Sprint first 10 sec of min	N/A	Sprint in the saddle (20 rpm faster) for the first 10 seconds of the minute.
56:00			Sprint first 10 sec of min		
57:00			Sprint first 10 sec of min		
58:00			Sprint first 10 sec of min		
59:00			Sprint first 10 sec of min		
1:00:00	39 × 27		End workout		Spin for a couple of minutes and head to the start line.

- The courses are normally flat or rolling, except in the instance of a hill time trial.
- The finish line is set by distance; the winner is the rider who posts the fastest time over the distance.

Who Is Suited for Time Trials

Time trialists need to put out large amounts of steady power over long distances—and they need to do this while holding an aerodynamic position. Normally, good climbers who are able to maintain the same power-to-weight ratios on the flats also make good time trialists. A very lightly built climber, though, may find time trialing difficult, especially on windy courses. It is no secret that the winner of the Tour de France is usually someone who can win or do well on climbs in the high mountains *and* can win or do well in time trial stages.

Time trialing rewards those cyclists who are equipment oriented, detail oriented, and focused on mastering technique. Repeatability, meaning the ability to perform similar wattages, speeds, and times, on similar courses in similar conditions, is of the utmost value in training, along with racing performance. Time trialing also rewards the self-motivated who can push themselves to the physical and mental limits. Expect this race to be a true mental test. In a time trial, you will push your body to your maximum sustainable aerobic heart rate and aerobic power thresholds and hold it there for the entire duration of the race. Expect yourself to be in an "arms race" to purchase the latest and fastest equipment. Buying the equipment and testing it are part of the fun.

Preparation for Time Trials

Athletes need to perform power workouts to build their sustained power output over long periods. They also need to perform position workouts to improve their comfort in the aerodynamic position. Time trialists should perform equipment testing to ensure that they are comfortable and in control when using aero equipment. Solid warm-up routines ensure that the time trialist hits the line ready to work hard from the start. Table 3.2 provides a sample time trial warm-up workout to follow.

TABLE 3.2

Time Trial Warm-Up (One Hour)

Time (min)	Gear	rpm	Instruction	Heart rate	Comment
0:00-29:00	39 × 27	60-70	Spin easy	Below 75% of MHR	Loosen up the legs. Grab water.
30:00	53 × 19	50-60	Push big gear	Below 80% of MHR	Get all those muscle fibers activated.
31:00	53 × 17	50-60	Increase one gear		
32:00	53 × 15	50-60	Increase one gear		
33:00	39 × 27	60-70	Rest	Below 75% of MHR	Let the legs recover.
34:00			Rest		
35:00	39 × 27	90	Spin-up: increase rpm each minute		Don't look at HR.
36:00		95			
37:00		100			
38:00		105			
39:00		110			
40:00		115			
41:00		120			
42:00		125			
43:00		130			
44:00	53 × 19	90-120	Sprint first 10 sec of min	80% of MHR	Sprint in the saddle (20 rpm increase) for the first 10 seconds of the minute.
45:00			Sprint first 10 sec of min	81% of MHR	
46:00			Sprint first 10 sec of min	82% of MHR	
47:00	53 × 19	90-100	2-min interval	83% of MHR	Use a TT gear. Build up through the interval to the target HR.
48:00					
49:00			Rest		
50:00	53 × 17	90-100	3-min interval	87% of MHR	Use a TT gear. Build up through the interval to the target HR.
51:00					
52:00					
53:00			Rest		
54:00			Rest		
55:00	53 × 15	90-100	3-min interval	90%+ of MHR	Use a TT gear. Build up through the interval to the target HR.
56:00					
57:00					
58:00			Rest		
59:00			Rest		
1:00:00	39 × 27		End workout		Head to the start line dripping wet and ready to go!

Time Trialing Position and Equipment

Although it is not required, having special equipment is beneficial for a racer in a time trial. When starting out in time trialing, you may simply modify your road bike with aerobars; this is suitable for getting your feet wet. As you become more acquainted with time trialing, a specific bike with specific equipment will become crucial.

Figure 3.1 Aerobars help cyclists create a streamlined form by shifting the body forward and flattening the back against the wind.

Equipment

- Aerobars: Aerobars allow racers to extend their body out on the bike and position themselves lower to reduce *drag* (see figure 3.1).

- Rear disc wheel: This type of wheel provides a smooth surface (as opposed to spokes) in order to allow the wheel to reduce drag. The wheel also acts as a sail, pushing or pulling the rider along in windy conditions.

- Deep-dish wheel: This type of wheel provides a deep rim in order to allow a bicycle to cut through the wind. Front wheels in time trials should be deep dish, while deep dish rear wheels are sometimes preferred to disc wheels in overly windy conditions.

- Time trial frame: This frame is designed to reduce drag; the frame has a lower profile, tubing in the shape of drag-reducing airplane wings, a steeper seat tube angle to move the body forward and open up the hip angle even when the cyclists is in the aero bars, and a wheel base designed for stability at high speeds while in the aerobars.

continued ⇒

- Aero helmet: An aero helmet reduces drag caused by the racer's head.
- Skinsuit: A skinsuit reduces drag caused by excess clothing catching the wind (see figure 3.2).

Figure 3.2 Wearing a close-fitting skinsuit will help eliminate drag.

Body Position

- Extended on aerobars: This forces the cyclist into a flattened, lower position.
- Back flat: This places the racer lower, reducing drag.
- Head up: Aero helmets are designed to be most effective with the racer looking up.
- Seat forward: Moving your saddle forward prevents the loss of power that can occur when the upper body is in a closer angle to the lower body. When the seat is forward, this keeps the hip angle open and in a similar angle to regular road riding.

Stage Races

The excitement of working through a multiple-day event that has a variety of one-day races, or stages, cannot be topped. For example, a four-day stage race may contain a time trial on the first day, a circuit on the second, a road race on the third, and a criterium on the fourth. Essentially, stage races are a chance to race the same competitors in individual races spread across continuous days. Stage races usually do not have category 5 or beginner categories, but they will most likely have category 4, or intermediate categories. Stage races provide a great opportunity to garner upgrade points not only for individual races, but also for the overall stage race. Upgrade points for the stage race are based on the rank you receive in general classification (GC). GC is your overall place based on cumulative time (or sometimes based on points) over multiple days or events; lowest cumulative time or most cumulative points earn first place on GC.

Stage races are exciting and challenging. In a stage race, you are challenging your competitors for first place on individual stages, and you are also tactically attempting to achieve your best overall performance—lowest cumulative time or most cumulative points—through the entire event. Stage races usually draw large community support, large crowds, and heavy regional competition. These races involve well-planned-out courses. Whatever your strength—whether it's time trialing, climbing, or sprinting—entering a stage race is an exciting endeavor that enables you to test your mettle against regional competition.

A stage race can be considered the culmination of your ability to use all the fitness elements highlighted in this book—physical skills, mental skills, tactical skills, and nutritional strategies.

Track Racing and Cyclocross

Track and cyclocross races are two other types of racing in which cyclists may participate. These types of racing require additional specific bikes. Track racing is the only cycling sport for some, but for road riders, it may be a way to gain additional fitness. The exciting aspects of track include short, fast races; the ability to enter multiple events in a single day (learning from each event and applying what you learn to the next race); and the variety of events. The various types of events may include the following:

- Points races: This is a mass-start race where points for first, second, and third place are given on set laps, such as laps 5, 10, 15, 20, and so on. The winner is the racer who accumulates the most points.

- Scratch races: These are mass-start races of a set amount of laps where the winner is determined by who makes it to the finish line first.

- Miss-n-outs: This is an elimination race in which the racer who crosses the start (finish) line last on each lap is eliminated from the race.

- Win-n-outs: This is a race of set laps where first place is determined by who crosses the finish line first on the first lap (this racer then leaves the track). Second place is determined on the next lap, and third on the next lap.
- Madisons: This is a race of set laps with two-person teams where one athlete races and is then relieved by his or her teammate. Reliefs are in the form of bike throws—the racer grabs the hand of the relieving teammate and swings the teammate into the racing action to maintain speed and momentum.

Another benefit of track racing is that it provides an excuse to buy another bike!

Cyclocross racing has grown in popularity to the point where it is the only cycling sport for some riders. Cyclocross is an excellent way to maintain or work on fitness in the cooler months of the year (i.e., autumn). One of the exciting aspects of cyclocross is that racers will be dismounting and running with their bike over obstacles, and then remounting. In addition, these races provide challenging, technical courses; fun, rowdy crowd support; and again, an excuse to buy another bike!

Exploring these types of events is worthwhile because they will help your overall fitness, allow you to work on specifics such as bike handling and sprinting, and provide a mental break from the rigors of road racing. Plus, crowds and racers at these two types of events are usually more fun loving, more easygoing, and even a bit less serious.

Entering Your First Race

You have the equipment. You've worked through some physical training. You can make it to the end of the local group ride with the lead group. Now's the time to make the leap to racing.

Your first task is obtaining an annual license or deciding to buy a one-day racing license. Then, the next step is tapping into your local bike shop or team members for upcoming race dates. Luckily, there are many Web sites dedicated to advertising and providing registration services for racing, making it easy to locate races and register for them. Finally, it's just a matter of getting to the race—and then you're off.

Obtaining a Racing License

Racing federations offer an annual license that racers need to have in order to compete in the governing body's sanctioned events. As mentioned, in the United States, the main sanctioning body for races is USA Cycling. The other main national sanctioning body in the United States is American Bicycle Racing. Most regional sanctioning bodies for races defer to the rules of these national bodies.

In the United States, competitive racers usually have at least a USA Cycling annual license. The cost of the license is around US$60.00. However, if you are just starting out as a racer, purchasing an annual license is not necessary. In most races sanctioned by national cycling federations, there will be a beginner or citizen category in which any racer can enter by purchasing a one-day license (usually for US$5.00).

The advantage of the one-day license is that it gives you the ability to try out racing without committing to an annual license. On the other hand, the advantage of an annual license is that it allows you to avoid the US$5.00 one-day charge at each race, and it gives you the ability to accrue points and race completions toward a category upgrade. An annual license also allows the licensee to take advantage of discounts on a variety of professional, personal, and cycling services from companies that sponsor the national cycling federation. Once you move into an intermediate category or above, you need to purchase an annual license to race in your category.

Locating Races

Talking to the other riders on your local group ride is a good way to find out when and where races will be held. Usually, as the weather warms, racers on your group ride will start talking about what races they will attend, what training they have done or will do before the event, and how they are going to fit into a team role at the event. Local bike shops often have an inside ear on when and where races will be held. They usually have race flyers on hand as well.

Finding Races Online

Many Web sites are available that provide race listings, including the following:

- www.usacycling.org
- www.TrueSport.com
- www.BikeReg.com
- www.SoCalCycling.com
- www.obra.org
- www.active.com
- www.SportsBaseOnline.com
- www.ffc.fr
- www.federciclismo.it
- www.fmc.com.mx

The more common way to locate races (and a fast way to register for races) is by searching the Internet for providers of regional racing listings. A quick Internet search using your geographic location and the keywords *bicycle* and *racing* will yield results. At races, you will most likely receive flyers for upcoming races. The road cycling community is a small one, but it is growing at a rapid rate, and it is very organized.

Registering for a Race

Once you've located a race, the next step is registering. If registering online, just put in the necessary information per the Web site's instructions (e.g., your name, your category, your emergency contact information, and the races you are entering). Be sure to fill out the information accurately to ensure that you are properly credited for any race placing you attain (and in case the race organizers need to access your emergency contact information). Follow the instructions for making payment. Most one-day races are priced between US$20.00 and US$55.00; criteriums and time trials are usually US$20.00 to US$30.00. Stage races have varying prices based on the number of event days and event types. If you choose to register for a race with a one-day license, you can usually purchase the license online. Many races allow for walk-up registrations on the day of the race.

Gearing Up for Your First Race

The following is a good checklist of necessary and important items to bring to a race:

- Helmet
- Shoes
- Jersey (short sleeve; sleeveless not allowed)
- Shorts or bibs
- Socks
- Gloves
- Wind or rain jacket
- Sunglasses
- Sunscreen

Before the Race

Be sure to bring a form of personal identification, such as a driver's license, along with your annual racing license (if you are an annual member) to the race. At registration, you will need to confirm your identity, age, and category. You will also sign any necessary waivers. This could include releases of liability required by the city, town, county, or race promoter, along with the release form required by the race sanctioning body. These forms require a wet signature. Again, write legibly in order to ensure that you will be credited for placing (and in case the race organizers need to access your emergency contact information). After confirming your registration, the race organizer will give you a race number to be pinned on your jersey.

Although seemingly a simple task, pinning on a race number does involve some tricks—and more important, some regulations. Be sure to ask at registration which side of the jersey the number should be pinned on. Race cameras will record the fast finishes, and your number needs to be placed on the proper side and in the proper position to be picked up by the camera. Obtain a minimum of four small safety pins from the registration table. Grabbing six safety pins is even better.

The race number should be on your middle back and to the designated side, but not low enough that it covers any jersey pockets you may need to access. The number should also be located to the camera-designated side. Pin one corner, and then work your way around to the other corners, ensuring that the number will be snug when you wear the jersey. If you have more than four safety pins, use the extras to pin the center top of the number and the outside side of the number to your jersey. These areas can catch wind, and a couple of extra pins will keep your number from becoming a wind-capturing parachute. A good option is to have a friend or teammate pin on your number while you're wearing the jersey. This will help ensure that the number is snug to your jersey and properly placed.

In some instances, you may have multiple numbers. Ask race organizers, or refer to the race guide or flyer, to find out how the organizers want the numbers placed. Organizers sometimes want the numbers on both sides of your back. Other times the organizers want the smaller number on your shoulders. For some races, especially stage races, organizers want additional numbers attached to your bike via zip ties. In time trials, the numbers are often placed on the middle of the back so that the spotter at the finish line can see your number once you cross the finish line.

At the Start Line

Reconfirm with the registration table that the races are being held at the times designated on the race flyer. Find a race official, preferably the chief referee (who is usually located at the starting area), and ensure that your watch is synchronized to the official's time. The chief referee watches for racer infractions, reports infractions to the chief judge, and oversees the starting, continuation, and completion of the racing. Synchronizing your watch will help ensure that you do not miss the start because of time discrepancies. It also ensures that you will be at the start line in time to obtain a good starting position.

You should end your warm-up five minutes before your race. Make sure that your water bottles are ready. Ensure that you have food in your jersey pockets for the race. Head to the start line. Not everyone can be on the start line in the first position, but you should make it your goal to be on the front line at every race. Race starts are unpredictable, and you do not want to be caught out or in a bad position before the race even begins.

Listen carefully to race rules and announcements, because the following items can be changed or modified on the fly: the length or time of the race, the finish line location, the road rules (such as the rule regarding double yellow lines, which specifies that you must stay to the right of the line [for races in the United States]), safety issues (such as road obstructions), and the number of placings or the prize amounts. Once the race gets under way, slot yourself in the top 10 to 20 racers to ensure that you are ready for any early attacks or technical challenges, such as hills or corners. Further discussion of strategic slotting can be found in chapter 6.

After the Race

After the race, if you have a race protest, you should immediately head to the chief judge's table or area, which is usually located near the finish line. The protest may be about illegal riding by a competitor (e.g., cutting corners, going over the double yellow line, veering off the racer's sprint line) or about the race itself (e.g., poor course marking that caused you to make a wrong turn, dangerous obstructions, improper or verbally abusive competitor behavior). You must lodge protests within 15 minutes of race completion. The chief judge determines penalties based on infractions observed by referees or reported by racers.

Avoid rash behavior toward other competitors. If you have a problem, calm down and defer action to the chief judge and race referees. At the end of a race, emotions are high, energy may up from adrenaline, and aggression is at its peak. Avoid arguing with judges or referees, and certainly do not have altercations with other competitors. Overall, keeping a calm demeanor before, during, and after a race is to your benefit. Before a race, remaining calm will allow you to focus on race tactics, a proper warm-up,

Postrace Gear Checklist

- Ice-cold water on hot days
- Hot, noncaffeinated tea on cool days
- Water and soap or wet wipes to clean your face, arms, legs, and crotch
- A towel for drying and wiping (or to provide cover when changing into street clothes)
- Recovery food or drink
- Light, loose clothing to prevent chafing of your skin and to allow your skin to dry (which helps prevent saddle sores)

and your overall enjoyment of the racing experience. During the event, staying calm will allow you to remain focused on the tasks at hand, such as preparing for a race-defining hill or finding position for the sprint. After the event, staying calm will allow you to assess maneuvers that worked or did not work during the event. It will also allow you to focus on cooling down properly. If you need to lodge a complaint, maintaining a calm demeanor will help you express a well-thought-out and rational complaint

A Pro's Experience: Picking Races

Sylvain Chavanel (French National Champion, Stage 19 Winner of the 2008 Tour de France)

Sylvain Chavanel, an extremely talented rider who exhibited all-around ability early in his career, was hailed as a future winner of the Tour de France. The pressure on Chavanel was high, because the Tour did not have a French winner in over 20 years. Each year, with the Tour as his big goal, Chavanel struggled to find his form and a good overall placing.

At the start of 2008, Chavanel knew he had other talents besides contending for an ever-elusive Tour title, so he convinced his director sportif to give him a chance at other races—ones that he had never ridden. Although racers usually have their own individual coaches, the director sportif is the person responsible for deciding the race strategy on and off the race course for the team.

Chavanel entered Dwars door Vlaanderen, an extremely popular, heavily stacked semi-classic race with a list of storied winners. He won the race, using a daring maneuver to drop his breakaway companions in the final kilometers to roll in for a solo win. As Sylvain said, "The fact that I started in this race has to do with a bet that I started with the director sportif. I wanted to prove that I can do well in Flanders and wanted to reinforce the team." He was referring to one of the monuments of one-day cycling classics, the Tour of Flanders.

Sylvain's surprise win was not to be doubted, because four days later in another semi-classic, Brabantse Pijl, he won again. This time Chavanel attacked from farther out, and he held off the peloton to the line for another solo win. "Just like [Dwars door Vlaanderen] I didn't know this course, as these are all races in which I've never competed, but apparently they suit me quite well." For a long time, Sylvain had no idea that he might not be suited for an overall victory in the Tour de France—and that he was better suited for the tough, harsh weather and courses of the Belgian road races.

What Can You Learn?

Picking your races is important. When you first start out, you should try all types of races to see how you fare—hilly races, windy races, flat races, technical races, long races, short races. Based on how you finish in the races, and more important, how you feel in these races, you can begin to determine what races suit your ability, talents, and style. Once you find your niche, you should play to it by choosing races, race courses, weather conditions, and times of year that suit you.

to the chief judge. Other competitors will appreciate your professional conduct as well—nobody likes a hot-headed racer who is continuing to act aggressive or confrontational after the race has run its course.

After a cool-down spin on the roads or on your stationary trainer—20 to 30 minutes of extremely easy rolling and riding—change out of your cycling clothes immediately. Clean and towel off your hands, face, and crotch with water and soap. Wet wipes can be very handy for cleaning up quickly. Change into loose-fitting clothing, which will allow your body, especially your crotch, to breathe. This type of clothing allows drying and decreases chafing; therefore, it helps prevent saddle sores. Grab something to drink that contains easily digestible calories (preferably a cool drink on hot days or a warm drink on cold days). Another option is to drink water or tea along with eating something solid that is easily digestible. Make this routine no longer than 10 or 15 minutes.

Head back to the finish area to see the posted results. If you think the posted results are incorrect, you have 15 minutes from the time they are posted to lodge a complaint. Lodge complaints with the chief judge. Being polite and stating the facts will give you a better chance to win your case than using overaggressive or obnoxious behavior.

Always go home and log your race results. This information is crucial when applying for category upgrades, and it is important when assessing your season at the end of competition.

Chapter 4

PREPARING YOUR BODY FOR COMPETITION

Always remember that the other chap is suffering just as much as you are.

—Fausto Coppi, two-time winner of the Tour de France and five-time winner of the Giro d'Italia

To quote a friend, Butch Richardson, "Training is the best part. Sometimes it's more fun than racing." Although racing is the reason why we train—with its excitement rolled into a short, intense period—training is the backbone of bicycle racing. Part of the joy of competitive racing is finding yourself growing stronger as you move through training cycles within the year.

This chapter provides guidelines for improving each element of your physical fitness for cycling. You'll learn how to perform training for specific elements, as well as how often you need to do so. Actual workouts are also provided, giving you the tools you need to train all of the individual physical elements.

Training Physical Elements of Cycling Fitness

Many amateur athletes concentrate on training their strengths year-round, and they ignore the development of their weaknesses. Others focus mainly on weaknesses in the off-season, allowing their strengths to flounder. A more efficient method that yields more tangible results is training all aspects of the physical elements of cycling progressively throughout the year. As Arnie Baker, MD—U.S. masters national champion and coach to world-class professional cyclists—said, "It is valuable to know about the elements of cycling fitness, because knowing what elements are important helps us decide how to train."

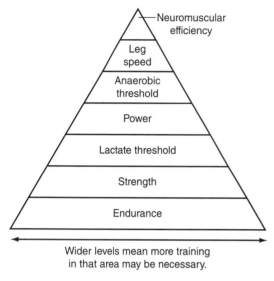

Wider levels mean more training in that area may be necessary.

Figure 4.1 Physical elements of cycling fitness.

Although this chapter focuses on the physical elements of cycling fitness, other elements exist as well—mental fortitude and nutrition can also be trained. By training and isolating individual physical elements—your strengths and your weaknesses—you will become a more well-rounded rider, and you will see measurable improvements. Your strengths will continue to improve, and your weaknesses will become strengths.

The physical elements of cycling fitness include endurance, strength, lactate threshold, power, anaerobic threshold, leg speed, and neuromuscular efficiency (see figure 4.1).

Before setting up training plans or workouts, you should know the general training guidelines for the various levels of competition. The physical training guidelines specify the yearly amounts of time, distance, and feet climbed that are recommended in order to be competitive at certain racing levels.

Table 4.1 identifies the commitment you will need to make in miles, time, and feet climbed for each category as you begin and advance in racing. The amounts listed may be considered general guidelines for success at each level. Meeting these guidelines does not reduce the need for other nonphysical aspects when racing, such as strategy, tactics, instinct, mental toughness, and luck. It takes time—months and even years—to reach some of these guidelines, so don't be discouraged when you first undertake training.

TABLE 4.1

Minimum Training Requirements for Each Racing Category*

	Miles (kilometers) per year	Hours per year	Feet (meters) climbing per year
Beginner (U.S. category 5)	5,000 (8,000)	400	350,000 (107,000)
Intermediate (U.S. category 4)	9,000 (14,000)	700	500,000 (152,000)
Expert (U.S. category 3)	12,000 (19,000)	1,000	750,000 (228,000)
Semipro (U.S. category 2)	15,000 (24,000)	1,300	1,000,000 (304,000)
Pro (U.S. category 1)	18,000 (29,000)	1,500	1,250,000 (381,000)
Worldwide pro	22,000 (35,000)	1,800	1,500,000 (457,000)

*These are general guidelines and not absolutes. Note that even though there are mileages, hours, and climbing amounts listed, the most important aspect is not *how many* but *how* you achieve these targets.

Beginning racers should expect to enter 10 to 20 races during a season. Doing more or less is fine, but 10 to 20 is the average. Intermediate and expert racers may also enter 20 races a season, although some enter as many as 50 races. Semipro and pro racers often enter 50 or more races a season; Worldwide pros may enter 70 or more races per season.

Planning a Workout Program

When you are planning a workout program, the best strategy is to think in cycles of varying sizes. The largest cycle is the *macrocycle*, which is one year or one season in length (sometimes longer). The macrocycle is divided into *mesocycles*, which are weeks or months in length. The mesocycles are divided into *microcycles*. Microcycles are weeks in length, and you develop your weekly workouts from these microcycles.

You should have specific goals for each cycle. Be sure to set measurable goals that are challenging yet attainable (independent of race results) for all macrocycles, mesocycles, and microcycles. Once you get into the rhythm of seasonal racing, you can stack macrocycles to create multiyear plans or even five-year plans.

Pick a race event as your target and count back four to six months. From this four- to six-month starting point, you will be able to lay out your training cycles. A sound method is to select two events separated by a few months during a racing season. Then develop plans that enable you to achieve your peak racing shape for these two events during that racing season. The closer you get to the peak, the more importance you can place on achieving your best performance in races—preferably independent of results. In between peaks, you can use races as training or learning experiences.

Mesocycles of Physical Fitness for Cycling

In training plans for achieving physical fitness for cycling, five mesocycles are commonly used: base, development, taper, race, and transition (see figure 4.2). In the base mesocycle, physical training is focused on the aerobic endurance element of physical fitness, along with preparing the body for the rigors of harder, more intense efforts. In the development mesocycle, the focus of training is improving all other elements of physical fitness: lactate threshold, anaerobic threshold, leg speed, neuromuscular efficiency, strength, and power. During the taper mesocycle, the athlete reduces volume while fine-tuning specific elements of fitness necessary for success in specific events. In the race mesocycle, physical training is focused solely on intensity—with reduced training volume and possibly frequency—to maintain elements developed in other mesocycles and to keep the athlete fresh for racing. The transition mesocycle is a period of recuperation, both physically

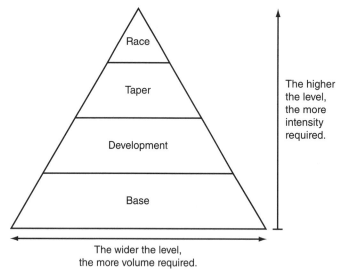

The higher the level, the more intensity required.

The wider the level, the more volume required.

Figure 4.2 Commonly used mesocycles for cycling.

and mentally, in order to prepare the athlete for tackling another season of training. Table 4.2 shows what the author's typical workout week late in the base cycle or early development mesocycles looks like.

Base

An old adage in bicycle training compares building an aerobic base to building a pyramid. The larger you build the base of the pyramid, the higher you can build the peak. Similarly, the larger you build your aerobic base, the higher you can build your racing fitness. After a postseason transition period, cyclists should begin a base mesocycle.

Beginning cyclists usually find it easy to push themselves physically. Each workout is a hard effort. Conversely, many beginners find performing endurance miles—which are easy aerobic efforts (e.g., less than 80 percent of maximum heart rate or less than 75 percent of 20-minute power [further explained on pages 76-77])—difficult, because riding easy does not "feel

TABLE 4.2

Sample Workout Week During the Late Base or Early Development Mesocycles

Day	Scheduled ride	Actual ride	Distance (mi)	Time (h)	Climb (ft)	Perceived effort (scale of 1-10)
Monday	Recovery ride	La Jolla to Encinitas	36	2.5	1,200	1
Tuesday	Strength workout in the mountains	Alpine to Julian	78	5.5	7,290	7
Wednesday	Endurance workout	North Park to La Mesa	27	3.6	3,700	5
Thursday	Strength workout in the mountains	Alpine to Mount Laguna	84	5.8	7,200	8
Friday	Leg speed workout	Fiesta Island	24	2.0	300	2
Saturday	Group ride	Team Saturday ride	43	2.5	2,180	5
Sunday	Off	Off	0	0.0	0	0
Weekly total			**292**	**21.9**	**21,870**	**28**

Macro-, Meso-, and Microcycles

Each cycle, no matter the size, will have increasing intensity or volume throughout the cycle. This is called *periodization*, whereby each cycle, or period, builds on the past period to provide ample and constructive development of physical elements. For example, if your base period (a mesocycle) is scheduled for three months, you may divide it into two or three segments (microcycles) that are each four to six weeks long. Each month, or microcycle, you will increase the overall volume of miles for the base mesocycle. Working a bit of recovery into each segment (e.g., in a three-month mesocycle, a week of rest every four weeks at the end of a microcycle) will be necessary as you transfer from segment to segment. Chapter 9 contains a table for planning out cycles for the race season. The following terms, attached to various cycles, will help you develop a solid training plan.

Macrocycle

One year, one season, or longer

Macrocycles can be stacked. For example, if you have a five-year goal, you would stack five macrocycles; the overall five-year period would still be considered its own macrocycle.

Mesocycle

Two weeks to three months

- Base mesocycle: one to three months
- Development mesocycle: one to two months
- Taper mesocycle: two weeks to one month
- Race mesocycle: two to three weeks
- Transition mesocycle: one month

Microcycle

One to six weeks

Within each mesocycle, you will set up segments, called microcycles, to provide a platform for increasing intensity or volume (and recovery). From the microcycles, you develop daily workouts.

like working out." Base miles will prime your aerobic engine and allow you to perform harder work in the development, taper, and race mesocycles.

Here is a good rule to follow: The longer the racing season, the longer the base mesocycle needs to be. For example, if your active race season is six months long and includes a couple of race mesocycles, this warrants a three-month base mesocycle.

Table 4.3 shows what a typical training week might look like during a base mesocycle. Specific workouts for each type of training appear later in this chapter.

TABLE 4.3

Sample Training Week During a Base Mesocycle

Monday	Tuesday	Wednesday	Thursday	Friday	Saturday	Sunday
Day off	Strength workout	Endurance workout on rolling hills	Neuromuscular workout	Day off	Endurance workout on a group ride	Long endurance workout

Development

After the base mesocycle, athletes move into a development mesocycle. During the development mesocycle, athletes perform specific structured work to develop the various physical elements: lactate threshold, anaerobic threshold, leg speed, neuromuscular efficiency, strength, and power. The athletes use structured *interval* work. The intensity (and possibly frequency) of training increase incrementally. Volume sometimes remains the same for experienced athletes, but often is reduced to allow for recovery from the ever-increasing intensity of efforts.

When you are planning the development mesocycle, knowing your target events is important because it will guide you on fine-tuning your training to concentrate on specific physical elements. For example, if your main event is a time trial, you should focus more effort on developing your lactate threshold. This element allows the athlete to put out more sustained, steady power over specific distances. Again, training all elements is important, but a training focus will provide the specific fitness necessary for target events.

If two race mesocycles are scheduled for a season, two development mesocycles should be incorporated. The first development mesocycle will be longer and will target all physical elements. The second development mesocycle will focus on elements specific to the second target event for the season.

Table 4.4 shows what a typical training week might look like during a development mesocycle. Specific workouts for each type of training appear later in this chapter.

TABLE 4.4

Sample Training Week During a Development Mesocycle

Monday	Tuesday	Wednesday	Thursday	Friday	Saturday	Sunday
Day off	Anaerobic threshold workout	Endurance workout OR lactate threshold workout	Strength workout OR power workout OR lactate threshold workout	Leg speed workout OR neuromuscular workout OR sprints	Racelike group ride	Strength workout

What Is Specificity?

Specificity means training specific elements at specific times to achieve a specific state of fitness. Attending group rides is a beneficial and necessary part of training; however, on these rides, you are at the mercy of the whims of the group for what type of training you receive. To achieve specificity, you need to perform most of your bicycle training solo or in small groups with similar targets. For example, if you are preparing for a criterium, you would specifically want to develop your sprinting and jumping skills, instead of, say, working on your steady tempo.

As Bob Kaplan, silver medalist in the U.S. Masters National Time Trial, says, "Every time you go out on your bicycle, even if you are going on a group ride, you should have a specific training purpose." Specific purposes include easy rides too, not just hard efforts.

Taper

After the development mesocycle, the athlete begins a taper mesocycle. During the taper mesocycle, the athlete fine-tunes specific areas of fitness that are necessary for success in the athlete's particular event. The volume of work decreases (frequency may also decrease), while the intensity of work remains the same or may even increase. Before all race mesocycles, a taper period is necessary in order to ensure that the athlete is fresh for the rigors of racing. Races entered during this mesocycle may be considered secondary target events; the overall focus remains on the primary target event that takes place during the race mesocycle.

Race

After the taper mesocycle, the athlete enters a race mesocycle. Reaching race fitness can sometimes seem magical and elusive; however, if this period is approached with a solid effort in the previous mesocycles (base, development, and taper), race fitness should last a couple of weeks to a month. The athlete should feel that all elements are at the best achievable peak for that particular time of season. Race mesocycles can be targeted for a couple times of year, focusing on a group of specific events.

Table 4.5 shows what a typical training week might look like during a race mesocycle. Specific workouts for each type of training appear later in this chapter.

TABLE 4.5

Sample Training Week During a Race Mesocycle

Monday	Tuesday	Wednesday	Thursday	Friday	Saturday	Sunday
Day off	Anaerobic threshold workout	Endurance workout	Power workout	Leg speed workout OR day off	Race	Race OR power workout

Transition

After the final race mesocycle of the season, the athlete enters a transition mesocycle. During the transition mesocycle, the athlete does not ride for at least one week, if not two weeks, depending on the length and intensity of the season. Skipping the transition mesocycle is a mistake because it could lead to a drop in performance months or even a year later. The body needs to recuperate physically and mentally in order to perform another macrocycle. Recuperation takes the form of active recovery (shorter, less intense riding) or complete recovery (no riding at all).

During the transition mesocycle, an athlete begins weight work and participates in other low-intensity aerobic sports (e.g., hiking). This is also a good time of year to set up "coffee rides." On these rides, a group of cyclists ride to a selected destination that is within an hour or so; the group then takes a long break before riding back.

Training With a Power Meter

Training with a power meter is the current gold standard for measuring improvement in performance and setting standardized goals for workouts. A well-calibrated power meter provides an absolute measurement (in watts) of the power generated by the cyclist.

For comparison purposes, wattage is paired with body weight, normally taken in kilograms. For example, a 140-pound (64 kg) rider who produces 300 watts can be said to produce 4.69 watts per kilogram (W/kg; that is, 300 W divided by 64 kg). Similarly, a 170-pound (77 kg) rider who wants to achieve the same 4.69 watts per kilogram needs to produce 361 watts. Table 4.6 provides a list of the target wattage needed for each category of racing.

TABLE 4.6

Watts per Kilogram Power Training Targets for Each Racing Category and Age Group*

	5 sec (W/kg)	1 min (W/kg)	5 min (W/kg)	20 min (W/kg)
Beginner (U.S. category 5)	13.7	7.1	3.8	3.0
Intermediate (U.S. category 4)	15.3	7.8	4.3	3.6
Expert (U.S. category 3)	17.0	8.6	4.9	4.1
Semipro (U.S. category 2)	18.6	9.2	5.5	4.6
Pro (U.S. category 1)	20.2	10.0	6.2	5.2
Worldwide pro	22.9	10.9	7.1	6.0

*These are general guidelines and not absolutes.
To convert pounds to kilograms, multiply by 2.2.

When you first start training and racing, owning a power meter may not be necessary. During the early stages of learning to race, you can perform workouts with a heart rate monitor and cadence sensor, or you can just ride by feel. These methods may be sufficient to help you show large gains in fitness. As time passes, gains in fitness may diminish without the use of outside methods for workout management, such as a power meter. Incremental improvements in cycling are known as "dialing it in." Power meters are an excellent tool for helping athletes dial in their fitness as they mature in the sport. To see what a power meter looks like, refer to figure 4.3

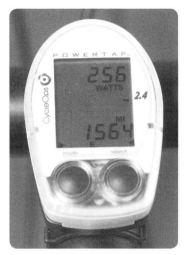

Figure 4.3 Power meter.

Purchasing a power meter is an economic investment. You may find power meters that cost around US$400, but some may cost as much as US$2,500. Only a few companies develop power meters. Some power meters use the bottom bracket as the source for extrapolating power, others use the rear wheel hub to extrapolate power, while still others use wind velocity and rider drag to extrapolate power. Higher price does not necessarily mean a better power meter. Explore the available options by talking with other riders who own power meters, local bike shops, and your coach. This will help you find out which system works for you.

Power Training Zones

Knowing your sustained power (wattage) at a select time interval will give you guidelines for specific workouts. Standard time periods include 5 seconds, 1 minute, 5 minutes, and 20 minutes. Using a 20-minute sustained power test is the most common way to determine training zones. The five zones identified in table 4.7 will provide an effective platform for structured training.

TABLE 4.7

Sustained Power Training Zones*

Zone number	Zone label	% of 20-min sustained power
Zone 1	Active recovery	<50%
Zone 2	Aerobic	50-75%
Zone 3	Lactate threshold	76-85%
Zone 4	Subanaerobic threshold	86-100%
Zone 5	Anaerobic	>100%

*These are general guidelines and not absolutes.

The test described in this section will estimate your 20-minute sustained power (SP). Your 20-minute SP number may increase throughout the season as your fitness increases, or the way you achieve your 20-minute SP may change throughout the season (e.g., at 95 rpm instead of 85 rpm). Although not covered in this book, if you want to fine-tune your fitness, you can perform 5-second, 1-minute, and 5-minute SP tests. With this information, you can choose workouts that target and cover these time periods. For example, you can use sprint workouts to improve 5-second SP or intense on-the-bike strength workouts to improve 1-minute SP.

You must be fully rested before performing the 20-minute test. Make sure you read the instruction manual for your power meter to determine how to mark each interval; you can then review and record the data and wattages later. The best conditions for performing the test are on a flat road (or a road with a slight rise) with steady wind and limited traffic, traffic lights, and stop signs. A closed park road with few pedestrians is ideal. The test can also be performed on a stationary trainer (if the trainer provides even resistance throughout the duration of testing).

Before performing any maximum efforts, you need to be in good physical health as confirmed by a medical professional.

Test for 20-Minute Sustained Power

Warm-Up: 20 Minutes

Ride steady and easy in the warm-up with heart rates at less than 75 percent of maximum for 30 minutes. Near the end of the warm-up, perform one 5-minute (1 × 5 min) effort at 95 percent of what you estimate to be your time trial heart rate. Then perform active recovery—rolling at cadences between 70-85 rpm at < 75 % of maximum heart rate (MHR)—for 5 minutes. (A discussion of MHR follows in the next section.) Next, perform three 1-minute (3 × 1 min) high-cadence (> 100 rpm) efforts in the easiest gear. Perform active recovery for 1 minute between the 1-minute intervals. After the three 1-minute efforts are complete, perform active recovery for 4 minutes.

Actual Test: 20 Minutes

Mark interval and start a 20-minute all-out time trial effort with cadence at 85 to 95 rpm. For the first 3 minutes, ease into a time trial pace.

Record all test conditions, including the course, weather, wind, and temperature. Also record your diet for the day before and the morning of the test. During the test, you need to remain mentally focused. Pacing during testing is crucial—meaning building by increasing power throughout, as you would in intervals. Attempt to maintain the highest average watts for the test period.

Review your test using your power meter software. Label the test interval for the appropriate time period. The average wattage for the 20-minute time period is your SP for that time period.

Learning how to do the test is part of obtaining maximum results. Repeat the test after a few months in order to ensure accurate and timely data.

Training With a Heart Rate Monitor

The heart rate monitor provides a fairly accurate measure for workout goals and improvements in fitness. Heart rate can be affected by weather, temperature, recovery, dehydration, altitude, motivation, and medication. As a result, heart rate data can vary. For example, it is not uncommon for racers to achieve the same effort (absolute power) in training as they achieve during races—however, on race day, they may achieve that same effort at heart rates up to 10 beats higher than their heart rate during training.

When training with a heart rate monitor, use percentages of MHR (see figure 4.4). The importance of percentage of MHR lies in the relative nature of heart rate. In the past, a rough formula of 220 minus your age was used to discover your MHR. However, this formula is inaccurate. Many cyclists aged 40 and above can achieve maximum heart rates of 200 beats per minute (bpm) or more. Conversely, many cyclists aged 30 and below cannot achieve heart rates of 175 bpm or more. The focus is not how high your maximum heart rate is, but how much of your maximum you can use for a given period. All things being equal, the athlete with the MHR of 200 bpm who can hold 90 percent of MHR for 10 minutes will most likely be beaten by the athlete with the MHR of 175 bpm who can hold 92 percent of MHR for 10 minutes.

Figure 4.4 Heart monitor displaying percentage of MHR.

Heart Rate Zones and Your Maximum Heart Rate

For setting your training zones, a simple system is best. The five zones identified in table 4.8 will provide an effective platform for structured training.

These zones provide a good estimate for performing specific workouts; however, you should note that as you build fitness and mature in cycling, you may be able to do more work at similar or lower heart rates. For example, early in the season, you may only be able to perform 20-minute lactate threshold workouts at 80 percent of MHR. When you are at your

highest racing fitness, you may be able to do the same workout at closer to 83 percent of MHR while feeling as if you are training at 80 percent of MHR.

To find your training zones, perform a maximum heart rate test. You will need a heart rate monitor and a bicycle computer that displays cadence. The best conditions for performing the test are on a flat road (or a road with a slight rise) with steady wind and limited traffic, traffic lights, and stop signs. A closed park road with few pedestrians is ideal. This test can also be performed on a stationary trainer (if the trainer provides even resistance throughout the duration of testing).

Before performing any maximum efforts, you need to be in good physical health as confirmed by a medical professional.

TABLE 4.8

Heart Rate Training Zones*

Zone number	Zone label	% of MHR
Zone 1	Active recovery	<75%
Zone 2	Aerobic	76-80%
Zone 3	Lactate threshold	81-85%
Zone 4	Subanaerobic threshold	86-90%
Zone 5	Anaerobic	>90%

*These are general guidelines and not absolutes.

Intensity Versus Volume

Intensity refers to the level of effort. *Volume* refers to the amount of time spent performing any effort. Volume always affects intensity, but intensity does not always affect volume. For example, a four-minute interval at 90 percent of your maximum heart rate (MHR) is considered an intense effort. In addition, doing six of these four-minute intervals is considered a very intense workout. On the flip side, a leisurely ride at 75 percent of your MHR may be considered low intensity if it lasts only an hour or two. Yet, a ride at 75 percent of your MHR that lasts for seven hours is considered very intense for most people.

Set intensity and volume parameters before workouts. Without parameters, you may perform work that is too intense or work that is too easy. Do not get caught in the middle, where you are always working "kind of hard" or "kind of easy." When you go hard, go really hard. When you go easy, go really easy.

Test for Finding Maximum Heart Rate

Warm-Up: 20 Minutes

Ride steady and easy in the warm-up at an estimated 75 percent of MHR for 30 minutes. Near the end of the warm-up, perform one 5-minute effort (1 × 5 min) at 95 percent of what you estimate to be your time trial heart rate. Perform active recovery—rolling at cadences between 70-85 rpm at < 75 % of MHR—for 5 minutes. Next, perform three 1-minute (3 × 1 min) high-cadence (> 100 rpm) efforts in the easiest gear. Perform 1 minute of active recovery between the 1-minute intervals. After the three 1-minute efforts are complete, perform active recovery for 4 minutes.

Actual Test: Variable Time Length

Mark the interval. Starting at 80 rpm, increase the cadence by 2 or 3 rpm or increase your gearing by one gear every 2 minutes. When you cannot hold your cadence for the 2 minutes, perform an all-out sprint for 30 seconds. Look at your heart rate monitor at this point; the value should be a good estimate of your maximum heart rate.

Compare the test value to the MHR values you see when racing in order to find the most accurate estimate.

Workouts

The following workouts train various physical elements. Integrating the various workouts at the indicated time of the year is part of periodization. At a minimum, to perform these workouts properly, you will need a heart rate monitor and cadence monitor. The gold standard for monitoring performance both in real time and in analysis is a power meter.

Intervals

An important concept in bicycle training is the *interval*. Simply stated, an interval is a set period of defined work followed by a set period of recovery. By doing intervals, the athlete is able to achieve more overall work because the work is broken into smaller segments. A good metaphor is moving items from one house to another. People do not pack all of their belongings into the biggest box that will possibly fit through the front door. Instead, people distribute their belongings into small boxes that are all approximately the same size; this way, a person can lift the boxes individually, carry them to a truck, and stack them. Intervals are the same—the work is broken into smaller, similarly sized, organized segments. Here is a sample interval prescription: 4 repetitions of 4-minute efforts at 90 percent of MHR with 4 minutes rest in between (4 × 4-min 90% MHR × 4 min).

Performing intervals properly will allow you to achieve the greatest fitness from an interval session. Figure 4.5 shows actual heart rate and power data for an athlete who performed an interval improperly.

The athlete has an uneven start (as shown by the power line) and then proceeds to push too hard too early, thereby going beyond the power threshold and steadily losing power from the halfway point to completion. The white dotted line shows the power target, which the athlete does not maintain. In addition, the technique has caused the athlete's heart rate to climb quickly and rapidly, pushing it over the threshold heart rate target (black dotted line) early and throughout the last half of the interval. Figure 4.6 shows actual

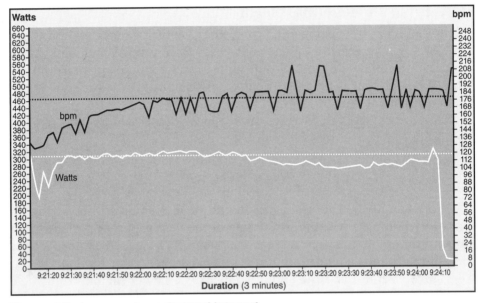

Figure 4.5 Improperly performed interval.

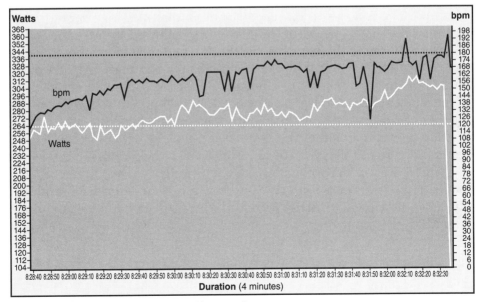

Figure 4.6 Properly performed interval.

heart rate and power data of a different athlete who performed an interval properly.

The athlete shows even power at the start of the interval and then an even rise beyond target power. The athlete also shows an even heart rate distribution to a peak at the target heart rate threshold near the end of the interval. A proper interval provides an even ramp of power and heart rate, thereby producing the most work with the least amount of wasted effort.

Warm-Up and Cool-Down

Warming up and cooling down are essential to performing exercises properly and without injury. Plunging right into hard work is never a good idea because you will most likely not achieve workout targets. A proper warm-up opens capillaries, activates neuromuscular systems, regulates breathing, activates biological cooling systems, and warms up muscles. A cool-down relaxes muscles, stretches muscles, and allows your heart rate to efficiently return to resting rates. Warming up should involve riding at recovery heart rates or power at first, then progressively adding in short, intense efforts as the workout or race nears. Cooling down should involve riding at recovery heart rates or power for the entire cool-down period.

As a general rule, the shorter, more intense your workout, the longer your warm-up and cool-down should be. For example, a sprint or power workout will require a 20- to 30-minute warm-up with a 20-minute cool-down, whereas an endurance workout requires a 10-minute warm-up and cool-down. Sample time trial and criterium warm-ups are available in chapter 3.

Understanding "Threshold" Terminology

Anaerobic threshold—The point at which you begin working your muscles almost exclusively without oxygen. Little to no fat burning occurs because your body relies almost solely on carbohydrate sources.

Lactate threshold—The point at which blood lactate begins to accumulate beyond lactate clearance. When lactic acid builds up in muscles, it causes feelings of fatigue. Lactic acid is converted into energy via the lactate shuttle, but the body relies more and more on carbohydrate sources as the lactate threshold is crossed.

$\dot{V}O_2max$—The highest rate of oxygen consumption achievable during exhaustive exercise. At $\dot{V}O_2max$, it is possible for exercise intensity to increase without the associated rise in oxygen consumption for short periods of time, but this effort may be unsustainable.

Endurance Workout

The following endurance workouts will build your aerobic base. A strong aerobic base enables you to hang in and attack in long races. It also enables you to work harder later in the season so you can reach a higher level of racing fitness.

Period: Base, development

Endurance workout 1: Warm up for 20 minutes. Ride for 2 to 3 hours in HR zones 1 and 2 or at 50 to 75 percent of your 20-minute SP on a rolling course. Use a cadence of 90 to 100 rpm. Keep your hands on the tops or hoods. Ride in the saddle by equipping your bike with proper gearing. Use mainly a small chainring on hills and a big chainring on flats.

Endurance workout 2: Warm up for 20 minutes. Ride for 2 hours in high HR zone 2 or at 75 percent of your 20-minute SP on a very hilly course. Use a cadence of at least 80 rpm on hills and at least 100 rpm on flats. Keep your hands mainly in the drops, even on hills. Ride in and out of the saddle on climbs, without causing surges in heart rate or power.

Lactate Threshold (LT) Workout

LT workouts will improve your ability to clear and utilize lactic acid within your system when maintaining steady, tempo efforts (such as in break-aways, while chasing breakaways, or in time trials).

Period: Development, race

LT workout 1: Warm up for 10 minutes. Ride for 30 minutes in HR zone 3 or at 75 to 85 percent of your 20-minute SP on a flat or slightly rolling course. Use a cadence of 80 to 90 rpm. Alternate your hands on the hoods and drops. Add this workout into the middle section of a longer endurance workout.

LT workout 2: Warm up for 15 minutes. Perform three or four intervals of 15 minutes in high HR zone 3 to low HR zone 4 or at 85 percent of your 20-minute SP on a flat or slightly rolling course. Do 2 minutes of active rest (HR zone 1) between intervals. Use a cadence of 80 to 90 rpm. Keep your hands on the hoods or drops. In each interval, build from the higher part of HR zone 3 to the lower part of HR zone 4, or build up to and through 85 percent of your 20-minute SP. Build by increasing gear while maintaining cadence.

Anaerobic Threshold (AT) Workout

AT workouts will improve your $\dot{V}O_2max$, thereby raising your anaerobic threshold and allowing you to go harder for longer periods.

Period: Development (late), taper, race

AT workout 1: Warm up for 30 minutes. Perform six intervals of 4 minutes in HR zone 5 or at 100 percent (or higher) of your 20-minute SP. Perform these intervals on a flat and windy course or on a hill with a sustained 3 to 5 percent gradient. Do 4 minutes of active rest between intervals. Use a cadence of 90 to 100 rpm. Keep your hands in the drops. In each interval, build from the upper part of HR zone 4 to HR zone 5, or build up to and through the SP zone. Build by increasing gear or cadence.

AT workout 2: Warm up for 30 minutes. Perform eight intervals as follows: 1 minute, 2 minutes, 3 minutes, 4 minutes, 4 minutes (again), 3 minutes, 2 minutes, 1 minute. Perform these intervals in HR zone 5 or at 100 percent (or higher) of your 20-minute SP. The intervals should be performed on a flat and windy course or on a hill with a sustained 3 to 5 percent gradient. Do 4 minutes of active rest between intervals. Use a cadence of 90 to 100 rpm. Keep your hands in the drops. In each interval, build from the lower part of HR zone 5 to the zone limits, or build up to and through the SP zone. Build by increasing gear or cadence.

Leg Speed Workout

The leg speed workouts will improve your ability to change cadences rapidly. This skill is especially important in sprints, during hill attacks, and when coming out of corners.

Period: Development, taper, race

Leg speed workout 1: Spin in the easiest gear, starting at 60 rpm and increasing 5 rpm every minute until reaching maximum attainable cadence. Good sprinters can achieve cadences of over 140 rpm. Bouncing in the saddle with uneven cadence indicates that you have reached your maximum. Repeat this drill three times with 2 minutes of active rest between the sets. Perform in HR zone 1 or at 50 percent or less of your 20-minute SP. This workout should be performed on a flat course. Alternate your hands on the tops, hoods, and drops.

Leg speed workout 2: Spin in the easiest gear, starting at 60 rpm and increasing 5 rpm every 15 seconds until reaching maximum attainable cadence. Hold maximum attainable cadence for 1 minute. Good sprinters can achieve cadences of over 140 rpm. Bouncing in the saddle with uneven cadence indicates that you have reached your maximum. Repeat this drill four times with 5 minutes of active rest between the sets. Perform in HR zone 1 or at 50 percent or less of your 20-minute SP. This workout should be performed on a flat course. Alternate your hands on the tops, hoods, and drops.

Neuromuscular Workout

Neuromuscular workouts will improve your body's ability to pedal efficiently, which will allow you to waste less energy for each pedal stroke. In effect, you are teaching your brain to fire your legs in a coordinated fashion in order to develop the most power with the least loss of energy.

Period: Base, development

Neuromuscular workout 1: Warm up for 10 minutes. Perform isolated leg training (ILT) by unclipping one foot and pedaling with the other leg at 80 rpm in your *easiest* gear for 3 minutes. Clip back in and switch legs. Repeat this exercise three times for each leg with 1 minute active rest between sets. Perform ILT in HR zone 1 or at less than 50 percent of your 20-minute SP. The drill should be done on a flat course. Alternate your hands on the tops, hoods, and drops. This drill takes skill and practice, but it has a quick learning curve. Make sure you can control your bike effectively before unclipping and pedaling with one foot. This drill should not be performed on active roadways or on roadways with uneven surfaces.

Neuromuscular workout 2: Warm up for 10 minutes. In this drill, one leg does 90 percent of the work until fatigue, then the other leg does 90 percent of the work until fatigue. Perform for 4 to 6 minutes. Pedal in an easy gear at 80 to 90 rpm. Repeat three times with 1 minute active rest between sets. You need to really concentrate on pedaling smooth circles with the active leg and "turning off" and floating the inactive leg. Perform ILT in HR zone 1 or at less than 50 percent of your 20-minute SP. This drill should be done on a flat course. Alternate your hands on the tops, hoods, and drops.

Strength Workout

These on-the-bike strength workouts will build your leg strength, allowing your body to withstand repeated jumps and sustained hard efforts in races.

Period: Base, development

Strength workout 1: Warm up for 20 minutes. Perform isolated leg training (ILT) by unclipping one foot and pedaling with the other leg at 50 to 60 rpm in a hard gear for 3 minutes. Clip back in and switch legs. Repeat this exercise three times for each leg with 1 minute active rest between sets. Perform ILT in HR zones 1 to 2 or at 60 to 75 percent of your 20-minute SP. This drill should be done on a flat course. Alternate your hands on the tops, hoods, and drops. Concentrate on pushing down hard on the downstroke and letting the momentum carry your foot through the upstroke. Do not pull up when bringing your pedal up over the top. Make sure you can control your bike effectively before unclipping and pedaling with one foot. This drill should not be performed on active roadways or on roadways with uneven surfaces.

Sample workout 2: Warm up for 20 minutes. Climb long steady hills that take at least 5 minutes to climb. The hills should have a 4 to 6 percent gradient. Use a cadence of 50 to 70 rpm. Perform in HR zones 1 to 2 or at 60 to 75 percent of your 20-minute SP. Do not ignore heart rate zones just because the objective is building leg strength (i.e., not working on cardiovascular capacity). Protect your knees by watching your pedaling form and not pulling up too vigorously on the upstroke. Alternate 5-minute climbing sections with standing and sitting.

Power Workout

Power is defined as work divided by time. To improve power, you either perform more work—that is, you apply more force over a given distance of a pedal stroke—or you reduce the time—that is, you increase your pedaling rate to apply the same force but more rapidly. These workouts will build your body's capacity to develop the most work over short periods of time. This will improve your sprinting as well as your ability to surge and break away.

Period: Development (late), taper, race

Power workout 1: Warm up for 30 minutes. Perform five jumps of 10 to 12 revolutions of the crankset, alternating in-the-saddle jumps with out-of-saddle jumps. Jumps are different from sprints in that jumps focus on acceleration based on the maximum cadence attainable. (Although sprints involve using a maximum cadence as well, sprints include an element of strength because you are using a larger gear.) Use a cadence greater than 120 rpm. Repeat this exercise three times. Actively recover for 1 minute between jumps and for 5 minutes between sets. Perform the exercise in a moderate sprinting gear. Each jump and each set should be progressively more intense. There are no HR or SP zones for this exercise.

Power workout 2: Warm up for 30 minutes. Perform four sprints of 15 seconds. Repeat this exercise three times. Actively recover for 3 minutes between sprints and for 5 minutes between sets. Perform the exercise in a moderate sprinting gear that allows you to finish each set with the same gear. Even though this is not a sprinting exercise, you should practice good sprinting form while in the moderate gear. There are no HR or SP zones for this exercise.

Stationary Trainers

Most workouts can be performed on a stationary trainer (see figure 4.7). Trainers provide a road feel by using a wind, fluid, or magnet mechanism attached to the roller. Wind mechanisms usually provide the best road feel and progressive resistance, but they are usually very loud. The resistance

Figure 4.7 Bicycle on stationary trainer with front wheel elevated to simulate on-the-road placement.

of a wind trainer comes from a fan attached to the trainer, which attaches to the rear wheel of the bicycle. Fluid mechanisms provide similar road feel to wind trainers, and they are quieter; however, when the fluid heats up, it may affect the consistency of the resistance. The resistance of a fluid trainer comes from a fluid-encased fan or rudder attached to the trainer, which attaches to the rear wheel of the bicycle. A trainer with a magnet mechanism is the quietest but provides the least road feel; this type of trainer may not provide enough resistance to enable you to perform workouts to their maximum.

Purchasing a trainer is recommended for all racers. Racers who live where winter can be severe will find trainers to be an invaluable training tool during winter months. Others will find the trainer to be a great alternative to suiting up and heading out on the road if time is prohibitive. For races, a trainer is usually necessary for a proper warm-up because roads that are adequate for warm-ups are often not available.

The benefits of performing workouts on a stationary trainer are many:

● Conditions are repeatable.

● The trainer is located conveniently at your home.

● The indoor location eliminates the need to worry about rain, snow, or cold.

● The focus is on training and not on stoplights, cars, or pedestrians.

● Using a trainer is safer than riding on the road.

● Workouts are concentrated, because coasting on the bike gets you nowhere.

● A trainer is the perfect tool for a repeatable and concentrated warm-up or cool-down for a race.

Always place a large fan in front of you when on a stationary trainer to replace the cooling effects of windchill. Keep a towel handy to wipe your face and hands. Keep cold drinks nearby. To prevent saddle sores, change shorts for trainer workouts over 2 hours. Stand occasionally to relieve pressure on the crotch and to simulate actual road riding.

If you perform some or all of your interval sessions on the stationary trainer, you are guaranteed to have accurate and repeatable measurements of performance. At a minimum, a stationary trainer should have a cadence monitor and a heart rate monitor. These are necessities for tracking performance and performing workouts. A trainer with a power meter is the gold standard.

A Pro's Experience

Johan Museeuw (World Champion; Winner of Tour of Flanders, Paris-Roubaix, and Tour de France Stages)

A man who knew how to train properly to overcome adversity was Johan Museeuw. He was known for his gradual approach to training, his belief in his training plans, and his ability to focus on training so he could return to racing when his cycling career seemed to be over—a couple of times.

A wicked crash on the slick cobblestones of the Arenberg Forest in the 1998 Paris-Roubaix, the queen of one-day bicycle racing classics, almost ended his career. Gangrene set in because of improper cleaning of a knee wound by medical personnel, and they almost had to amputate the leg. As it turned out, they didn't amputate the leg, and Museeuw responded by recovering, training, and coming up with a win in the 2000 Paris-Roubaix. Tragedy struck again when he crashed on his motorcycle in the summer of 2000. He fought back yet again for another Paris-Roubaix win in 2002, among other victories.

Museeuw's glory started in a small way, but he kept stretching his personal limits. In his first race outside of Belgium, the Tour of Austria, Museeuw finished the first stage 30 minutes behind the winner. He was alone, numb from the cold, and reportedly crying on his bike. He did not abandon the race though. In the same manner, he would continue to break down barriers during the remainder of his career—with dogged determination.

Museeuw was infamous for training alone for periods as long as 4 months. He knew his specific training goals would not be achievable in large groups. He would ride ruthlessly into the wind for hours on end. When he adopted heart rate training later in his career, he took himself into the red repeatedly on hard days, for unbearably long periods. He would impose kilometer per hour "basements" on some training rides—on the order of 43 kilometers per hour (about 27 mph)—and he'd refuse his body when it told him to slow down.

Museeuw's good friend and teammate (and world-class racer in his own right) Wilfried Peeters says of Museeuw, "Out of 100 pros, 95 won't be able to deal with Johan's training rhythm. A young rider who tries to constantly keep up with him will, so to speak, destroy his body. Johan has both the body and the willpower to work those heavy training schedules. He sometimes has some riders that live in his region ride with him, but very few can keep up for a few days in a row."

Peeters explains that after brutal group training rides, Museeuw would ride another half hour extra, because it was mentally very important to him.

What Can You Learn?

Although Museeuw's superhuman feats are not to be replicated or attempted by amateurs, you can learn many things from him—including the value of always having a plan, believing in the plan, and building gradually through your bicycle training and racing. You will experience low physical and mental points, but you need to stay focused on training and building properly. You will overcome adversity and become a better, more seasoned racing cyclist. Museeuw always kept his eye on the prize, and he used proper, focused, and well-laid-out training to beat his competitors—and his training partners.

Physical Development Curve

Gaining fitness does not occur linearly. Fitness is gained via stair steps. Initially, by working through a set training program, you will achieve large gains. This is a function of performing measurable and repeatable tasks. After this initial large gain, you should be prepared for fitness plateaus. More important, you should be prepared for drops in fitness at the end of the race season, when you are tired and need a break.

The good news is, for every plateau, there is usually a gain. The gain will not happen quickly, but it will occur, and you will be paid off for all of your focus and training. Similarly, if you take a proper transition period of recovery—in which your fitness will drop a bit—you should be paid off with greater fitness during the following race season.

Tracking Your Progress

In addition to writing out yearly, monthly, and weekly training plans, you should also keep a daily log of completed workouts. Note workout statistics, such as duration, distance, total elevation gained, average speed, average power, average heart rate, interval heart rates, and interval wattages. Include a brief comment on the ride course and any observations about the workout. You will also find it useful to track your morning weight, hours of sleep, and level of stress (on a scale of 1 to 10, with 10 being the most stress). By keeping the log, you will be able to pinpoint which workouts and workout sequences worked and did not work. In addition, you will be able to deduce what factors contributed to great or poor performance. The appendix contains a sample format for a daily log.

Recovery

Recovery is important on all levels. On a large scale, you need to recover completely from each macrocycle—meaning, at the end of the season, you should take time off the bike or participate in other low-intensity endurance sports. Recovery from mesocycles and microcycles is also necessary.

For each mesocycle, an athlete should plan a microcycle of active recovery; this microcycle should last a week to a week and a half. *Active recovery* means you continue to train (maintaining frequency), but you cut intensity by 30 to 50 percent, and you cut volume by 20 to 40 percent. Within each microcycle, recovery is important as well. If, for example, you are performing a microcycle containing intervals during the development mesocycle, you will need to work in some active recovery days of easy riding in easy gears (i.e., low wattage or low percentage of heart maximums). Further, within each workout, you will need to include active recovery between intervals.

Finally, recovery off the bike is important too. An old adage says, "You become stronger not in training, but in recovery." The point of training is to *overextend* by either intensity or volume of work. In recovery, you consolidate the gains made in overextending. Among other things, your body will repair damaged muscles (your source of force), replenish stored glycogen (your source of energy), and renew your mental state (your source of motivation). Recovering off the bike means eating well-balanced and well-timed meals, remaining well hydrated, attaining adequate sleep each night, staying off your feet, and reducing external stress.

Chapter 5

MASTERING THE SKILLS

Smooth, predictable riding when you're in a group isn't just a matter of style. It's a matter of survival.

—Geoff Drake, former editor at *Bicycling* and *Velonews* magazines

High speeds coupled with the close quarters are part of the excitement of bicycle racing—shoulder to shoulder, racers dive into corners, descend down mountains, and dash for the finish line. To succeed in these common situations, a racer needs to have a fundamental understanding of cycling skills. These skills will also make bicycle racing safer and more fun. Often overlooked, rarely practiced, and wholly necessary, bicycle-handling skills are a must in competitive racing.

This chapter gives you the basics of riding wheel to wheel and shoulder to shoulder in large packs, teaches you communication skills to let other riders know your intentions, and gives you the know-how to beat compatriots who are only inches away. You will learn the skills (through practice drills) that will help you make it to the finish line in the number one slot and in one piece.

Group Ride Etiquette

Many cyclists learn group riding skills or etiquette through a trial-and-error method. They show up for the ride, do something dangerous or socially frowned on—such as swerving around an obstacle into other riders—and are chastised for the behavior. In this way, they learn not to do it in a negative atmosphere. The problem with this method is that less obvious etiquette-based behaviors—such as not pointing to a slot in a fast-moving pack before moving to fill the slot—may not be learned. Cyclists may be scolded for such behavior, but they are often not aware of what they are being scolded for.

Cyclists safely holding their lines in an all-out group sprint.

Even though bicycles are listed as vehicles in most national and state jurisdictions, no mandatory licensure or education is needed to ride a bicycle on the road. As you know, the common practice is to buy a bike and then head right to the streets with little or no education on the rules of the road—and more alarmingly, little or no education on how to operate the vehicle.

Although it may be socially and administratively impossible for governments to set such rules, they have done just that with motor vehicles (such as motorcycles). Improper use of a bicycle could have similar consequences to its motorized counterparts—bodily injury or death to yourself or others or damage to property. The solution is twofold: (1) providing cyclists with the tools to practice on their own and in groups, along with positive encouragement to learn skills; and (2) recommending that cyclists understand the rules of the road by reading and providing current information from the Department of Motor Vehicles regarding road rules. When in doubt, assume that bicyclists must follow the same rules as those for automobiles, except in sanctioned races where course marshals or local authorities provide a dispensation.

Fundamentally, if you are new to a group ride, you should treat everyone with courtesy. Let others know you are new so they will point out left and right turns and areas in which the group conducts specific drills. Never be on the front if you do not know where you are going. The key to group riding is communication—being verbal about your intentions (e.g., turning, moving into pack spaces, speed changes). Do these things and you will be a welcome member of the group.

Alerting Cyclists Behind You of an Approaching Obstacle

Often, cyclists directly behind you in a race or fast group ride cannot see the same obstacle you can see. If you are approaching an obstacle—such as narrowing road, a slower rider, a pedestrian, or a parked car—put one arm out behind you and wave the cyclist away from the obstacle. For example, if a parked car is on your right, put your arm behind you and wave the cyclist away from the car and to the left. If removing your hands from the handlebar is prohibitive, you can announce the obstacle—for example, call out "Car right!"

You should alert cyclists to the rear of other common obstacles such as potholes, road-dividing curbs, traffic cones, sewer grates, cattle guards, water, sand, gravel, rocks, and any other obstacle that you think could injure a cyclist making contact (see figure 5.1). Use discretion though, because announcing avoidable obstacles or minor obstacles can cause cyclists in the rear to brake or swerve unnecessarily.

Figure 5.1 Rider pointing out a road hazard to trailing cyclists.

Alerting Cyclists Behind You to Changes in Speed

Surging and slowing are part of group riding and racing. This is the nature of having a group of cyclists spread over one-eighth of a mile of road. For example, when the front cyclists hit the base of a climb, they prepare by changing gears, changing to a climbing position, and settling into a climbing tempo. The riders behind them have a slower reaction time, because they cannot see the climb or have not yet felt the pull of gravity of the climb. The information is being telegraphed more subtly with each row of riders back from the front. The riders at the very back only know that they were cruising at 25 mph and now they are suddenly at 10 mph. A typical response from the riders closer to the front is to say, "Slowing," which alerts riders behind them of the impending change in speed.

Being able to predict these changes will help you flow better in the pack and prevent an accident. Places where speed will decrease include the following:

- Bases of climbs
- Upcoming corners
- Narrowing roads
- Changes of direction into the wind

Places where speed will increase include the following:

- Over the top of climbs
- After corners
- Widening roads
- Changes of direction with a tailwind

Keep your head up and try to predict these changes. This way, you will be ready to shift and change your cycling posture as necessary when the peloton slows. Conversely, you will be ready to make the necessary adjustments when a gap immediately opens as the speed ramps up.

Alerting Cyclists Behind You to Move Through

A common amateur mistake is to move to the front and remain there until exhausted—then, when the pace slows, someone rides around. This slows the pack and burns your precious energy. The bigger the group, the shorter the *pull* (meaning the time spent on the front) should be. If you are on the front and want to get off—while maintaining your pace—look to the side to which you want to pull off and make sure the space is clear of cyclists and obstacles. Shake the elbow of the arm on the opposite side (the side that you want the cyclist to move through on),

Figure 5.2 Using his elbow, the lead cyclist signals the riders behind to pull through.

and then move to the pull-off side—the cyclist behind moves straight up (see figure 5.2). By shaking your elbow, you're telling the cyclist which side of your body he or she should come through on; however, you are the one who moves to the side (the opposite side) while the other rider moves straight up.

Alerting Cyclists in Front or to the Side of Your Presence

You will sometimes find yourself in a position where the *hole* is closing because of a narrowing of the road, a tightening of the pack, or a competitor moving into another position. The hole refers to an empty space in a pack in front of you that you are entering. When the hole closes, you are usually being pushed into the gutter, an obstacle, or other riders by the pack closing in on one of your sides. A good way to remedy the situation is to reach out and gently touch or tap the person in front of you and to the side—that is, the person who is unwittingly cutting you off. A light tap will do the trick, nothing to throw the person off balance. If possible, the person will usually give you room and stop his lateral movement. Similarly, if you feel a light touch on your leg or lower back, this indicates that you should hold your position to avoid running someone into an obstacle.

Before executing a touch maneuver, you should review the section titled "Steer With No Hands" later in this chapter.

Fundamental Cycling Skills

As stated earlier, a bicycle is like any vehicle, so learning some "driving" skills is necessary. The following sections cover a few elementary cycling skills, along with some drills that can be used to practice the skills. You should always approach skill drills with caution. When practicing skills in groups, ensure that everyone understands the goals of the drill. Practicing skills on a well-mown grassy area is highly recommended. This will lessen the chance of injury in case of a fall. Practice skill drills a minimum of twice a year, especially within a few weeks of the start of the race season.

Keep Your Head Up

Keeping the head up may sound simple, but many cyclists do not do this, especially in pack situations. Their focus falls on the back of the person in front of them or on the person's rear wheel, crankset, or cassette. These things should actually be in your peripheral vision. Your main focus should be beyond the rider in front of you to see what is coming up on the road. This means looking over the rider's shoulders (see figure 5.3). Many find this uncomfortable at first, believing that their main focus should be on the closest object because that's what they would crash into. Mastering the proper technique takes practice.

By looking ahead, you can modulate speed, avoid obstacles, line up for upcoming corners, change gears for upcoming hills, and see the motions of the front of the pack. You will be able to anticipate evasive maneuvers more quickly. If you can anticipate pack movements, you will most likely save energy by not having to brake hard or accelerate quickly to recover from changes in direction or speed.

Heads-Up Drill Perform the drill on a well-cut, grassy field. If you are alone, choose an object in the distance, such as a tree. Ride slowly (under 10 mph) toward the tree, keeping your eyes on the tree. If you can see the hub of your front wheel directly, you need to look farther in the distance. Your front wheel may be in your periphery, but never in

Figure 5.3 Cyclist in back practicing heads-up cycling by checking the road in front of the pack.

your line of sight. Try this drill in the drops, hoods, or tops. If the drill is done in a group, riders should line up and roll one behind the other as if pacelining on the road. Instruct everyone to look beyond the first rider in the group to an object in the distance.

Hold Your Line When You Turn and Look Back

It is a natural tendency for your body to steer your bike toward where you look. This is a good thing when turning, cornering, and descending properly. However, you need to overcome this tendency when looking behind you or to the left or right side when riding in a straight line (see figure 5.4). When you look left, your body will naturally steer your body in that direction; the same is true with the right. Overcoming this natural tendency is important on the roads so that you can avoid swerving into traffic when training. In races, this skill will enable you to avoid swerving into competitors and causing a crash. When you are in breakaways, this skill allows you to look back and gauge the distance of the pack without wasting precious energy swerving all over the race course.

Hold Your Line Drill Perform the drill on a well-cut, grassy field. If you are alone, pick an object in the distance, such as a tree. Ride slowly (10 mph) toward the object in a large gear. Alternate looking left for a couple of seconds and looking right for a couple of seconds. Then look straight ahead to see if you are still headed toward the tree. Practice this until you can turn your head and not veer off your direct line to the tree. Try easier gears as you improve. Try this drill in the drops, hoods, and tops. If the drill is done in a group, riders should go one at a time or with enough distance between them to not overlap wheels.

Figure 5.4 The lead cyclist is holding his line while he looks back.

Steer With No Hands

Pros sit up on their bikes while they remove or put on wind or rain jackets and grab snacks out of their musettes (special bags designed to provide food and drinks to racers in a feed zone). This behavior is not recommended in the amateur ranks, because despite your possible ability to ride with no hands, you never know the bike-handling skills of those around you. With your hands off the handlebars, you are very vulnerable to having your bars *hooked*—that is, hit to the side suddenly by a competitor's handlebar. Yet, learning how to ride with no hands is a necessary skill for building general balance while riding. This skill helps when you have to take one hand off your handlebars to touch other riders during the race.

When removing your hands from the bars, you are essentially unweighting the front of the bike and using your lower body through the saddle to steer the bike (see figure 5.5). Being able to steer the bike with your lower body will allow you to unweight the front bars when hitting unexpected rough road, and it will allow you to relax your upper body. In fact, your bike should be set up so that you can easily unweight your hands and steer—you still have your hands on the bars, but you do not need them to prop up your upper body.

Figure 5.5 When riding with no hands, use the lower body to steer.

No Hands Drill Caution: This drill can cause unexpected falls. Perform the drill on a well-cut, grassy field. This drill is best practiced individually or one at a time. Pedal slowly in a big gear (about 10 mph) and gradually unweight your hands for one second. Do not remove your hands from the handlebars, just unweight them. Then reweight your hands. Repeat the drill, increasing the time of unweighting your hands. With your hands unweighted, practice steering the bike by moving your weight in the saddle. When you feel comfortable, lift your hands off the bars and sit up, moving your weight completely into the saddle. Bringing your hands toward your body makes balancing easier by slightly reducing the center of gravity. Again, practice steering the bike by moving your weight in the saddle. Move to an easier gear and repeat the drill.

Riding Rollers

Riding rollers may improve your pedal stroke and provide another mode for neuromuscular training, but the real benefit is that rollers teach you balancing skills—especially lower body steering. Starting and balancing on rollers take practice. Most beginners set the rollers up next to a sturdy, stationary object that they can lean on; this allows them to clip in before they start riding. Using a large gear (such as a 53 × 14) will help you in the beginning, because the harder pressure on the pedals will improve your ability to balance.

Riding rollers takes balance and concentration.

When starting out, make sure you have room to fall. Riding on a carpet or rug, or near a couch or cushions, is a good idea. Riding in a doorway is a popular technique, because you can grab onto the wall on the right or left and use your elbows against the door jam to keep you on the rollers. Holding the front brake as you clip in one foot is helpful. Release the brake, push down with your clipped-in foot, and move your other foot onto the other pedal while pedaling. Clip in the other foot as you keep pedaling. Keep your eyes focused ahead, although your instinct will be to look at your front wheel. Avoid any true steering with your hands. If you need to adjust your position on the rollers as you roll, use your lower body to control and move the bike laterally.

Once rolling, ride for 15 to 30 minutes, slowly increasing your cadence every minute by 5 rpm until you get to a comfortable maximum. Hold cadence for one minute, then recover by pedaling slowly for another minute. Then repeat the drill. Try moving to easier gears as you become comfortable.

Stopping on rollers is another trick. Hold on to the stationary object, slow your cadence, stop pedaling to allow the bike to roll to a stop, and unclip and put your foot down in one motion. Without a stationary object, slow your cadence to below 30 rpm, unclip one foot and put it down, allowing the wheel to slow, then apply the front brake.

For some cyclists, riding rollers is more of a thrill than racing.

Fundamental Contact Skills

Cycling is not classified as a contact sport, but you will likely make contact with other cyclists or their bike during races or group rides. The key to having the best chance to survive such situations is holding your line and remaining as calm as possible. The way to achieve these two survival skills is by practicing bumping and wheel touching.

Bumping

In cycling terminology, this skill is called *bumping*, but the term *leaning* is a more apt name. Most cycling governing bodies frown on aggressive contact, although you will encounter it in racing. In essence, when you make contact, you want to lean into the contact. Your instincts may make you pull away from the perceived danger, but that will have poor consequences—a swerve or even a fall. Think of it this way: When you are standing in a crowded line or train or bus, if someone leans on you, you lean back. The reason you do this is to prevent yourself or the other person from falling. This is the same for cycling.

In cycling, you will encounter bumping in sprints, on corners, on narrow roads, or where either the terrain changes or cyclists around you bunch up.

Bumping Drill Caution: This drill can cause unexpected falls. Perform the drill on a well-cut, grassy field. Choose training partners whom you can trust to follow the guidelines. With their hands in the drops, two cyclists ride slowly across a grassy field, and they slowly veer toward each other

Controlling Your Opponents With Skills

By mastering skills, you become a more complete racer. Being confident in your skills can help you control your opponents in tight situations.

Many races, especially at an amateur level, end in bunch sprints. Although speed and power are necessary to reach the line first, good bike-handling skills are equally important. Sprints contain bumping, possible wheel touching, and cornering, which are all opportunities to control your opponents.

To control your opponents, make sure your front wheel is ahead of your opponent's front wheel. Being in front means that your front wheel is protected. A protected front wheel has a lower risk of being swiped. If you are comfortable with your bumping drills, you will not be spooked—and thereby lose speed—by the bit of contact it takes to maintain your pack position. Once in position, you can be confident in your wheel touching skills, knowing that if a wheel touches, you may be able to recover (or knowing that you can at least maintain a good line to avoid any wheel touching). Keeping your head up, as practiced, prepares you for a change in speed or direction. From your no hands drills, you can be confident that you are balancing and controlling your bike at high speeds. As the sprint approaches, bring all those skills together, and line yourself up for a fast and safe push for the finish line.

Racers riding shoulder to shoulder through a corner.

to make very light contact shoulder to shoulder. The object is to just lean on each other—not push each other. Suppress the instinct to pull away suddenly. Once contact has been made a few times, try leaning on each other for extended periods. Next, try contacting the partner's thigh with your shoulder. Then try contacting the side of the partner's handlebar. Your hands need to be in the drops to avoid hooking each other's handlebars. Try all the drills on the hoods next. Watch out for hooking. Increase the speed of the drills and try to lean on your partner enough to control his or her direction of movement. A simple rule in cycling is that the person with his or her front wheel farther ahead can control the direction of two riders.

Wheel Touching

Wheel touching—one cyclist's front wheel contacting another cyclist's rear wheel—is part of bicycle racing. There are just too many people trying to fit into too few holes for an occasional wheel touch not to occur. Usually, the person in the front will not fall, because the weight of the person's body on his rear wheel prevents it. Many times the person in the back may be out of luck, because this person's front wheel is turned by the other cyclist's rear wheel. By keeping a cool head and good control, you may survive your front wheel touching. The following drill will help you in those situations.

Wheel Touching Drill   Caution: This drill can cause unexpected falls. Perform the drill on a well-cut, grassy field. Choose training partners whom you can trust to follow the guidelines. With their hands in the drops, two cyclists, one in front of the other, ride slowly across a grassy field. The rear cyclist slowly veers his front wheel toward the front cyclist's rear wheel in an attempt to make light side contact, meaning the sidewall of the tires touch. Watch out for the rear derailleur. The object is to just touch tires—not push tires together roughly. The person in the front will most likely feel no contact with his rear wheel. The person in the back needs to suppress the instinct to pull away suddenly. Pulling away suddenly will turn the front wheel and cause a crash. The best strategy for the person in the back is to maintain the contact, hold the handlebars straight, and decelerate. In most cases, but not all, the person in front will naturally glide away from the front wheel, either speeding up or moving away.

Fundamental Turning Skills

As an isolated skill, turning is rarely practiced by amateur racers. Most learn as they go. This is not wise. By learning turning skills, you will be more confident in your ability to avoid obstacles, to corner, and to descend.

Turning comes in three forms: leaning, countersteering, and steering.

Leaning

Leaning is the method for turning that is most often applied by cyclists. This method is suitable for wide corners in which you can see the exit. In leaning, both the bike and the cyclist are angled in the same direction. The handlebars are not turned; they are just angled with the bike and body (see figure 5.6).

To lean, approach the corner from the outside. Angle the bike toward the corner as you move from the outside to the inside through the corner and back to the outside on the exit of the corner (see figure 5.7).

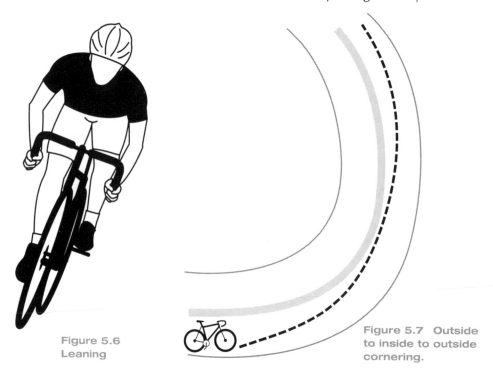

Figure 5.6
Leaning

Figure 5.7 Outside
to inside to outside
cornering.

Countersteering

Countersteering is a slightly more advanced cornering technique than leaning. This technique is good for corners in which you cannot see the exit, off-camber turns, or decreasing-radius turns. It is also useful in changing the line of cornering in the middle of a turn. In countersteering, the cyclist is leaning the bicycle more than himself (see figure 5.8).

To countersteer, lean the bike more than your body, putting positive pressure on the inside hand as you extend it. The positive pressure is to be directed down into the handlebar, not forward to turn the handlebar. Increasing the lean of the bike with more inside hand pressure tightens the cornering; decreasing the lean of the bike with less inside hand pressure widens the cornering.

Steering

Cyclists are constantly steering their bicycles. By shifting their weight to the right or left of the saddle and putting pressure on the left or right side of the handlebar, they steer the bike around obstacles. These are often slight movements, but at slow speeds they can be large movements of the handlebar.

As a specific cornering skill, steering is an advanced technique not to be tried until you have mastered leaning and countersteering. Steering through corners is beneficial on wet roads, because the more vertical nature of your bike keeps more tire in contact with the ground. To steer, keep your bicycle vertical, and move your weight and body slightly forward and to the inside of the turn. Straighten your outside arm, pushing with slight pressure down and forward to steer the bike around the corner (see figure 5.9).

Figure 5.8
Countersteering.

Figure 5.9
Steering.

Tripod Method for Cornering With Confidence

For better turning, you can employ the tripod method. The idea is to make three contact points of a tripod with your body and the bike. By adjusting the length or pressure of these tripod contact points, you can control the bicycle through turns. The three contact points of the tripod are the hand, the lower body, and the leg.

Arm and Hand Position The first contact point of the tripod is your hand in contact with the handlebars. The best position of your hands for control is in the drops. By being in the drops, your hands (a) are closest to the brakes, (b) provide more force for control of the front wheel, and (c) place the most pressure on the front tire, giving you the most traction. A firm but relaxed grip should be used. Arms should be loosely bent at approximately 120 to 150 degrees at the elbow. This position allows for absorption of shock from rough roads and prevents handlebar hooking in tight quarters. Keep your back flat and your head up; your eyes should be scanning the road as far into the distance as possible. Keep your knees close to the top tube, if not locked on the top tube. The farther you look into the distance, the more in control of the bike you will be, because you will feel confident that you can adjust your direction (see figure 5.10).

To turn, the inside hand should place light pressure on the handlebar. This light pressure will help steer (or more specifically, countersteer) you through the corner, and it will enable you to keep good front tire contact

Figure 5.10 Rider using the tripod method to lean through a corner.

with the road. When cornering on descents, you will use very little (or no) handlebar turning; instead, you will lean the bike to cause it to carve a corner. For example, when turning right, you place light pressure with your right hand on the handlebar.

Body Weight in Saddle The second contact point of the tripod is your buttocks on the saddle. Sliding slightly back in the saddle will provide more stability because the rear tire will have more grip. Sliding slightly back will also allow you to flatten your back. Maintain contact with your saddle, but do not overweight the rear end of your bike. Instead, float over the saddle and allow your outside leg to get the crank in the down position, thereby lifting the inside portion of your buttocks.

Leg Position The third contact point of the tripod is your leg. The leg to the outside of the corner should be fully extended; in other words, the crank on the outside of the corner should be in the down position. You must also apply large pressure to this down pedal. The pressure will transfer to your rear tire, providing more traction and forcing it to carve the turn. For example, when turning right, you extend your left leg and place pressure on the left pedal. For more pressure, roll your buttocks on the side of the extended leg so that you lift more of your weight from the saddle and place it over the pedal.

Braking in Cornering and Descending

In some instances, especially instances where you cannot clearly see the corner or road ahead, moving slowly is safer. Yet, moving slowly does not always mean more control. Look at cornering this way: It is better to be in control, no matter what your speed. Using your brakes in conjunction with the cornering techniques previously described will allow you to corner with confidence.

If you need to brake, do so well in advance of the corner. In actuality, it is not the speed with which you enter a corner that determines your overall cornering speed, but the speed with which you exit the corner. Braking in the middle of a corner is never a good idea, unless you are drifting into the other lane or off the road. The angle of your bike, the shift of your body weight, and the contact of the brakes on a leaning wheel can cause a skid, which may result in a crash.

Using both brakes, slow down to a safe speed before you enter the corner. Release the brakes and roll through the corner. Once you have leaned far enough upright, you should pedal. If you need to avoid a crash in a corner, it is better to use the rear brake instead of the front brake. If you use the front brake, the front wheel may skid or lock up in the turn, sending you to the ground instantly. A rear-wheel skid is easier to recover from, because the bike usually stays upright. If you are in a life-threatening situation, use both brakes.

Pacelining

A rider is approximately 30 percent more efficient when sitting in the *draft* of another rider. The draft is a position behind or to the side of a rider that enables another rider to stay out of the wind. Air resistance is an exponential function of speed, meaning that it becomes exponentially harder to ride when speed increases because of wind resistance. Therefore, as you ride harder, sharing the work by *pacelining* makes sense. In pacelining, a group of cyclists are organized to efficiently take turns riding in the wind and "sitting in" protected from the wind.

Pacelining is a necessary skill for maintaining and increasing speed on group rides, chasing down or driving breaks in races, or working together to move through a windy section quickly. Pacelining should be practiced. A chain is only as strong as its weakest link, and this is the case in pacelining. Learn the skill and be a strong link in the chain.

All of us who have participated in any group cycling have inadvertently participated in pacelining. Cyclists in a paceline ride inches apart front to back (and side to side in some instances). The paceline works toward the good of the whole, meaning that it allows riders to move more quickly than on their own, while also expending less energy. If you learn to properly pull off and pull through, pacelining will be enjoyable. Pacelining is illegal in individual time trials, where drafting is not permitted.

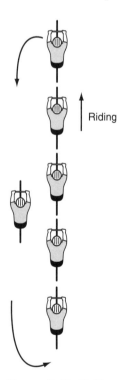

Riding

Figure 5.11 Pulling off to the left in a single paceline.

Pulling Off

If you are in a *single* paceline, do not wait until you are exhausted to pull off. The rule is, the greater the amount of riders, the shorter the pull. For example, in a single paceline of four riders, you might each take 30-second to 1-minute pulls. Try to verbally agree on how long you each will pull based on either time or miles. When pulling off, do so *into* the wind. For example, if the wind is from the left, then pull off to the left (see figure 5.11). By pulling off into the wind, you momentarily protect the rider moving into the lead position from the wind. Always look over your shoulder, without decreasing your speed, to ensure that your path is clear before pulling off. This is especially important on roads with traffic and little room for bicycles. Do not decrease speed until you are clear of the line, but remain laterally very close to the paceline, because riders will benefit from your draft even though you are off the front. Once clear, decrease speed evenly, and move to the back of the line as quickly as possible without braking. Sit on the back and move up the line accordingly.

A Pro's Experience

Cody Stevenson (Adageo Energy Professional Cycling Team)

Using Skills to Position for a Sprint

Cody Stevenson is a sprint specialist for the Adageo Energy Professional Cycling Team. Having raced in the United States, Australia, China, and Europe, Cody knows what it takes to seize the right opportunities to make a solid dash for the line among the world's best. The key to executing Cody's sprint techniques comes down to using the skills discussed in this chapter. Without bike-handling skills, it would not be possible to attain the right position, as described by Cody, to take a shot at winning the race.

As Cody says, "The key to winning sprints is not just natural ability. It certainly goes a long way, but you also need position and the ability to protect that position. Positioning is the most fundamental part of a sprint and determines the outcome before the sprint has even started."

Cody continues, "If you have a lead-out, then the best position is behind your last lead-out man. This diminishes the need to fight—I do mean fight—to stay on a wheel. You will have less pushing, shoving, and elbowing to contend with, allowing you to concentrate on your final explosive effort." A lead-out or lead-out train is a team performing a high-speed paceline in the closing kilometers of a race to prevent attacks from other teams and to ensure that their sprinter is near the front before the dash for the finish line. In amateur races, you will often not have a teammate lead you out. You will have to pick someone, a competitor, who will be a good lead-out. You will know who the good sprinters are from previous races or from group training. Lock into position behind the selected sprinter, and when he starts his sprint, it will be a lead-out for your sprint.

Cody explains the situation in smaller groups and amateur events: "Positioning is once again critical, but you also have to be more flexible with your positioning. This means following the wheel in front or switching to another. Sitting in the middle does not give you the opportunity to 'get out' or 'hit out' if there is a hesitation." Cody gives examples of colleagues. "Robbie McEwen and Oscar Freire use other teams' lead-out trains to their advantage. They are rare riders who have the ability to accelerate twice in a sprint or to accelerate in the final 100 meters."

Being confident in your skills means knowing how to use them instinctively. Cody explains, "Instinct is an equally important factor in sprinting. Instinct helps make split-second decisions in the heat of the sprint and helps you to protect your position. Sprinting can be dangerous, chaotic, and physical, and you must be prepared to take a shove from time to time. If you are not confident to do this, then get out of there; you are potentially endangering yourself and other sprinters. Rely on your instinct to defend yourself, to go through a gap, and to start your sprint if there is a hesitation in the final 500 meters."

Cody will explain specific instances of sprinting in the Achieving Sprinting Success section in chapter 6.

What Can You Learn?

As an amateur bike racer, you will most likely be faced with many sprint finishes. This is a function of race categories, which contain cyclists of very similar abilities. Most amateur racers only prepare their bodies for the hard physical efforts. Be ahead of the curve by integrating bike-handling skills into your training plan. As Cody explains, you should take your position entering the final sections of the race seriously. Use the skills you have learned—cornering, bumping, pacelining, and wheel following—to hold your position in the pack and to give yourself a good shot at powering to the line for the win.

In a *rotating* (or, *double*) paceline, each rider comes to the front in an ascending line and then moves back in a descending line. Once a rider coming to the front is clear of the descending line, the rider pulls into the descending line (see figure 5.12). As you reach the front, the lead rider in the descending paceline should say "Clear" when your rear wheel is far enough in front of her front wheel to allow you to leave the ascending line and enter the descending line. Turns in a rotating paceline are extremely short, because you are either descending or ascending at all times. Mirror pacelines (figure 5.13) and echelons (figure 5.14) are more advanced double-paceline techniques, and they should only be practiced by and with experienced riders.

Pulling Forward or Pulling Through

When pulling through, do so at the same speed that the paceline was traveling before your move to take the lead. Never accelerate into the lead position. It is the responsibility of the rider who has pulled off the front to stop pedaling and slide back into the rear position. For example, if the paceline is traveling on flat ground at 25 mph, you should apply power to maintain that pace as you pull through; do not apply more power to increase the speed to 26 mph to pass the lead rider pulling off. This is a waste of your precious power, and it causes the paceline members to accelerate in order to hold your wheel, wasting their power. In essence, a pull-through

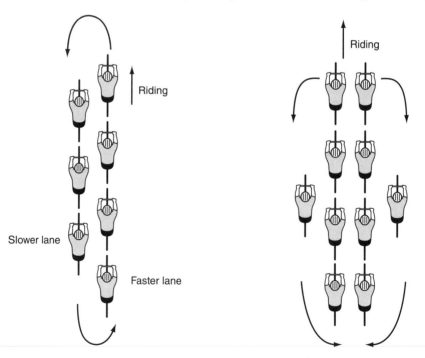

Figure 5.12 Rotating paceline.

Figure 5.13 Mirror paceline.

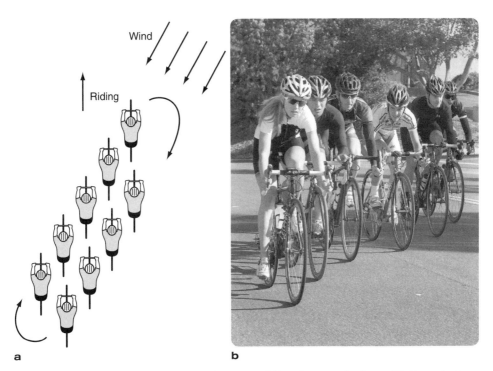

Wind

Riding

a

b

Figure 5.14 In parts *a* and *b*, cyclists are riding in an echelon with the wind approaching from their right-hand side.

is just passively maintaining the pace, while the actual action is taken by the lead rider actively pulling off.

It is always a bad idea for a rider who is not in the second position to race to the front to lead the paceline. This will leave gaps, change the paceline speed, and force people to decelerate or accelerate. Instead, encourage your fellow riders to continue pacelining properly by saying "Pull through," "Even pace," and "Pull off." Encouragement always works better than negative ranting or aggressive moves to the front to take over the pace.

If you are tired in a single paceline, do not just pull off behind the lead rider as that person pulls off. Doing so would leave the person in third position in the lurch and would obstruct the lead rider's ability to return to the back of the line quickly. Instead, let the lead rider pull off and descend; then you can immediately pull off and descend, maintaining the paceline integrity.

Maintaining Consistent Power in a Paceline

The key to paceline success is a constant level of power—notice that it is not a constant level of speed. In most instances, the wind will ebb and flow, and the terrain will pitch and flatten; therefore, a constant speed is nearly unattainable, but a constant power is attainable. If riding without a power meter, you should just measure your effort by not increasing or reducing miles per hour quickly; ride smoothly and consistently.

When on the front and entering a hill, you should maintain your pace as you hit the bottom of the hill so that the paceline does not bunch up; however, you should maintain your power and subsequently decrease your speed as you climb so that you are not forcing the riders to work any harder than they were on the flats. When on the front and going downhill, you should pedal to maintain your power and speed (or increase your speed only to the point of the previous power on flat land). Avoid having riders behind you hit their brakes, which sometimes occurs because they are speeding up in your draft on a downhill and you are being slowed by wind resistance.

When moving in the paceline, ensure that you leave no gaps to the rider in front of you. Gaps cause different speeds and accelerations within the paceline, causing riders to waste precious energy. If a gap forms, slowly close it; closing the gap quickly only leaves the rider behind you in the lurch as you accelerate unexpectedly.

Skipping Turns

Although it is not recommended, you may sometimes need to skip turns in a paceline. In race situations, this can cause friction, because other racers may think that you are not doing your share of the work. In group ride situations, it is more acceptable. Keep in mind that if you feel too tired to share pace, pulling out of the paceline and sitting on the back may be tougher than just sitting in and taking very short pulls—that is, rotating up to the front and off immediately. When sitting on the back, you may have to accelerate and decelerate to hold on to the back as the paceline rotates, thereby wasting your energy.

If sitting on the back of a paceline, you need to announce your intentions. This alerts descending riders to go in front of you—not behind you—when they head to the back of the line. A good cue you may use in this situation is to move out into the descending path as the rider approaches and to call out "Sitting on" or "You're last." This leaves a clear indication of the space you just vacated on the back of the paceline. Follow the descending rider onto the back of the line, preventing gaps between you and him as much as possible. After a few rotations, the other riders will realize you are sitting on.

If you have a rider sitting on your group, do not chastise the rider. Sitting on the back is the rider's prerogative in group rides, and in most instances, the person is truly too fatigued to work. If entering the end of a race or sprint, you may not be so kind, and you may encourage the rider to start sharing the work.

Wheel Following

When following wheels in a paceline, make sure you do not leave any gaps. Try not to overlap wheels, meaning that your front wheel should not be to the immediate left or right of the rear wheel of the rider in front of you. Keep your head up, looking to the riders in the lead of the paceline, because their movements will dictate changes in speed or direction for the paceline. Stay laterally close to the riders either ascending or descending as you move through the paceline; this will help your draft and their draft. Never brake or stand in a paceline, unless you are the rider on the back. Save your eating and drinking for when you are on the back of the line. When descending down to the back of a paceline, move quickly into the draft of the last rider—each second out in the wind is a waste of your energy.

Chapter 6

USING RACING STRATEGIES AND TACTICS

Perhaps the single most important element in mastering the techniques and tactics of racing is experience. But once you have the fundamentals, acquiring the experience is a matter of time.

—Greg LeMond, three-time Tour de France winner and two-time World Road Race champion

The pure physical energy of bicycle racing is an important motivation for entering cycling competition; however, one of the most challenging and gratifying aspects of the sport is executing strategies and tactics that put the racer or his or her teammates on the top step of the podium.

Cycling can be described as a rolling chess match. Not only are competitors trying to outmuscle each other, but they are also trying to outwit each other. In fact, one truism in cycling is that the strongest cyclist does not always win, but the smartest does. Developing a prerace strategy that plays to an individual's or team's strengths—and putting that strategy into action via tactics—is a sure way to be ahead of the curve in amateur racing.

This chapter covers how to develop strategies based on course analysis, competition analysis, and self-analysis. It also covers the tactics necessary for employing those strategies. Once a strategic plan is in place, racing will have another level of excitement, especially if the planned strategy and tactics work. The underlying current of the chapter is position. Just as in business where location (or position) is everything, position is vital to success in bicycle racing. For each strategy or tactic, note the proper position for success.

Analyzing the Course

To develop a race strategy, you need to perform an analysis of the "battle-field," or the race course. When analyzing a race course, you should be looking at these elements: elevation gains and losses, technical turns, wind direction and windy areas, changes in road conditions, and the finishing straight (i.e., the last few hundred meters in a race).

The best method of preliminary course analysis is riding the course. A first run-through of the course should be completed at a slow, endurance pace. This enables you to concentrate on looking for landmarks and evaluating the primary elements listed previously. The slow pace also allows you to have the energy to concentrate on preliminary strategies. Print out the course map and bring it (along with a pen) to the run-through so you can mark any important course notes, such as a rapid change in elevation. A quick review of these notes will be helpful on race day.

A second run-through of the course should be performed at near race pace. It is amazing how a road that does not seem like much of a climb at endurance pace seems like a mountain at race pace. A corner may not seem technical when riding at slow speeds, but flying through it at race pace may cause it to be technical. The run-through at race pace is best done with teammates or riding comrades in order to help increase the validity of the simulation. It is a good idea to run through unfamiliar courses with comrades who have racing experience.

A *strategy* is a plan for achieving a specific goal during a race or event. You develop strategies from the two run-throughs (endurance and race pace). A *tactic* is a method that allows a strategy to be employed. You develop tactics by talking with teammates or individually visualizing how to execute those strategies. A race strategy may be to attack on the last climb. A tactic would be how the hill attack is employed: At the bottom? At the top? By launching teammates to draw out competitors, and then countering the attack? By increasing the tempo and steadily "burning off" the competition?

Elevation Gains and Losses

Climbs and descents make or break races. Even climbs that are small can make a difference as the race miles pile on. In this way, climbs are additive, meaning that a 50-foot elevation gain may not seem like much in the first few miles, but near the finish, it can seem like a mountain.

When reviewing climbs, note all hills on the course, no matter their size. Take special note of hills toward the end of the race. These last few hills usually split the race into two groups: the leading group going for the win and the chasers trying to pick up the remaining places (see figure 6.1). Note hills that are immediately after corners. These hills will require you to be in good position—toward the front of the pack—to keep from getting

Figure 6.1 Late race attack on small rise in road.

gapped as the ascent starts. At a corner leading into a hill, a typical scenario is that those entering the corner last are gapped off the back because of an *accordion effect* caused by the initial surge up the hill.

Note all the descents. Long straight descents may require work to stay in the draft. Twisty or narrow descents may require technical skills. If the descent seems technical in review, it will definitely be technical at race speeds. Perform practice runs down the hill, because knowing the corners and steeper sections of a descent will make it less difficult.

Here are some good tactics for hills:

- Be near the front for corners that are followed immediately by hills. This will help prevent you from being gapped.

- Shift to easier gears before approaching hills in order to prevent dropping your chain off the front chainrings when you shift from the big front ring to the small front ring. Quickly go around riders who drop their chains.

- Close gaps on hills immediately, but with an even, steady pace. Once the group starts riding away on a hill, it is nearly impossible to bring them back.

- Keep your pace high over the crest of the hill, because the leaders will be increasing speed faster than the riders at the tail of the group.

- Relax and breathe deeply to control your heart rate on climbs.

- Dig deep to stay in contact on shorter climbs, because once the group clears the top, you will find it very difficult, or impossible, to catch back up on the descent.

- On longer climbs, ride at a pace that ensures that you will not *crack* or *blow up* (i.e., overexert yourself to the point where you can no longer ride hard). Be confident in your ability to reel back in other riders who go too hard, too fast.

- Always start climbs near the front. That way, if the pace becomes too high, you will be able to drop through the pack and still recover without losing contact with the pack.

- Keep in mind that hills are a good place to attack. Know the hill's distance and location in the course before setting out on an attack or covering an attack by a competitor.

- Try to descend near the front, but not on the front. Being near the front will give you a greater probability of avoiding crashes than being in the back.

Technical Turns

Turns are the bread and butter of criterium racing, and they are also a factor in road races. On flat courses, turns are usually the determining factor for who is in position for the sprint or who is able to "break the chain" of the pack and form a break.

When reviewing turns, check their turning radius and their location in the race. For a sharper turn—one with a decreasing radius—you need to have technical skill and familiarity. Identify a good entry (remember, outside to inside; see chapter 5) and exit from the turn, taking into account race pace and the probability that the pack will prevent a perfect line through the turn. Be near the front to take advantage of any opportunities to attack or to cover an attack. Increasing-radius turns may provide an opportunity for you to break away, because you know that you can exit much faster than you enter. If you enter an increasing-radius turn—that is, a turn that starts sharper and finishes straighter—at high speed and then pedal rapidly out of it, this can slingshot you off the front (or up positions in the pack if you are near the back).

Note the location of the turn in the race both in terms of distance and specific location. For example, you need to be vigilant about a turn before a hill, a turn before a narrowing road, a turn before a change in wind direction, or a turn before a change in road condition. Be sure you are near the front or at worst in the middle with the ability to pick your way through riders who are unprepared for the turn.

Here are some good tactics for technical turns:

- Ride near the front when entering the turn. This puts you in the best position to defend or launch attacks (see figure 6.2).

- Know the race speed of the turn and the angle of the turn. Use this knowledge to move up in the pack or to move off the front of the pack.

Figure 6.2 Racers taking advantage of a turn by attacking prior to the turn and pushing the pace through and after the turn.

- Attack before a technical turn. The confusion of the peloton in the turn will give you much needed time to establish a break off the front.
- Find the rhythm of the turns in races such as criteriums. This will help you conserve energy during the race. For example, many criteriums require a nice smooth coasting turn, followed by 10 or so powerful pedal strokes to hold pack position.
- Try to have good position for turns that come within 300 meters (328 yards) of the finish line. Normally, the athlete's position when he enters this last turn will be the position in which he finishes the race. There is simply not enough time or road left to come around more than a few competitors. Try to come through the turn in the top three in order to be in line for the win.

Wind Direction and Windy Areas

Most racers do not like windy races or windy sections of courses. Racing takes tremendous physical energy if you are exposed to the wind, and it takes tremendous mental energy to fight for and hold a pack position that is out of the wind. This is good to know so you can take advantage of it. A headwind or sidewind, especially on narrow roads, can actually split the peloton (just as a climb can). A headwind can also dampen the peloton's willingness to chase a breakaway. Conversely, a tailwind can assist a peloton in chasing a breakaway or lining up for a sprint.

Windy Time Trials

The art of time trialing (TT) is about reducing wind resistance via aerodynamic equipment. When analyzing a windy time trial course, note the wind direction and speed. If the wind is from the side, a disc wheel or deep-dish wheel should act as a sail pushing and pulling you along. When encountering headwind sections, set a manageable pace, slightly above threshold; recovery will be available in less windy sections.

On an out-and-back course with a headwind on the outward bound leg, you should push through this leg at a pace over threshold. Think of the TT as ending on the outbound leg, because with the tailwind on the return leg, recovery is possible. With a tailwind on the outbound leg, push to just below threshold. Save a little bit of energy to push over threshold through the wind on the way back.

When reviewing courses, you should note windy sections, especially on exposed flats. Note the direction of the wind. Wind speed and direction can change from race to race, but most race courses have a wind pattern. For instance, near a body of water, the wind usually blows off the water. In valleys between climbs, the wind is usually from the rear or in front, but not the side.

Here are some good tactics for windy courses:

- Attack slightly before windy sections, and use the unwillingness of the peloton to chase into the wind to build a time gap.
- Never ride in the wind unless you are off the front in a break. Find the best draft. For example, if the wind is from the front, tuck into the middle of the pack. If the wind is on the right, position yourself on the left of the pack.
- Try to avoid breaking away with a tailwind. It is easy for the peloton to chase with a tailwind pushing them along.
- Know the wind in the finishing straight, and position your sprint from the draft side.
- If chasing, use tailwind sections to make up the most ground on the breakaway.

Changes in Road Conditions

Road conditions are less and less of an issue on modern road courses, but in select races, the road conditions can affect the outcome of a race. When reviewing courses, look for areas in which the road becomes rough or smooth, changes to dirt or to pavement, and narrows or widens. A rough road could affect the speed of the peloton, because riders will be more wary. If you are prepared for the rough sections, you can avoid the confusion that these sections place on the pack. Attacking before a rough section is always a good tactic; the confused peloton will be more worried about the road and less about chasing a breakaway (see figure 6.3).

In the rare instances when the road changes from pavement to packed dirt, you should be prepared for attacks. Some racers will attack to take advantage of the poor technical skills of their competition. Some racers will attack because they are nervous or have poor technical skills, and they want to make riding room away from competitors. If you are not near the front, you should be prepared to pick through floundering riders. If you know that a race course has a packed dirt section, practice on packed dirt at race speed before starting the race.

Narrowing roads are good locations to launch attacks. Racers become wary in narrow sections. In these sections, racers often become trapped in poor pack positions (i.e., the back or blocked on the inside), and they generally cannot move up as well. Be near the front when the road narrows to avoid being caught out.

Here are some good tactics for varying road conditions:

● Be near the front when road conditions change.
● Use road conditions for planning attacks.

Figure 6.3 Two-person attack, under the watchful eye of the peloton, prior to a rough section in the road.

- Practice riding the course at race speed to simulate dealing with changing conditions.
- Practice bike handling within a week of a race. This helps ensure that you are sharp and prepared.

The Finishing Straight

Always analyze the finishing straight. Use all of the items discussed in the previous sections—elevation gains and losses, technical turns, wind direction and speed, and road conditions—to make a qualified judgment about what the best pack position will be as the finish approaches. Back-track from the finish to uncover these primary elements. Be prepared to cover any winning moves before entering the finishing area, or be prepared to launch winning moves. Always enter the finishing straight with a plan, but be flexible because the race situation may force a change in the plan.

For a good placing in a race, sometimes your primary goal will not be the actual finish line, but some other element in the lead-up to the line. In these instances, you must convince yourself that your placing in the race is dependent on an imaginary finish line before the real finish line. For example, as discussed earlier, if a turn is within 300 meters of the finish, the athlete may need to race to that turn (imaginary finish line), because that will determine finishing position in the race. Another example is a hill within a few miles of the finish. In this case, the primary goal is to make it over the hill with the lead group, because that will determine which athletes are in position for the win (see figure 6.4).

Figure 6.4 Cyclist outclimbing the competition to a hilltop finish.

Analyzing the Competition

The more you race, the more you will learn about the strengths, weaknesses, and tactics of individuals and teams. To analyze competition, simply pay attention to what they do in races and group rides. Individual racers and teams employ extremely similar tactics from race to race and from group ride to group ride.

Athletes should be wary of this statement: "I only did that [tactic] because this group ride [or race] is just practice." What racers do in practice, they do in competition, because they have trained themselves to do such action. It is difficult to undo poor habitual tactics, especially in the heat of racing when you are reacting more than you are thinking. You should experiment but also exercise common sense. Through experience, you must learn to recognize common mistakes—your own and those of others. This will help you avoid making those mistakes in the future.

These questions will help you analyze and categorize individual competitors:

- Is this person a climber, sprinter, or breakaway specialist?
- Does this person make "suicide attacks"—attacks that have little gain—or does the person attack with purpose?
- Have you seen this person performing well in current group rides or races?
- Is this person a team player or individually motivated?
- Is this person willing to work in breakaways?
- Does this person position himself well in a pack?

These questions will help you analyze and categorize strengths and weaknesses of teams:

- Does the team participate in only hilly races or only flat races?
- Does the team show up with a large contingent?
- Are the racers for the team physically in shape?
- Does the team control the race either in the beginning or the end of the race?
- Does the team always work for one individual, or do they pick one as the race unfolds?
- What tactics do they employ as a team, and when, during group rides?
- What tactics do they employ as a team, and when, during a race?

Use these questions to formulate individual and team profiles. The answers will reveal patterns that you can take advantage of. By knowing these patterns, you will be able to attack and catch a team or individual off guard, and you will be prepared to cover attacks that a team or individual is going to launch.

A good tactic is to use competitors' strengths to improve your own personal strengths. For example, if you are a good sprinter and you know that one of the competitors is also a good sprinter, then you will want to be on that person's wheel for a good lead-out in the finish. Another tactic is to use a competitor's strengths to eliminate your own weaknesses. For example, if you are always finding yourself in poor pack position, you should make it your mission to stick onto the wheel of an individual or team who always has good pack position.

Exploring Strengths and Weaknesses

As an amateur, you need to be aware that this is a good time to experiment. Can you climb in a race? Can you sprint? Can you drive breakaways? Are you a good team player? Find out now and do not assume. One athlete whom I coached—and whom we will call Sam—was convinced that he was "not very fit for racing," because he was *dropped* each week on a local hill during a weekly group ride. Other racers used that hill as a benchmark of fitness, so Sam used it as a benchmark as well. On his own, Sam changed his bike position to better suit climbing, invested in lighter equipment, trained on hills every day, and lost a bit of weight. This resulted in improvement, yet he was still dropped.

This process drove Sam deeper into believing that he was not very fit for racing and that he should not enter races. In reality, the problem was that this athlete was not built to be a pure climber. Working together, we changed the focus of Sam's training. We would avoid training on that hill. We started planning for him to ease up when he hit the hill, letting the pack drift away, thereby saving energy for later in the ride when the pack regrouped. Sam was instructed to forget about losing weight, to forget about spending money on light bike parts, and to forget about different positions. Instead, he would now concentrate on power training and sprints, all on flat or slightly rolling courses. Sam was encouraged to try out track racing. Sam noticed that he excelled in those situations and was even at the top of his category. He started entering more criteriums and short circuits (especially ones without hills), as well as more track races. He even started placing on the podium. Sam realized that, in fact, he was a very good racer, but previously he had not been playing to his strengths.

The interesting outcome is that with renewed confidence and perspective, Sam started posting personal records on the local hill, week after week, on the weekly group ride. He was still getting dropped but by less and less, and the best part was, he accepted the fact and relaxed into the group ride. With his new confidence and energy, he was able to shine on other parts of the ride that involved sprints. In fact, he became the man to watch in those instances. He started to shine on the rolling sections of the course as well, which he used to struggle on. Now others on the group ride had to pay attention to him on all parts of the ride.

Sam learned that it is not enough to have complete course knowledge, to be trained specifically, and to know where the action in a race or group ride is going to occur. You also need to know what you are capable of doing in those situations. Experiment now. Try everything. Find out what works for you.

Performing Self-Analysis

Self-analysis will make analysis of other individuals and teams more effective. Pay attention to personal strengths and weaknesses when training. Use the tools in this book to help you uncover personal abilities—for example, chapter 4 lists common power-to-weight averages per category level. Find out where you stack up against the competition; this will be a good indicator of your performance on climbs.

When undergoing physical, mental, or skills training, you should note exercises that you excel at or find enjoyable and easy. If you enjoy power workouts but dislike lactate threshold workouts, this may indicate that you are the type of racer who should sit in for the sprint instead of trying to drive breaks. If you enjoy rides with many turns, near traffic, or down twisty descents, this may indicate that you should choose races that require above-average technical skills. Alison Dunlap—professional mountain biker, two-time Olympian, former world champion, and former national champion—says the following: "I like a power sprint much more than anything. I get freaked out in the big field sprints. I don't like bumping elbows with people." Alison knows her strengths and comfort level and plays to them.

Controlling the Race

The way to win at chess is by executing well-planned, unexpected attacks and by blocking the attacks of the opponent. In addition, you need to force opponents to make moves that they otherwise would not make. This is also an effective strategy for bicycle racing, especially the part about forcing others to make moves that they otherwise would not make, which is often overlooked by racers.

Making Others Work for You

In races, most cyclists focus on trying to manage their own energy—food intake, timing of attacks, pacing—but the real key to successful racing is turning that inward focus outward. Through an outward focus, you can find ways to waste the energy of the competition.

For example, many cyclists see a gap forming in front of them (or in front of the person in front of them) and think, *I better close that gap before I get dropped*. They close the gap as rapidly as possible. In some instances, such as climbing, this is a good move; however, in most other instances, it is not. Your rapid reaction to close the gap will burn your energy as you toil in the wind until riding up to the distanced wheel. Here's a better approach to try during a group ride or race: If a gap starts to open, do not close it immediately; just maintain the same pace. Suddenly, nervous riders will rocket around you and close the gap. As they pass, move on their wheel and use their draft to regain contact with the pack (see figure 6.5). This saves your energy, but most important, it wastes their energy.

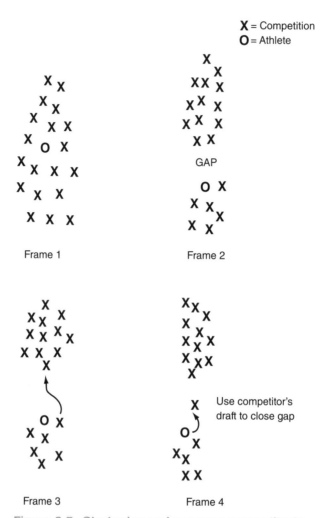

Figure 6.5 Strategize and use your competitor's energy to close the gap.

In the Peloton While riding in the peloton, you should use the knowledge gained from course analysis to waste the energy of the competition. Review the following examples and refer to figure 6.6:

● If the wind is from the right, stay on the left side, forcing the competition into the wind (see position 1). Cyclists in the wind work approximately 30 percent harder.

● When gaps form, let the competition close them. Take a free ride on the wheel of a competitor closing the gap (see position 2).

● When entering technical corners, carve the corner smoothly and then execute a few especially hard strokes on the exit, thereby forcing competitors behind you to close the gap you created.

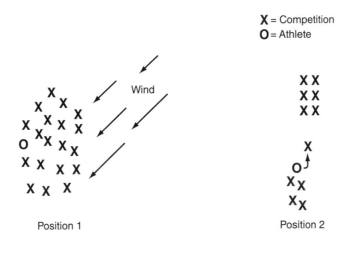

Position 3

Figure 6.6   Fortuitous pack positions.

- When climbing, throw in a couple of manageable surges. Do not surge to get away. The competition will hammer to close the gap. Recover as they approach. Surge again as they near, forcing them to hammer again and to waste energy at threshold.

- Move up within the peloton and not on the outside. Use the draft of competitors on either side (see position 3). To move up on the outside, wait for a free draft from a passing competitor and get on that person's wheel.

- Politely urge teams with no riders in the break to pull back the break, while you sit in.

In Breakaways   When you are involved in breaks, the best tactic is to actually work and not sit in. By sitting in, you waste energy—being on the back, moving in and out of the draft—as the breakaway pacelines. Yet, in racing, it is always best to do less work than others, meaning taking less powerful pulls or rotating through more quickly. This may not win friends, but it will win the race. The objective is to appear to be doing an appropriate share, even though you may not be.

The following are effective tactics to execute this strategy:

- Take position completely out of the wind when not contributing to pace making. If that means riding slightly off to the right or left, then do it.
- Take position behind the weakest rider. Taking a strong pull after a strong rider may actually force double work—once to stay on the strong rider's wheel as he pulls and once to take your actual pull, maintaining the stronger rider's pace. Reshuffle positions to gain position behind the weakest rider by skipping a turn or two on the back.
- Make deals with the other riders in the break so you can work toward your strengths. For example, if you are not a climber, take longer pulls on the flat. To stay in the break, suggest to competitors that they take it easier on the climbs, and in return you will work longer on future flats.
- When it gets close to the sprint, verbally urge other riders toward the front. Execute surges to break up the rhythm and to put the break on the best terms for your personal power management.

Attacking Effectively

As cycling legend Bernard Hinault says, "Attack and attack again till you get away or the rest give up." Although this quote has merit, a revision might say, "Attack *effectively* and attack *effectively* again till you get away or the rest give up." When, where, and how you attack are probably more important than *if* you can attack.

When to Attack Usually, in amateur racing, attacks that go early in the race are brought back by the pack. Unless teams are present who are willing and able to work to *block* or control the pace, individual riders will normally chase down attacks immediately. Attacking in the second half of the race increases the chances for success. By that time, individual riders who would be willing to chase are too tired to chase. You should attack when you are tired, because most likely the competition is just as tired. In this situation, you must mentally convince yourself to attack and stay away from a peloton that is equally physically and mentally tired.

Take advantage of lulls in racing to attack. Lulls occur when breaks are brought back or when the pack loses the impetus to keep pushing hard because of fatigue. Lulls may occur in the closing miles, because no one wants to lead out the field to the finish—everyone is attempting to save their energy for the sprint. When a break is brought back, be prepared to take advantage of the ensuing lull. Be prepared to follow other counterattacks, because they are sure to occur.

If a break has formed that contains a representative from the majority of teams in the race, an athlete must attempt to bridge the gap to the break. Other teammates of the riders in the break will block in order to prevent the pack from bringing back the break. A single rider may be allowed to bridge the gap, as long as he or she is not deemed a threat to the finish. However, if an athlete is known to be a good climber, for example, the blocking teammates might not let him or her bridge the gap if the race ends on an uphill.

If a break has locked up the race—meaning the pack will not catch it before the finish—you should attack in the closing miles. The pack has usually given up on the race mentally at this point. It is never wise to attack personal teammates; if your teammates are in a break, you should not attack. An attack will encourage the pack to chase you—and subsequently chase your teammates. Use the time when teammates are up the road to either passively sit in and save energy or block to aid their escape effort.

Where to Attack Analysis of the race course will help uncover good locations to launch attacks. For example, if you know that the course is turning into the wind in a mile, you should launch an attack. A lead into a wind will deter the pack from chasing. If a technical corner or series of corners is approaching, launch an attack so you can enter the corner first with a lead on the pack. The technical nature of the corners will most likely either slow the field or cause *splits*. The field may be too focused on the corners to actively chase. It is usually not a good idea to attack before hills, unless you know that you can outclimb the field. Packs usually climb faster than individuals. Yet, launching attacks *on* the hill is often a good idea. On a short hill, hit the bottom with good speed to provide momentum off the front and to help put you over the top first and with a lead. On a long hill, wait until halfway up or close to the top to launch the attack (see figure 6.7). Save a bit of energy to pedal through the long downhill on the other side; a pack descends faster than an individual.

Figure 6.7 Attack on the last half of a hill.

How to Attack Attack hard but silently. If the pack is traveling at 25 mph, an attack will need to be launched at 27 to 30 mph. Be prepared to maintain this pace in order to "snap the rubber band" to the pack. Once you have broken clear and a lead has been established, settle into a constant speed and rhythm. Attacks only survive with consistent speed, because the pack will be surging and slowing in an attempt to *reel the break back*—or catch the breakaway rider.

Attacking silently ensures that the pack is surprised and slow to react. To be silent, an attack should not be from the front. Instead, take position at least 10 riders back. As speed lulls, maintain your speed, moving up on the side away from the wind. It is best not to telegraph your intentions by standing up, *hammering*, rocking your bike back and forth, switching gears aggressively, or breathing hard. The idea is to slip off the front and then, once clear (in the saddle), pick up the pace to break clear (see figure 6.8).

Plan your attacks wisely. Do not write checks that you cannot cover. If you cannot go 25 mph on your own, why attack when the peloton is going above 25 mph? If you are not a sprinter, then you need to attack before the finish. Waiting may be too late and then you may be forced to sprint. If you are a good climber, you can use hills to attack. Do not wait for flat road.

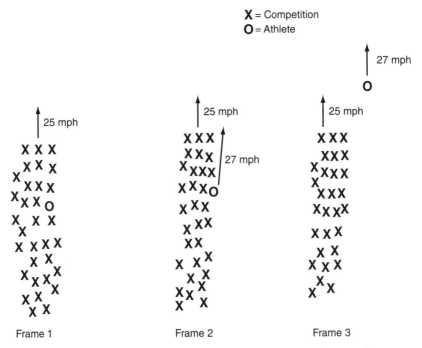

Figure 6.8 Rider attacks from a few places back in the pack, smoothly accelerating up to 27 mph.

Working With Teammates to Attack

Before the race, teammates should agree on when, where, and how they are going to individually attack. Although the race situation may dictate which attacks can be executed, having a plan puts the team ahead of most of the pack. If teammates know each other's plans, they can aid by attacking early to set up counterattacks and by moving into position to block.

If a team has more than one teammate in an attack or break, all teammates should initially work to establish the break. Once the attack has established itself, one teammate in the break should just sit in and recover, while the other teammates work. This cooperation will ensure that one teammate is fresh to attack the break in the closing kilometers or to power to the sprint win in the finale. If multiple teammates are in a break coming into a finish, they should "one-two" the competition, meaning one teammate should attack, and the other should sit in the wheels of the chasing competitors. As soon as the teammate is reeled in, the teammate sitting on should attack. Repeat this until the competition tires and one teammate can escape to the line.

Blocking Effectively

Blocking is an extremely effective way to establish breaks up the road. When blocking, you disrupt the rhythm of the chasers. Blocking always occurs near the front of the pack. This should never be executed in a dangerous manner—that is, bullying people into gutters, purposely braking, swerving, or sitting on the front indefinitely.

When and Where to Block   Whenever any of your teammates are off the front, you are responsible for blocking. As the teammate or teammates attack, move toward the front of the pack. This will give the teammates time to establish a break or maintain a break. If the break is certain to be reeled in, it may be advantageous for you to stop blocking, either to set up your own attack or to set up the attack of another teammate.

How to Block   The best way to block is by integrating into the chasing riders and disrupting their rhythm by not taking hard pulls or increasing the speed. For example, if a team or group of organized individuals are pacelining to chase, move into the paceline and neither contribute nor take away. If the group's average speed is 25 mph, then pull through and off at this pace. Never increase the speed, never slow the speed, and never sit on the front for any given length except to move up and off. This disrupts the rhythm of the paceline—because they will be attempting to pick up the pace or take longer pulls—but it will not aggravate chasing riders or cause dangerous conditions.

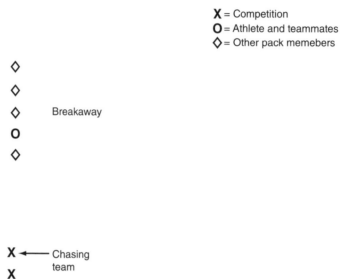

Figure 6.9 Blocking by gatekeeping.

Another method includes *gatekeeping*, whereby an athlete sits right on the wheel of the tail end of the pacelining chase (see figure 6.9). This athlete makes sure that other riders have a difficult time getting involved in the chase. By not contributing and by lessening the chance that others can contribute, the athlete ensures that the combined power of the chase is diminished.

Achieving Sprinting Success

Sprinting is an essential skill, especially in the amateur ranks where many races end in a mass gallop to the line. If sprinting is a weakness for an athlete, this does not mean that the athlete should not practice the skill or should avoid sprints. Even a little bit of practice will improve the chances for a win and will build confidence for future sprints.

Individual and Team

In most instances, sprinting occurs individually. If an athlete is fortunate enough to have an organized team, the team must be sure to practice lead-outs and sprints many times before executing them in races.

When sprinting, you should follow these tips:

- Know your competition. Find out who commonly wins sprints, and fight for the draft of that wheel in the closing miles.
- Line up your sprint position 3 to 5 miles (4.8 to 8.0 km) from the line. Many amateurs do not think about the sprint until the last mile. This practice will not get you to the line first.
- Remember that position is important. Make sure you are near the front so a clear shot at the line is available, but not so far forward that you find yourself on the front too far from the line.
- Know the finish. Know landmarks for timing a sprint. Be able to kick from an optimum position, usually within the last 300 meters (328 yards).
- In practice drills, find out how far you can sprint (where you are constantly accelerating toward and through the line). Measure this optimum distance from the finish before the race.
- Hold your pack position during the run-up to the sprint. This is no time to lose wheels, meaning getting gapped or blocked behind slower riders. In many cases, there is a sprint before the sprint, whereby the field splits. Be prepared for this initial sprint for position.
- When going for the win, look at the finish line and take a straight shot. Do not deviate from your line. Doing so may cause a crash.
- Do not hold back; put down the hammer and commit to the finish. A teammate once said, "When the sprint opens up and everyone is dashing for the line, you've got to pound [the pedals]."
- Keep in mind that sprinting can be a contact sport. Do not be a racer who initiates contact, but be prepared to fend off contact. Use the skills you acquired in bumping drills.
- Do not decelerate. Even a slight deceleration in the run-up will cost victory, either by having you lose momentum or by causing you to become gapped from the charging sprinters. Mario Cipollini—multiple Tour de France and Giro d'Italia stage winner and classics winner—says the following: "If you want to win sprints, don't touch your brakes."

Practice with your team numerous times before executing a lead-out in a race. Leading out is a carefully coordinated effort, and if it is handled sloppily, it can lead to crashes. A proper lead-out makes sprinting safer. In a proper lead-out, the speed is higher, providing an environment where there is less chance of multiple people crossing the line simultaneously. The lead-out needs to start miles from the finish and not in the finishing straight. Keep the speed high in the last few miles to deter attacks. Move lead-out teammates toward the front at least 8 kilometers (5 miles) from the finish, and start moving together in the pack and controlling the speed (see figure 6.10). Most racers are thankful for lead-outs; therefore, being courteous and asking for slots in the run-in by announcing a lead-out intention will win graces. Paceline the lead-out at a constant speed. Increase the speed as the finish line grows closer.

Within the final 2 kilometers of the finish, each lead-out person should do a hard, even pull that does not drop his teammates. The lead-out teammate should pull off after a hard pull and should move out of the peloton's way, dropping off on the side to the back. The sprinter, who is second to last, should be verbally directing his lead-out teammates, announcing which side to pull off on and telling them to increase speed as necessary. The last lead-out person should pull only a short distance (100 to 500 meters), and the effort should be a sprint. This lead-out person needs to pull off so the sprinter can launch within the last 200 meters. The last lead-out person often needs to keep sprinting to the best of his ability in order to avoid being swallowed up dangerously by a fast-moving pack. This is a safe way to finish. The last person in the group situated behind the sprint is the gatekeeper, who keeps other sprinters off the wheel of the team sprinter. This will lessen the chance of the competition using the lead-out team as a lead-out train that they can ride to victory. See figure 6.11 for illustration of a lead-out train.

Figure 6.10 Team setting up their sprinter with a lead-out train.

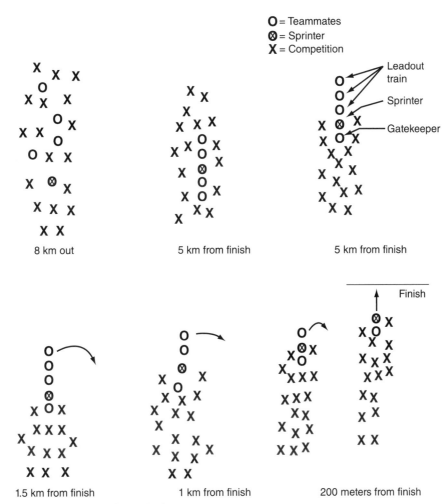

O = Teammates
⊗ = Sprinter
X = Competition

Figure 6.11 Lead-out train.

Executing a Sprint

To execute a sprint, place your hands in the drops with a firm grip and loose elbows. Having your hands in the drops prevents the bars from being hooked. The firm grip allows you to use your arms to power the body along in the hard effort. Keeping the elbows loose allows you to fend off bumping, cushioning the lateral bumps. Get low on the bike like a cat about to pounce. This keeps you aerodynamic and puts your legs over the pedals for maximum power.

Choose a gear that allows you to accelerate all the way to the line and also allows you to jump—that is, stand up and pound the pedals in the last 200 meters. Have the gear set before launching a sprint. Changing gears when the sprint is launched may cause a chain hop or skip, possibly causing a crash.

A Pro's Experience

Cody Stevenson, Adageo Energy Professional Cycling Team)

Lead-Out Train for the Win in the Tour of Hungary

It was the final stage of the Tour of Hungary in 2004—150 kilometers with a 5K finishing circuit that the racers completed four times. Cody says, "My teammates took control just before we hit the circuits, giving us the best opportunity to look at the circuit in the best position—the front—and also to keep us out of potential crashes. I had 3 guys rotate for the first 3 laps. After review, I could tell my team what I wanted in the finish."

With one lap to go, Cody planned to "hit out" halfway up the finishing straight. It was 350 meters from the last corner; however, it was into a headwind. He needed his teammate to take him through the last corner "full gas" and to keep sprinting on the exit. The final lap involved a lot of pushing, and coming into the last kilometer, Cody still had two teammates in front. Cody recalls, "With 700 meters to go, a team hit out over the top, and I yelled for my last lead-out man to switch to the back of their lead out. Coming into the last corner, my teammate hit out just before the corner, on the inside. I followed him through. He punched it through and out of the corner, allowing me to wait and then hit out with about 200 meters to go. I won, and as my team did a perfect job, I only had to hit the gas twice—once just before the corner, and then again with 200 meters to go."

Small-Group Sprint for the Win in Australia

As another example, Cody explains, "It is more common to have to sprint without a lead-out train." Cody was in a group of approximately 50 guys; it was a slight tailwind coming into the finish, so a lot of riders "fancied" their chances. Attack after attack took place in the final 15 kilometers; however, with the wind and the size of the group, Cody was confident that the group would stay together for a sprint finish. Cody had two teammates. As they came into the last 5 kilometers, Cody's teammates moved him toward the front, but on the edge of the "bubble," giving him room to move to another wheel if needed. Cody recalls, "The speed was very high, and I knew a few guys who like to hit out early, especially on a slight downhill tailwind finish. I told my teammate to take me a little closer to the front, around 10th wheel. There was a slight left-hand corner 350 meters from the finish, and a guy hit out there from behind me; as he went by, I jumped on his wheel and used him as a lead-out. I waited until the last 75 meters and jumped him right on the line. It was a bike throw that won it, but by waiting until the last second to do my kick I was able to just get him on the line."

What Can You Learn?

In both instances, team lead-out and competitor lead-out, Cody was confident of his skills to control the situation to his advantage. Cody learned these skills via many hours of individual and team practice. He analyzed the course in both instances and was prepared to jump at the opportune time. He used both his and his teammates' strengths, while taking advantage of his competitors' weakness (i.e., not knowing the course or the finish).

Leg speed is essential. Many top sprinters churn their gears at over 140 rpm. This allows quick acceleration to gap competitors to the line. Usually, the initial jump determines the finishing position.

When jumping, power the pedals using your arms to rock the bike back and forth. This rocking gives you a mechanical advantage. Always sprint with your head up to see the line and any competitor who may get in the sprint path. Think of the finish as 50 meters behind the finish line; this will help ensure that you accelerate through the line. Do not let up too soon, and be prepared for a bike throw.

Bike Throw

A bike throw may occur if competitors are neck and neck up to the line. To execute a bike throw, sprint to within a few meters of the line, and in one swift motion (pushing forward on the handlebars), drop your body low, push your buttocks back above and behind the saddle, and flatten your back (see figure 6.12). This will give you a slight edge to the finish line that could win the race.

Figure 6.12　Executing a bike throw.

Practice bike throws with comrades at slow speeds. Increase speed with each bike throw, practicing a seamless, split-second transition from hammering on the pedals to thrusting the bike in front of you.

Sprint Drills

Drill 1: Form Sprints

Form sprints are moderate-speed sprints that are used to practice transitioning from sitting to a jump, powering the bike while standing, and executing bike throws. Perform these on a closed road or a road with a large shoulder and little traffic. Perform 6 to 8 sprints, recovering for 3 to 5 minutes between each. Choose a moderate gear, such as 53 × 17 or 53 × 15. Heart rate and power are not monitored. Start the drill from a fast roll. Perform these form sprints alone. Riding with others may make it too competitive, thereby defeating the purpose of concentrating on personal form. Concentrate on a powerful smooth stroke, a smooth move to standing, and starting with a flat, low back as you power to the line. Also focus on throwing the bike within meters of the finish.

Drill 2: Overgear Starts

Pick a sprint gear. Come almost to a stop. Jump (i.e., stand and hammer) for 20 to 40 pedal strokes. Try to reach maximum speed in those strokes. Choose a moderate gear, such as 53 × 17 or 53 × 15. Recover for 4 minutes and repeat 6 times. Watch your knees. Be sure to warm up for over 45 minutes before performing this exercise. Heart rate and power do not need to be monitored.

Drill 3: Overgear Jumps

Pick one gear bigger than your sprint gear. Rolling at high speed (22 to 25 mph), jump for 20 to 40 pedal strokes. Try to reach maximum speed in those strokes. Recover for 5 minutes and repeat the drill 6 times, getting up to speed before jumping. Be sure to warm up for over 45 minutes before performing this exercise. Heart rate and power do not need to be monitored.

Practice these drills at least once a week during the development, taper, and race mesocycles. Perform the drills in both individual and group settings. Sprinting is such an essential part of bicycle racing—whether sprinting from a bunch or from a breakaway—that practicing it will give you an upper hand against the competition and will ensure that you have the skills to be safe in a fast finish.

Chapter 7

PERFORMING MENTAL TRAINING

The real race is not on the hot, paved roads, the tortuous off-road course or the smooth surfaced velodrome. It is in the electrochemical pathways of your mind.

—Alexi Grewal, 1984 Olympic road race gold medalist

The truth is, winning involves luck and other elements that are out of the athlete's control. But the saying "You make your own luck" is valid in the world of bicycle racing. Cyclists must attempt to limit elements out of their control by focusing on easily controllable elements.

To make your luck, you must understand how to complete the proper physical, technical, tactical, and mental training. Previous chapters focused on physical, technical, and tactical training. This chapter focuses on mental training. There is often little physical difference between individuals in races. The victory frequently depends on mental preparation. By using the concepts of cycling psychology presented in this chapter, an athlete can synergize all the aspects of physical training, improve and maintain motivation, and build confidence before and during competition. These factors can help put the athlete at the finish line first.

Thinking One's Way to a Better Season

All racers started out riding a bicycle for the pure enjoyment of the sport. As time passed, cycling became a large part of their extracurricular lives. They formed friendships, built a social network, or even worked in the cycling industry. For some, this initial enjoyment evolved into a career. The ones who are successful in this career are the ones who never lost sight of the original reason they started cycling in the first place—that is, they really enjoyed riding bikes!

Very few people who race will make it a full-time profession; however, an important lesson can be learned from the professionals—always keep sight of the enjoyment in cycling, even when it comes to stressful situations

© Human Kinetics

Mentally focused racers rolling out from a race start.

such as the buildup for and entry into races. Having this enjoyment focus through stringent training, aggressive group rides, and competition will keep the athlete in the sport and move the athlete to higher levels of physical aptitude in the sport.

Many racing cyclists start out by pushing themselves to train on the road, riding hour after hour. However, the best place to start is by taking a second to review *how* you approach bicycle racing mentally. In other words, identify what motivates you to reach goals. There are many approaches to motivation, but an easy-to-understand approach that works well in cycling is the achievement goal theory.

According to Nicholls (1984), two goal orientations—task goal orientation and ego goal orientation—lead to a person's own perceived ability. Naturally, a racer should have a high perceived cycling ability, because this means the person is confident enough to enter competitive situations and win. Studies have shown that a moderate level of ego orientation in tandem with a high level of task orientation yields the highest levels of perceived ability (Cox 2007). Understanding the interaction of these two goal orientations (task and ego) will start the aspiring racer off on the right foot to racing success.

Ego Orientation

For an ego orientation, perceived ability is measured as a function of outperforming others (Nicholls 1984). This is an important component in mass-start racing. In this type of racing, the athlete strives to win and outperform others to satisfy a need for a high perceived ability in cycling.

Ego orientation is usually how most promising cyclists enter the racing scene. They start attending group rides, and they discover that they can drop the other riders on climbs or in ad-hoc sprints. As a result, their ego tells them that they are more physically adept than the local competition. These cyclists notice that they are stronger compared to other riders—they can ride longer and faster, and they are less fatigued.

Unfortunately, an overreliance on this orientation can also be a negative trap. Jean-Paul van Poppel said, "In 1990, in every race I told myself you have to win, you have to win, you have to win. In this state, you make mistakes" (Strickland 2001). Although cyclists need to measure themselves against the competition, they must also have contingencies in case they find that they are rarely on the winning end of matchups. In a hypothetical example, a local racer sees promise in a local rider after a fast, hilly group ride—that is, the rider made it over all the hills with the lead group and even had enough energy to fight for the town-line sprint. The racer, in encouraging the rider to race, says, "You should really race. You are very strong." Then she pauses and says, "You learn a lot about yourself racing. It is very humbling." Racing is humbling, because many things have to go one's way to win (i.e., uncontrollable elements). In addition, after putting in months of training, if the athlete does not win, the athlete may feel humbled and discouraged by the experience. But the reality is that racers have off days, compete against unexpectedly stronger riders, and are sometimes ill-prepared for events, no matter how much training is undertaken. On those days, an ego orientation may stunt motivation by allowing thoughts of low perceived ability. Cyclists who continually have low levels of perceived ability will eventually create negative connotations toward training, competition, or the sport in general. These cyclists may drop out of the sport.

Many cyclists move through the lower categories having their motivation dictated by high race placings that serve as a measure of their perceived ability. This should be avoided. Eventually, these cyclists run into a category where they are outgunned. They may not have another motivation system set up, and they may drop out of racing altogether. Bicycle racing rewards those who have the mental fortitude to continue racing and training despite poor race placings and training setbacks. Therefore, athletes must have mechanisms that enable them to persevere under these circumstances. This is where task orientation steps in to help the athlete maintain motivation and focus.

Task Orientation

For task orientation, perceived ability is measured as a function of mastering a specific skill (Nicholls 1984). This is an important component of motivation in competitive events and training. The athlete strives to perform a task better each time, which satisfies a need for a high perceived ability in cycling. The task-oriented individual continues to work at the task, regardless of any setbacks, because the end goal is mastery of the skill. The athlete perseveres in training and racing by remaining focused on specific tasks that lead to overall improvement. This orientation is necessary and needs to be more dominant than ego orientation.

In all types of sports, athletes or teams sometimes have their ego deflated by a stunning loss in a competition that they should have won. Before the loss, their ego orientation told them that they were going to be the winners because they were ranked number one, had won the event before, or had undergone better preparation than the competition. After the loss, the athletes' response (perhaps after some pouting) is to focus on a task orientation. In other words, they analyze how they lost, determine what they could change in training to help reduce this deficit, and set training goals related to a new task that will repair the deficit.

The systematic nature of cycling training naturally draws task-oriented individuals. Their need to improve at a specific task drives them to success in the sport. The trick is balancing this with the ego orientation. When an athlete's ego steers her toward low perceived ability, it is time to assess the situation and to set about improving at specific tasks. This is truly the heart of training—identifying a series of tasks to master, and once those tasks are mastered, moving on to more advanced tasks.

Get started with task orientation by ensuring that every training ride has a specific purpose. Although the statement "I am going on the Saturday ride to win the sprint" is valid, it does not provide a base from which to build future improvement. The statement does not identify specific skills to be measured or improved. It is better for a cyclist to say, "I am going to the Saturday ride to achieve a higher sprint speed," or "I am going to the Saturday ride to work on starting my sprint from a farther distance," or "I am going to the Saturday ride to practice the best pack position from which I start my sprint." These statements identify measurable goals based on tasks. Whether winning or losing the sprint, the athlete can take count of success in improving the task and can attempt to improve it further in subsequent sessions. The athlete will be guaranteed to sprint better and faster as the weeks pass.

A task orientation can be used in racing as well. Of course, all racers who head to the starting line want to win, and they believe that they or their teammate can win the race. However, only one person will achieve this goal in the race. That's why you need to show up to races with tasks (i.e., working on a race-specific skill) at the forefront of your mind, rather than focusing on your ego (i.e., outperforming others). Racer-specific tasks can be as simple as attempting to stay in the top 10 for the entire race, which is actually very difficult, or performing the perfect lead-out for a teammate in the sprint. Tasks may also be specific to the race course. These

What's Your Plan B?

This advice is given to students facing the challenge of acceptance to a competitive graduate school: Always have a plan B, in case you do not get into graduate school. Some may question this approach, thinking that it may cause a person to take his eyes off the prize. In fact, the applicants who have a plan B are often the ones who are accepted into graduate school. Many who do not have a plan B do not get in. The reason for this is that those who have a plan B are also people who have thought through their motives for entering graduate school (i.e., Is it right for them? Are they choosing the right school? What are they truly looking to achieve by entering graduate school?). In setting up their plan B, they give a lot of thought to plan A. Thus, they approach getting into graduate school with focus and maturity. The students who neglect a plan B are often less focused and less sure of their motives. They often make application choices that do not suit their personalities.

When entering races, your plan A may be to win the race—this plan is based on your ego orientation. However, you should be sure to set up a plan B based on your task orientation. The plan B is a task, such as those mentioned earlier, and your focus on the task will likely put you in position to have a chance at winning the race. And if you do not win the race, you can review your performance to determine if the task was achieved or not. If yes, build on the task for your next race. If not, reevaluate your approach and training and try to achieve the task the next time. In essence, by working toward a task, you go home a winner, even if you do not cross the line first.

tasks can be as simple as knowing that the race is won in the last corner and trying to get to the last corner first. Another example is knowing that the hill is where you were dropped last year, but using your energy more wisely to make it over the hill this year.

Mental Training: Pre-Event and Competition Strategies

As stated earlier, winning requires luck and other elements that are mostly out of your control. These elements may include how you or your teammates are feeling that day, what position you are in at a certain time, whether you follow the right moves, the course environment, how poorly your competition is feeling that day, and so on. You should go into a race with a specific goal and plan. A specific goal or plan will enable you to place things in your control outside the confines of just winning or losing. By doing this, you will have more success in that race and will be better prepared for races you enter afterward.

A Pro Balances Ego and Task Orientations

Lance Armstrong spoke of finishing one of his early European professional races—the San Sebastian Classic—in last place. Lance, a phenomenal talent even in professional triathlon before entering cycling, was coming off dominating the U.S. racing scene. In Europe, at San Sebastian, this superstar was utterly humiliated. By the time he arrived at the finish line, they were tearing down the stage, stands, and barriers. His ego was crushed, but he did not pack it in. He did not do so during the race, where he could have just pulled off the course (which is not dishonorable in cycling once you are completely out of the action). Nor did he let this situation curtail his focus after the race; instead, he resolved not to have that happen again. His task orientation told him that finishing the race was the priority. He swallowed his ego and rolled in to face the humiliation at the finish. His task orientation also told him how to prepare for the event in the future, now that he had seen the course. He knew he had a series of tasks ahead of him to master. He also knew that once he mastered those tasks, he could return to the San Sebastian confident in his ability to win—and he did years later.

Lance knew that motivation to race could not be solely ego oriented. Without that knowledge, he would have quit that day, or worse, he would have continued racing with some resentment. Instead, by focusing on tasks, he kept his motivation up through this challenging time in his career, and he went on to further greatness.

Many myths about psychological preparation exist. Here are some examples: To do well, you need to be really psyched up; last-minute advice always gives the athlete an advantage; prerace pep talks are good motivators; nervousness is good before competition; and psyching techniques are the same for every athlete. The truth is that every athlete has her own level of anxiety and arousal when entering events. Some athletes should relax more, some athletes should "key up" more, and some athletes need extensive pre-event and event psychological routines, while some need the minimum (Martin and Lumsden 1987). The following sections provide the basics for finding a mental routine that works for you.

Controlling Distracting Thoughts Thoughts such as worrying about other competitors, losing, and personal or family problems can distract an athlete and reduce performance. Each athlete should take a mental inventory of any distracting thoughts before competition. *Centering* procedures should be employed to reduce these thoughts before and during competition.

Centering emphasizes muscle relaxation, a particular way of breathing, and thought control through self-statements. You should consciously relax the neck and shoulder muscles. Some people find that when they

Reasons for Mental Training

1. On the day of competition, there is little that can be done to enhance physical performance in terms of training.
2. What you say to yourself and how you think will affect performance.
3. Having a detailed plan for competition day allows you to see what factors positively or negatively influence performance.
4. Mental training minimizes the effects of the competition's psych-out attempts.
5. This training prevents excessive nervousness or tension, which may hinder performance.
6. Mental training techniques are applicable to everyday life as well as competition.

From Martin and Lumsden (1987).

relax these muscles, the muscles tighten up again instantly. If this occurs, force yourself to relax them again. You should breathe from very low in the abdomen, resisting the urge to breathe high in the chest. Another term for this is *belly breathing*. This is a technique of breathing from your diaphragm as opposed to your upper chest. As you inhale, think of filling your abdomen with air and expanding your belly. Outside of competition, this can be practiced by placing a light book or magazine on your belly when lying down. If breathing from the belly, you will see the book or magazine rise noticeably. It is helpful to think "relax" when belly breathing.

To achieve thought control through self-statements, you should write out positive thoughts in a script to recite before and during competition. The more specific these thoughts, the better. For example, the following statement is positive and may be relaxing: "I am not going to worry about the competition." However, a better self-statement would be as follows: "I am here to work on increasing sprint speed and not to worry about placing in primes or the overall win."

Another area that can be addressed with self-statements includes worrisome thoughts about losing. For these thoughts, a self-statement could be as follows: "Losing is a part of competition. Losing is not the end of the world. I am here to reach my own realistic, reachable goals. I have as good a chance of winning as everyone else." Many cyclists reach the line and suddenly start doubting the six months of training under their belt. A self-statement such as the following may help: "I believe in my training and training plan. I have shown improvement throughout. This competition is an extension of my training." Identify distracting thoughts and develop positive, specific statements to counteract these thoughts.

Write down the statements, and review them the night before or the morning before competition. Have them at your mental disposal so you can repeat them if distracting thoughts creep into your mind before or during a race.

Reducing Excessive Nervousness or Anxiety Excessive nervousness or anxiety has been linked to reduced performance. When an athlete is overly nervous, practice routines are less likely to occur in competition, response to environmental cues may be reduced, and physical energy may be wasted. This is another example of where centering can help the athlete cope. Centering self-statements that can be used to reduce anxiety include "Worrying never helps, so stop worrying" and "I have a goal and plan. It's time to review them."

In addition to centering, a prerace routine can help reduce anxiety. Practice the routine several times outside of competition, so you are just going through the motions on race day. The simpler the routine—that is, the less equipment or fewer personal tasks involved—the better. Here are some examples of tasks that could be included in a prerace routine:

- Choose a prerace eating time that allows you to digest before the start of the race—two hours of digestion is a good standard to follow.
- Lay your clothes out or pack your bag for the race the night before.
- Do a mechanical check and cleaning of your bicycle two days before competition.
- Write down a specific prerace warm-up routine (performed on a stationary trainer) and follow it. Review tables 3.1 and 3.2 in chapter 3 for criterium and time trial warm-up routines.

Psyching Up (if Needed) Some athletes may be too relaxed, disinterested, or complacent in the lead-up to and during the event. Being relaxed is associated with confidence; however, being too relaxed at the wrong time in cycling events may lead to missing the break, poor sprint positioning, or lack of attention in technical situations. Mario Cipollini says, "I don't fail to finish because I'm physically not up to it, but because I get mentally tired" (Strickland 2001). Some techniques for getting psyched up include bursts of physical activity (such as a hard workout on the trainer), rehearsal statements (such as "I'm going for it" or "I'm not holding back after all this training"), and listening to music with fast tempos. Practicing these psych-up strategies before group training rides is essential to having them established for race day.

Note that everyone's mental preparation is different, so pressing your techniques on others is unwarranted. For example, if fast music is your psych-up technique, you should use headphones; do not ramp up the car audio and open all the doors on your car for the entire field of competition to hear. Some find the group format a better method for psyching themselves up. For example, teammates sit on trainers and warm up together. This is a good technique if you do not find the group setting too distracting, intimidating, or anxiety inducing. You will notice that even though a group warm-up is occurring, many athletes have on headphones with individual music.

Handling Psych-Out Attempts From the Competition Competitors may do things that disrupt an athlete's preparation. Many times, the competitors are disruptive without intention or consciousness. The image of the blasting car radio is a good example of how the competition is not intentionally distracting to others; the competition's actions are just an extension of their own mental warm-up. A group of competitors simply warming up together could be seen as a distraction. Athletes may find this unnerving because the competition looks more official or in better team unison than themselves. The loudness of opponents talking about strategy over the sound of their trainers and music playing may also be intimidating.

Some racers psych themselves up with a hard workout on the trainer before a race.

© Human Kinetics

The key is to find out what aspect of your preparation is being psyched out. Psych-out behaviors usually fall under three categories: those that affect motivation, those that affect strategy, or those that affect mood. Motivation psych-outs disrupt the competitors from their focus and technique in competition. This can occur when seeing a team warm up. You may think, Wow. They look really good and strong. No matter how hard we try, they will still beat us. If you realize that the psych-out is affecting your motivation, then it is time to review your race goals and your purpose for being at the race. If you focus on these, the psych-out attempts will not matter. In fact, the more rehearsed your prerace and competition routine, the more likely you will be confident in your success, thereby maintaining high motivation.

Strategy psych-outs distract competitors from their cues for success in competition. Strategy psych-outs can come in various forms, but they predominantly occur in two situations: (1) you overhear another team's strategy and think your own strategy is inadequate, or (2) a powerful opponent unexpectedly shows up to race. You may even hear this from other competitors: "Bill is here. We are all racing for second." In this situation, you need to review your strategy and stick with it. Last-minute changes will most likely not affect the outcome positively. Having well-defined roles in the race for you or your teammates helps diminish the threat of the strategy psych-out. For example, if the strategy is to work to keep the race together for the sprinter, then stick with the plan, whether or not the local sprint winner from another team shows up. If you are racing alone, you are most likely following a looser plan, and you should adapt to reach your original goal as the race ensues.

Psych-out behaviors may also affect mood. These antics distract the competition from the main goal of fair sport. These are usually negative situations where the competition acts aggressive unnecessarily or at inappropriate times of the race (e.g., as you roll out). They may involve tantrums and yelling within the peloton. The best strategy is to move away from such ploys and not respond. Usually, such antics will extinguish themselves if left alone. In the case where some harsh words are exchanged or physical contact is made during a run-up to a sprint, you have to decide if it is excessive and unnecessary. If so, speak with the chief referee to resolve the issue immediately after the race.

Using Imagery Imagery is rehearsing a competitive scenario and outcome in your mind before or after the actual event. When using imagery, the concern is not with increasing, decreasing, or dealing with a particular behavior, but with providing a positive environment in which you can compete. Many times imagery is not something that is undertaken on race day or even the days leading up to the race; instead, imagery is done well in advance of the race. Imagery works best if you are in the moment rehearsing an outcome. Imagery can be broken into two categories: forward imagery (or envisioning future outcomes based on real-time training) and reverse imagery (or envisioning future outcomes based on previous training). For example, when practicing sprints, imagine beating other competitors to the line. This is forward imagery. When practicing climbing, imagine dropping competitors as the road steepens. Put yourself in a race moment. This is also forward imagery (Cox 2007).

On the day of the race, you should not imagine crossing the finish line first, because that is an arbitrary goal based on other uncontrollable elements. Instead, use reverse imagery. Imagine those moments in training when you were pouring on the power and your comrades were begging for mercy. Imagine the last town-sign sprint you won. Use reverse imagery to draw confidence in your abilities. Use reverse imagery to calm yourself and to know you are prepared for the competition. Reverse imagery helps you feel as though the race is nothing extraordinary, but just another training moment.

When using imagery, you need to be as specific as possible. When imagining dropping your competition, make the image complete: What do you hear? What do you see? What do you smell? How do your legs feel? How does the bike feel? How does the road feel?

Controlling Thought Content Cycling, unlike more explosive and reactionary sports (such as tennis), provides a lot of time for thought. Many cyclists find that controlling thoughts through rehearsal improves their performance. Classify thoughts as mood or technique, write down a detailed script, and rehearse the words before competition. For example, when sprinting, a cyclist may have a general mood thought such as "Pound," "Jump," "Go, go, go," or "Bam, bam, bam!" Here are some specific repeating mood thoughts: "Keep it in the 53-15. Keep it in the 53-15," or "Stay on that wheel. Stay on that wheel," or "Hold third position. Hold third position," or "Keep the power on. I'm dropping everyone. Don't let up. I'm dropping everyone." When climbing, technique thoughts may include "Keep the upper body relaxed and focus all energy to the legs" or "Stay in an easy spinning gear and resist pushing big gears." When the field is speeding along in single file, use technique thoughts such as "Stay low and in the draft with loose elbows to minimize drag" or "Pedal smoothly to save energy."

Rehearsing your thoughts and segmenting them into various areas of competition will help you get into the *flow* of competition (Csíkszentmihályi 1999). Part of being in the flow is finding the rhythm of the race—where you always seem to be in the right place at the right time and in much better condition than your competition. Part of getting to a flow state involves rehearsing a script to the point where it is so second nature that you do not even realize that you are saying the statements to yourself; you are simply acting out their commands.

The Moment in a Race All races come down to a moment. The moment defines who will be in a position for the win. Normally it occurs within seconds. For example, the moment might occur when you notice who starts the sprint first and then react. Or, it might happen when you observe a slowdown in the pack and then slip off the front. Or maybe the moment happens when you end up in a break. Usually after the race is finished, a rider can look back and remember the moment that made or lost the race. The key, though, is being able to react without much thought, instead relying on experience and instinct when the moment occurs. Some racers have a natural talent for this fast reaction, but many need to race extensively to learn how to recognize such moments.

A good place to start is the local group ride. Look for moments when the pack splits, the sprint starts, a tactical move is executed. Be ready. Be willing. React. This is not a physical skill, but a mental skill. Train yourself

A Pro's Experience

Janel Holcomb, USA Women's Bicycle Racing Team

Prerace and Race Routine

Janel Holcomb says the following: "The fact that I love racing and that I do this professionally doesn't preclude me from prerace nerves and excitement. When my emotions take over, I lose precious sleep, so I learned early on that I must conscientiously prepare myself so my head is in the right place and I can be relaxed when the start gun is fired."

Janel explains that mental preparation revolves around two things: visualizing the race and setting goals. Most of her attention is given to the race course. Janel says, "Knowing the course forms the framework for my thinking about the race. First I divide the race into three to four pieces based on time or distance. Then, I divide the course into consecutive pieces, such as flat areas, major climbs, and sprint or queen of the mountain (QOM) points. This methodology gives me something manageable to focus on during the race." Janel adds that no matter what point she is at in the race, she has something to keep her mind focused on down the road. Janel says, "This helps me through mental and physical fatigue, the hardest parts of the race, and gets me closer to the finish." She thinks beyond the most difficult parts if struggling, or she thinks about the parts of the course that play to her strengths in order to increase her confidence.

When Janel does not have the luxury of preriding a course, she uses the race's technical guide to learn everything possible. Janel remembers, "When stage racing in Germany in the summer of 2008, I made bar tape for every race: On a two-inch piece of medical tape, I wrote down the feed zones, sprint and QOM lines, and where the start and summit of climbs were. It's like virtual visualization!"

Setting goals is another trick used by Janel. She chooses a major goal and minor goals for every race. The major goal can be about a finishing place or a job for a teammate. Janel says, "During the race, if I feel stretched to the point where my goal hangs in the balance, I remind myself that, at the beginning of the race, I had an achievable goal. I change my thinking from negative to positive then refocus on what's coming up next in the course."

Janel continues, "Setting minor goals keeps me mentally engaged in the race. If my goal is to hold position near the front of the pack, I repeatedly check to see where I am and if I can move up. Alternatively, perhaps I decide to go for points in a QOM competition." During stage 1 of the Cascade Classic in a past season, Janel was set on meeting that goal, and it was not until three-quarters up the major climb that she realized that she was part of an incredibly selective breakaway. Janel was so focused on her goal that she did not have the opportunity to think, *There is a world champion in this group! I don't belong here!*

Realistically, Janel has days when she feels too exhausted to race, when stage racing has ruined her appetite, when the peloton is nervous and dangerous, or when things don't seem to be going as planned. Janel says this about those moments: "I find reasons to smile." When the pack gets nervous, she may sing a song to herself to relax. If she gets dropped, she will say to herself, "Janel, you're doing great! You are strong. It's OK. You can do this." And, when she crosses the finish line, whether first or in the pack, Janel thinks, *How lucky I am to be able to race my bike.*

What Can You Learn?

Janel balances both orientations—ego and task—along with using many mental training techniques while preparing for and participating in races. She sets large and small goals and maintains focus by constantly striving for them, regardless of the circumstances. Yet, she is adaptive as the prerace situation or race situation morphs. Her framework, backed by sound mental training techniques, allows her to remain competitive even when tired or momentarily distracted. This framework makes each race experience an opportunity to grow and improve as a competitive cyclist, regardless of the finishing outcome.

to mentally "switch on" when you see the moment and instantly move yourself into position to take advantage.

Taking Inventory During a Race   Races can be long and monotonous, so you must train yourself to be mentally acute at all times during an event. You should always be taking inventory of what you are doing in a race. It is very easy to become distracted by elements occurring inside the race—poor bike handling, aggressive yelling, fighting for position, suffering on a long climb—and elements occurring outside the race—bills, careers, family—so it's important to mentally train yourself to recognize these distractions and realign your attention to the race. It can be helpful to simply ask yourself the question: *What am I doing right now?* The answer may surprise you.

Following are some primary concerns you'll want to assess as you take inventory:

- Are you overlapping wheels, thereby increasing your chances of a crash?
- Are you riding on the windward side, providing everyone in your leeward side a free draft?
- Are you in the back of the pack, out of position to follow attacks?
- Are you drinking and eating enough?
- Are you grinding along in a big gear instead of keeping your legs fresh by spinning?

Some longer-term situations to assess include the following:

- Are you moving up in time to be in position for the start of the sprint?
- Are you executing your plan by preparing for attacks in the second half of the race?
- Are you helping protect a teammate before the big climb?
- Are you defending your position before a technical section of the race?

Postrace Focus

Once the race is run, the athlete should immediately accept the results (unless an infraction needs to be sorted out with the chief referee). The race is complete and is in the past, so dwelling on it, especially if the connotations are negative, is never a good idea. Just like your prerace and competition routine, having a postrace routine will help you prepare better for future training and racing.

You need to cool down after a race effort, which is usually a maximal effort even beyond the effort put forth in training. Head over to your stationary trainer or head off the race course and roll around easy for at least a half hour. The trainer works best, because when your stomach

© Human Kinetics

Postrace cool-down spin.

settles, you will be close to your packed cooler of recovery food; you can then begin to eat (to replace your energy stores) and drink (to rehydrate). If your trainer is not available, grab food and refill your water bottles so you can refuel and rehydrate on the roll. You should attempt to return to noncompetition levels of stress and anxiety; in other words, clear your head and do not think about the race.

Once your cool-down is complete and you have calories in your body (more information on postrace refueling is provided in chapter 8), you should start your postrace analysis. This is not an exercise in degrading yourself, your teammates, or your competitors. Instead, it is an exercise in finding the things that worked—these are things that you will want to do more of in training or in the next race.

Thinking about the following elements of the race will help you complete a postrace analysis properly:

- When was I holding a good pack position?
- When did I pace myself properly?
- When did I put down my best surge?
- When was I analyzing the race situation properly?
- When was I in the flow?
- When did I exhibit good technical skills?
- When did I exhibit good strategy?
- When and how did I bridge a gap?

By focusing on positive elements, you know what you can build on and improve in practice. If you focus on the negative elements, you may force yourself to focus on elements that you cannot build on or improve. For example, you may analyze a race in this manner: "I was pedaling smoothly, had a relaxed upper body, put out even high power, and responded to surges on the third climb of the race." This is better than analyzing as follows: "When I was getting dropped on the third climb, I had no power, was all over the bike, and could not respond to one surge." There is nothing beneficial or anything you can learn from the second analysis. Using the first analysis, you can head into training knowing what you want to continue to build on: smooth pedaling, relaxed upper body, even power, and response to surges.

Chapter 8

MAINTAINING PROPER NUTRITION AND HYDRATION

Our bodies are like a car. When you drive a lot and drive very fast, you need more oil than a normal car.

—Jean-Paul van Poppel, multiple stage winner in all three Grand Tours

For athletes to reach their potential in training and racing, they need to approach nutrition with the same attentiveness and eagerness as an interval session. Eating only to compensate for the calories burned will simply not do. Well-balanced diets in general—in addition to proper fueling before, during, and after exercise—are instrumental to cycling success. An easy trap for cyclists is to believe that they need to mainly eat engineered foods, drink mixes, and vitamins to achieve their potential. The simple fact is that athletes need a properly balanced diet of unprocessed foods. More portable foods—such as bars, gels, or mixes—are useful during racing and long training, but their makeup should again be only natural ingredients.

This chapter provides athletes with the know-how to review their current nutritional intake and to properly modify their nutritional intake while training and racing. Athletes will also learn how to use long-term nutritional strategies to help ensure that they reach their potential throughout the cycling season.

General Nutritional Needs for Endurance Athletes

An endurance athlete's diet—like everyone's diet—can be thought of in broad terms as needing to include fat, carbohydrate, and protein. The difference between the nonathlete and athlete is that the majority of an endurance athlete's nutrition should come from carbohydrate. This ensures the replenishment of glycogen stores after bouts of exercise, and it provides the quick-yield energy needed for intense racing and training. Protein serves to rebuild muscles and other cellular structures of the athlete's system and provides building blocks in order to maintain physical systems. Fat provides the longest lasting and most calorie-dense energy source for an endurance athlete. Fat also provides the bases for many cellular structures and hormones.

A gram of carbohydrate contains 4 calories, a gram of protein contains 4 calories, and a gram of fat contains 9 calories. Fat and carbohydrate are both burned during endurance exercise. Fats are mostly burned at endurance paces of heart rates lower than 75 percent of maximum heart rate (MHR); carbohydrate is mostly burned at near anaerobic or anaerobic efforts of greater than 88 percent of MHR. Simply put, the more intense the effort, the greater the ratio of carbohydrate versus fats burned. Protein is rarely metabolized as an energy source, and this usually occurs only in the direst of circumstances. Your body stores approximately 2,500 calories of

Energy Source Needs for Endurance Athletes

Carbohydrate

- Athletes need 3 to 5 grams of carbohydrate per pound of body weight daily.
- A 150-pound male athlete needs 450 to 750 grams daily.
- Carbohydrate should make up approximately 60 percent of total calories daily.

Protein

- Athletes need 0.55 to 0.75 grams of protein per pound of body weight daily.
- A 150-pound male athlete needs 82.5 to 112.5 grams daily.
- Protein should make up approximately 15 to 20 percent of total calories daily.

Fat

- Athletes need half a gram of fat per pound of body weight daily.
- A 150-pound male athlete needs 75 grams daily.
- Fat should make up at least 20 percent of total calories daily.

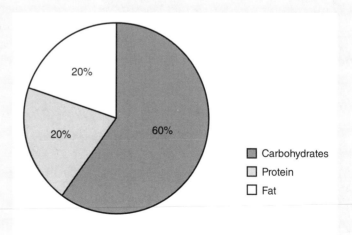

carbohydrate (in the form of muscle and liver glycogen) when completely topped off. Astonishingly, your body stores over 100,000 calories of fat. As an endurance athlete, fat provides an essential part of your energy production (Eberle 2000; Baechle and Earle 2000). Endurance training (less than 75 percent of MHR) may train the body to tap into using fat stores and is the foundation of training in the base mesocycle.

Everyday Nutrition Using the Food Pyramid

Like nonathletes, endurance athletes benefit from a high-fiber diet that is low in saturated fat and contains a wide variety of foods, focusing mainly on fruits, vegetables, and whole grains. One difference between nonathletes and athletes is that endurance athletes need more calories in general to compensate for calories burned during exercise. In addition, endurance athletes tend to need a greater ratio of carbohydrate than the average population.

© ega/fotolia.com

Food pyramid illustrating good dietary balance.

The U.S. Department of Agriculture and Department of Health and Human Services provide an excellent example of a well-balanced diet at MyPyramid.gov. Their food pyramid divides the diet into (a) fats, oils, and sweets; (b) milk, yogurt, and cheese; (c) meat, poultry, fish, and beans; (d) vegetables; (e) fruits; and (f) bread, cereal, rice, and pasta. This provides a perfect framework for athletes to ensure that they are eating properly and healthfully. The serving amounts in the food pyramid yield a total daily caloric intake of 1,600 to 2,800 calories. Although this may be well below the daily calories needed by an endurance athlete, the concept of a percentage of each section of the pyramid is applicable. Table 8.1 lists the recommended daily amounts of vitamins and minerals, along with their sources and indications.

Special note on sodium: A low concentration of sodium in the body is associated with weakness, fatigue, and seizures. The average intake is 2 to 5 grams daily. The body loses approximately 1 gram of sodium per quart of sweat. The daily average intake may be inadequate for heavy sweating athletes or athletes performing multiple-hour intense training rides, especially in hot conditions. Athletes, who are not in the salt-sensitive majority—meaning that high sodium intake correlates with high blood pressure—can consume up to 1 gram of sodium (about 0.5 teaspoons) per quart of fluid lost during exercise. Salty snacks (such as tomato juice, salted crackers, or low-fat salted pretzels) can aid in salt intake, but salty sports drinks are recommended. Most sports drinks do not provide enough sodium, because they are unpalatable for the general public. Putting table salt in a water bottle is the method I employ. In cooler weather, I place 0.125 teaspoons in a water bottle along with a carbohydrate solution of maltodextrin. In warm to hot weather, I place 0.25 teaspoons in water bottles with a carbohydrate solution.

Modifying the Food Pyramid

Cycling is a demanding sport in that you have to spend many hours on the bike to note improvements. Instead of the 1,600 to 2,800 daily calories recommended by the USDA's food pyramid, you may need closer to 3,000 to 5,000 daily calories when racing or training. To figure out your daily caloric needs, use a basal metabolic rate (BMR) calculator and multiply in an activity factor.

Approximating Basal Metabolic Rate (BMR)

The gold standard for truly testing a personal BMR is a laboratory that tests metabolism via respiration. Basal metabolic rate is the *approximate* amount of energy (in calories) that an individual burns each day at rest. Long-term activity factors are applied to a BMR to create an adjusted result; the initial BMR calculation does not take into account activity above and beyond normal daily functions. If you expend more calories beyond your

TABLE 8.1

Recommended Daily Amounts of Vitamins and Minerals

Vitamin	Dietary reference intake	Function	Sources
Vitamin A	900 mcg	Growth and repair of body tissues, bone formation, healthy skin and hair	Liver, egg yolk, whole milk, butter
Beta-carotene	1,000 mcg	Antioxidant	Carrots, sweet potatoes, spinach, turnips
Vitamin D	5 mcg	Aids in absorption of calcium and helps build bone mass	Tuna, shrimp, milk, fortified breakfast cereals
Vitamin C	90 mcg	Cell development, wound healing, and resistance to infections; makes iron available for hemoglobin synthesis	Sweet peppers, broccoli, strawberries, oranges
Thiamin (B_1)	1.2 mg	Normal functioning of nervous system and muscles; coenzyme for carbohydrate metabolism	Fortified breakfast cereals, peas, pork, pecans
Riboflavin (B_2)	1.3 mg	Coenzyme in red blood cell formation, nervous system functioning, and metabolism of carbohydrate, protein, and fat	Wheat germ, almonds, whey protein, yogurt
Niacin	16 mg	Coenzyme for carbohydrate, fat, and protein metabolism and proper nervous system functioning	Soy protein, peanut butter, textured vegetable protein, fortified breakfast cereals
Pyridoxine (B_6)	1.3 mg	Synthesis of hormones and red blood cells; coenzyme for protein metabolism and nervous and immune system function	Bananas, tuna, potatoes, alfalfa sprouts
Cobalamin (B_{12})	2.4 mcg	Blood formation and healthy nervous system	Shellfish, lamb, poultry, eggs

Mineral	Dietary reference intake	Function	Sources
Calcium	1,000 mg	Developing and maintaining healthy bones and teeth; assists in blood clotting, muscle contraction, and nervous system transmission; reduces risk of osteoporosis	Fruit juices fortified with calcium, sardines, yogurt, kale
Magnesium	400 mg	Enzyme activation; assists in nerve and muscle function	Bran, sunflower seeds, soybeans, almonds
Iron	8 mg	Red blood cell formation and function	Pork, cashews, clams, kidney beans
Potassium	4.7 g	pH balance, water balance, muscle growth, healthy nervous system and brain function	Raisins, dates, bananas, beans
Zinc	11 mg	Part of enzymes involved in digestion, metabolism, reproduction, and wound healing	Oysters, chicken, lima beans, white beans

adjusted BMR because of heavy physical activity, your calorie demands will increase in accordance.

The following calculation available from the American College of Sports Medicine (Israel 2001) is an approximation based on studies of varied populations. First, convert weight in pounds to kilograms by dividing by 2.2 (lb / 2.2 = kg). Second, convert height in inches to centimeters by multiplying by 2.54 (in. × 2.54 = cm). Use these converted amounts in the following gender-based BMR calculation:

Men

$$\text{BMR} = 66 + 13.8 \times (\text{weight in kg}) + 5 \times (\text{height in cm}) - 6.8 \times (\text{age})$$

Women

$$\text{BMR} = 655 + 9.6 \times (\text{weight in kg}) + 1.8 \times (\text{height in cm}) - 4.7 \times (\text{age})$$

Adjusting Your BMR With an Activity Factor Take the BMR result and multiply it by a long-term activity factor:

- 1.2—bed rest
- 1.3—sedentary
- 1.4—active
- 1.5—very active

Equation: BMR × activity factor

An activity factor is not a daily measure of activity, but a long-term measure of activity based on your lifestyle. A competitive cyclist would be considered active or very active in parts of the off-season and very active most other times of the year. *Active* means participating in a light exercise routine (such as walking) each day for more than 30 minutes while continuing to perform other activities. *Very active* means performing vigorous activity (such as a 1-hour ride) on a daily basis in addition to other activities. The BMR multiplied by the activity factor is an adjusted BMR and signifies how many calories one burns in an average day—it *does not* factor in additional exercise.

Adding in Daily Physical Activity On certain days, an athlete may expend more calories in training than on other days. For example, on one day, a cyclist may go for a 1-hour endurance ride. On another day, this cyclist may go on a 3-hour group ride at race pace. Logically, the latter will cause more calories to be burned. The calories you burn during this exercise must be added to your adjusted BMR. That will provide a good approximation of how many calories were burned on that given day.

Many heart rate monitors provide ways to measure calories burned via algorithms from height, age, and weight data. Power meters provide an almost direct link to calories burned in that they show total kilojoules expended. A kilojoule equals approximately 0.24 calories. The body is approximately 24 percent efficient in converting energy to work (Baker 2006). Thus, the kilojoule is a good estimate of calories burned.

Add the total kilojoules expended to your adjusted BMR to calculate how many calories you burned in a training day.

BMR Results: A Case Study As stated previously, adjusted BMR shows *approximately* how many calories your body burns in a day for basic functions. Let's look at an example of a 125-pound female athlete, 5 feet 6 inches tall, who is 32 years of age and cycles an average of over 2 hours a day (i.e., activity factor = very active). First, convert body weight in pounds to body weight in kilograms:

125 lb ÷ 2.2 = 56.8 kg

Second, convert height in inches to height in centimeters:

66 in. × 2.54 = 168 cm

Apply the converted amounts to the BMR calculation for women:

BMR = 655 + 9.6(56.8) + 1.8(168) – 4.7(32)

BMR = 1,352 calories

To adjust the BMR for activity level, multiply the calculated BMR by the appropriate activity factor:

1,352 × 1.5 = 2,028 calories per day

The approximate calories per day (2,028) identifies the amount of calories that this female must consume to maintain weight, as long as she continues her 2-hour-per-day cycling routine. In addition, she must factor in the calories actually burned while cycling, which is approximately 1,000 calories (i.e., about 500 calories per hour). Therefore, this female should consume about 3,028 calories on a 2-hour training day; she should consume less if she misses her 2-hour ride. On a 4-hour riding day, she may burn an additional 1,000 calories, which brings the total to approximately 4,028 calories needed for that training day.

Fat, Oils, and Sweets

Fat, oils, and sweets should be consumed sparingly. Many sweets contain carbohydrate in the form of simple sugar, but it is better to attain this form of carbohydrate from whole grains, fruits, and vegetables because these foods provide more nutritionally complete complex carbohydrate. A nonfat diet is unacceptable for the athlete, because fat is the precursor for many cell structures and metabolic functions. Yet, athletes should be wary of unhealthy fat such as trans fat (found in fried foods) or an abundance of saturated fat (found in fatty animal meats). These are often referred to as "empty calories" because they are high in calories but low in nutrients.

Fat is nearly impossible to avoid, and it should not be avoided because it provides necessary calories and has nutritional value. The goal is choosing foods that contain more healthful fat, such as nuts or olives—the unsaturated fat in these items is better than the saturated fat found in meats, which can lead to atherosclerosis and digestive distress. For example, it is better to use olive oil than butter, and it is better to choose lean cuts of meat such as sirloins as opposed to T-bones. If fat is on meat (e.g., chicken skin), remove it before cooking.

Omega-3 fatty acids—docosahexaenoic acid (DHA) and eicosapentaenoic acid (EPA)—found in dietary fish or fish oil supplements may reduce the risk of death, heart attack, dangerous abnormal heart rhythms, and strokes in people with known cardiovascular disease. In addition, these substances may slow the hardening of the arteries and may lower blood pressure slightly. An additional omega-3 fatty acid is alpha-linolenic acid (ALA), which is found in some nuts (e.g., English walnuts) and vegetable oils (e.g., canola, soybean, flaxseed or linseed, and olive) (Mayo Foundation for Medical Education and Research 2009).

If you are someone who enjoys sweets, removing them from your diet altogether is not advisable; however, you should curb your consumption of sweets. Candy should essentially be removed from your diet. If you enjoy fruit pies, try not to eat large slices or to eat pie every night with dinner. A better choice might be to eat a small slice in the morning before training—when it is certain you will burn those calories off. I enjoy cookies, but I avoid eating them at home. I do, however, carry them with me when I ride so I can eat them as a treat. I always choose healthy cookies, though, such as fig bars, which are low in fat, usually dairy free, and made from natural ingredients. Be wary of caloric sweeteners—sugar or syrups added to foods during processing or preparation. Consume little of these nutritionally poor items, which are identified on food labels as brown sugar, corn syrup, dextrose, fruit juice concentrates, high-fructose corn syrup, invert sugar, malt syrup, raw sugar, or sugar (refined) (Johnson et al. 2009). Current guidelines recommend that (1) women consume fewer than 100 calories of processed sugar daily (6 teaspoons or 25 grams) and (2) men consume fewer than 150 calories (9 teaspoons or 38 grams) (USDA 2005).

Examples of foods in this category (fat, oils, and sweets) include coffee, tea, soda, alcohol, butter, margarine, salad dressing, mayonnaise, jelly, condiments, candy, sugar, honey, syrup, sauces, and gravies. Others that are in both this category and other categories (i.e., protein and carbohydrate) include bacon, french fries, onion rings, chips, buttered popcorn, ice cream, sherbet, cookies, doughnuts, cakes, and pies.

Milk, Yogurt, and Cheese

- Two to three daily servings of milk products are recommended by the USDA's food pyramid.
- For an athlete needing about 3,000 daily calories, four daily servings are recommended.

- For an athlete needing about 4,000 daily calories, five daily servings are recommended.

Dairy provides many benefits, mainly calcium and vitamin D. In addition, dairy provides a very balanced (i.e., carbohydrate, protein, and low fat), easily digestible, and easily obtained calorie source. Examples of this food category are milk, cheese, yogurt, and ice cream. Dairy-containing products include the cocoa found in milk chocolate and chocolate milk, smoothies, and lattes. Puddings, custards, and even some breads contain milk in the form of dried whey. The goal is to choose dairy products that are low in fat or fat free. Because dairy is an animal product, the fat it contains is saturated. Choose skim (or fat-free) milk or low-fat yogurt. Dairy alternatives include fortified soy or rice milk, although these often contain less protein than regular milk. You should avoid cheese. Cheese is usually calorie dense (because of high fat content) but low in nutritional value, and it often contains additives for flavor, coloring, or texture. In many cases, cheese is not easily digestible and thus can cause irritation when training.

A Pro's Experience

Food Sensitivities

As training increases, your body may become more sensitive to foods—that is, foods that do not affect you at lower activity levels will affect you at higher activity levels. A regional professional racer spoke of his intolerance to lactose as a stumbling block to training and racing. He found success in using milk and other dairy products that included the lactase enzyme to break down the indigestible lactose. He says, "While dairy with lactase added is a bit sweeter tasting, the change is barely noticeable after a few tries." He uses lactose-free milk in cereal, smoothies, or even for a quick calorie source after a ride or with his meal at dinner.

He says, "I have found yogurt—a good source of necessary digestive bacteria—to be somewhat low in lactose and thus digestible. Many frozen yogurts are similar, although I consume it sparingly." He avoids ice cream, with its high levels of lactose, as well as most cheeses. He found that hard cheeses (such as parmesan) sit fairly well, but most other cheeses (especially creamy cheeses) are inedible for him.

What Can You Learn?

If you have a food sensitivity or allergy, such as lactose intolerance, finding the right foods may take some detective work. You will also need a bit of patience and perhaps humility in giving up well-loved (and tasty) foods. But by finding the appropriate foods for you, you will feel more healthy in general and will avoid any uncomfortable situations in training and racing. As you become more attuned to your body and place it through more intense rigors of racing and training, you should learn to listen to your body's signals for what foods provide nonirritating, proper nutrition and what foods put you on the sidelines.

Meat, Poultry, Fish, and Beans

● Two to three daily servings of meat and its alternatives are recommended.

● For an athlete needing about 3,000 daily calories, four to five daily servings are recommended.

● For an athlete needing about 4,000 daily calories, six daily servings are recommended.

Meat, poultry, fish, and beans provide nutrients to rebuild muscle and develop precursors for enzymes. In addition, this food category is a major source of iron (for hemoglobin) and zinc (for fighting infections). This food category includes beef, lamb, chicken, turkey, shrimp, scallops, lobster, tuna, mackerel, halibut, salmon, pinto beans, green beans, black beans, lentils, green peas, and other legumes. Many of the choices are animal based, so avoiding saturated fat is important. Choose lean cuts of meat (such as rounds or loins), or cut the excess fat from fatty cuts of meat. If the meat is streaked with fat (i.e., marbleized), it is best avoided. Choose boneless, skinless cuts of poultry. When cooking meat, choose to bake, broil, or grill (instead of frying or sauteing) in order to allow fat to drip off. Keep in mind that a serving of meat is three ounces, which is only the size of a deck of playing cards.

Foods in this category provide protein. Protein is an important component of the athlete's diet, yet it can contain many unhealthy pitfalls. To avoid pitfalls, follow these tips: Eat more fish, but be wary of fish containing heavy amounts of mercury. Fish with lower levels of mercury include wild salmon, albacore tuna, and sardines. Eat more beans, which are low in fat and high in fiber as well. Mix beans with whole grains to achieve the same complete protein profile as lean meat. Eat up to four eggs a week, but better yet, only eat the egg whites or choose low-cholesterol egg substitutes. Add tofu to pastas, noodles, or soups. Tofu provides high-quality protein, fiber, and minerals with little saturated fat.

Vegetables and Fruits

● Three to five daily servings of vegetables and two to four daily servings of fruit are recommended.

● For an athlete needing about 3,000 daily calories, six daily servings of vegetables and five daily servings of fruit are recommended.

● For an athlete needing about 4,000 daily calories, seven daily servings of vegetables and six daily servings of fruit are recommended.

Whole grains from the bread, cereal, rice, and pasta group are a relatively inexpensive and convenient way for an athlete to consume carbohydrate; however, athletes cannot overlook the need for vegetables and fruits in their diet. Fruits and vegetables not only provide carbohydrate calories, but also provide much needed fiber for gastrointestinal health. In addition, they provide most of the necessary vitamins and minerals for proper bodily functioning. Obtaining the appropriate amount of fruits and vegetables can be time consuming, and it takes some planning, but the payoff may be great. In fact, it is safe to assume that fruits and vegetables contain additional healthful nutrients whose benefits we have yet to discover.

Foods from this category include apricots, cantaloupe, carrots, kale, collards, romaine lettuce, spinach, sweet potatoes, winter squash, broccoli, cabbage, bell peppers, grapefruit, kiwi, oranges, strawberries, tomatoes, bananas, cherries, dates, figs, and pears. Strategies that can help you eat more veggies and fruit include drinking vegetable juice, eating vegetable soup, and buying ready-to-eat, precut vegetables in bags or from salad bars. You should avoid iceberg lettuce (which is low in nutrients) and instead choose spinach salad (which is high in nutrients). Other strategies include keeping frozen and canned vegetables on hand, trying lots of different vegetables to find the ones you like, drinking 100 percent fruit juice, keeping dried fruit (such as dates, raisins, or dried plums) on hand, and keeping frozen berries for cereal or smoothies.

Bread, Cereal, Rice, and Pasta

- The recommended daily amount of bread, cereal, rice, and pasta is 6 to 11 servings.
- For an athlete needing about 3,000 daily calories, 18 daily servings are recommended.
- For an athlete needing about 4,000 daily calories, 24 daily servings are recommended.

This group of foods is a relatively inexpensive and convenient way for all endurance athletes to obtain carbohydrate, the main source of energy for extended intense endurance exercise. As exercise intensity increases, the percentage of fuel that comes from carbohydrate increases. When the person's heart rate moves above endurance levels (greater than 75 percent of MHR), the percentage of carbohydrate burned begins to increase. As the athlete approaches 88 percent of MHR, the percentage of fuel coming from carbohydrate approaches 100 percent. Carbohydrate replenishes your glycogen stores. Your body taps into those stores during exercise to retrieve necessary fuel.

Foods from this category include breads, tortilla, pita, rolls, biscuits, muffins, small bagels, English muffins, dry cereal, cooked cereal, pasta, rice, crackers, pretzels, nonbuttered popcorn, and oatmeal. Obtaining calories from this group is easy because serving sizes are small; however, obtaining high-quality foods from this category can be a challenge. The goal should be *nutritious* carbohydrate, meaning more whole grains. Here are some tips for finding whole grains: Choose products whose first ingredient listed is

Serving Sizes

You may be thinking, *24 servings of carbohydrate! That seems like a lot!* Understanding a serving size is essential to learning how to properly fuel your body. Table 8.2 will help you to know exactly what counts as a serving for each of the food groups.

TABLE 8.2

Sample Serving Sizes per Food Group

Group	Item	Single serving
BREAD AND CEREALS		
	Bread	1 slice
	Tortilla	1 tortilla (6-inch diameter)
	Muffin	1 small muffin (<2 oz)
	Small bagel	1/2 bagel
	Dry cereal	1 oz
	Cooked cereal	1/2 cup
VEGETABLE		
	Raw leafy	1 cup
	Cooked raw	1/2 cup
	Vegetable juice	3/4 cup
	Potato salad	1/2 cup
	Potato	1 medium-size potato
	Spaghetti sauce	1/2 cup
FRUIT		
	Whole fruit	1 medium-size piece
	Cooked or canned	1/2 cup
	Melon	1/4 cup
	Banana	1/2 banana
	Fruit juice	3/4 cup
	Dried fruit	1/4 cup
MEAT AND BEANS		
	Cooked lean meat, poultry, fish	3 oz
	Cooked beans	1/2 cup
	Tofu	3 oz
	Egg	1 egg
	Nuts	1/3 cup
	Egg whites	2 egg whites
	Peanut butter	2 tablespoons
DAIRY		
	Nonfat milk	1 cup
	Yogurt	1 cup
	Natural cheese	1.5 oz
	Cottage cheese	1 cup
	Fat-free or low-fat frozen yogurt or ice cream	1 cup
	Processed cheese	2 oz

100 percent whole grain, such as whole wheat, oats, barley, quinoa, spelt, or brown rice; choose whole-grain breakfast cereals such as oatmeal, shredded wheat, or bran cereals; and choose whole-grain crackers. Whole grains tend to make a person feel more full than processed white flour does. As a result, you may need to train yourself to eat these foods because of the sheer volume needed when training and racing.

Fluids

The importance of hydration—even off the bike—cannot be emphasized enough. Water helps digest food, lubricates joints, cushions organs, transports nutrients, removes waste products, and helps regulate body temperature via sweating. Sweat losses of as little as 2 percent of body weight (only 3 pounds for a 150-pound athlete) can impair performance dramatically by causing exponentially increased heart rates for a given workload.

Everyone should drink at least 8 to 10 cups of water per day, but athletes need more fluid if exercising in hot weather. In addition, athletes may need electrolytes such as salt, potassium, and magnesium the more they hydrate. A good practice is to drink at least one 24-fluid-ounce (720 ml) bottle per hour. On hot days, drink two or more 20- to 24-fluid-ounce bottles per hour. Bottles should contain energy drink with electrolytes, as tolerated. Although caffeine, if tolerated, may improve performance, you should try to avoid caffeinated beverages while riding because they act as diuretics (i.e., they cause your body to excrete water in the form of urine). Alcohol should be avoided, even though many people find pleasure from the occasional drink. Alcohol serves no athletic benefit, and conflicting evidence exists for its health benefits even in small amounts with food. If drinking alcohol or caffeine, you should have a large glass of water with it.

Prerace and Training Nutrition

Whether you head out for your training rides first thing in the morning or you perform training rides later in the day, the morning is the best time to get your training day off to a good start. It may sound cliché, but breakfast *is* the most important meal of the day. Be prepared to start eating breakfast at least an hour (or better yet, an hour and a half) before the day's training begins. Try this trick—start a training ride when you are a little full, because this forces you to complete a proper (easy) warm-up while finishing digesting. There is no specific calorie guideline (because everyone has different caloric demands), but a 150-pound rider may shoot for approximately 800 to 1,000 calories for breakfast. It may take your body some time to adjust to ingesting this amount of calories early in the day, so you shouldn't go from a 100-calorie breakfast straight to 1,000 calories. Train your body over months to ingest more calories, choosing foods that your body enjoys.

Glycogen Depletion on the Go

Muscle glycogen is necessary for endurance training. In fact, when you are training for bouts of three hours or more, your body needs muscle glycogen to function properly through the entire exercise period. Figure 8.1 depicts how various fuels are used to attain 100 percent of your energy when exercising (Coyle et al. 1986).

As you can see, muscle glycogen starts off providing nearly 50 percent of your fuel at time zero and is almost depleted after three and a half hours. Note that the exercise bout is at 70 percent of $\dot{V}O_2$max as well, which many people would consider a recovery pace. The graph makes an excellent point of showing that you can substitute the energy expenditure from depleted glycogen with carbohydrate ingestion.

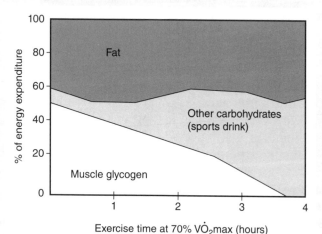

Figure 8.1 Fuel consumption during exercise.

Compared to runners, cyclists are better able to fend off "the wall" or "the bonk" because cyclists can simply cruise and eat. This is not always the case, though—for example, you may not be able to do this at high intensities or when out for more than four hours of endurance training. In these instances, you have to train yourself to eat before exercise, during exercise, and after exercise.

Figure 8.2 shows what happens to muscle glycogen over repeated bouts of exercise over repeated days (Burke et al. 2004).

Notice in the graph that training volume is the same over a three-day period. Athletes ingesting a high-carbohydrate diet are able to almost completely replenish their glycogen stores for the next exercise bout. Athletes ingesting a low-carbohydrate diet are unable to replenish their glycogen stores, and they start the next exercise bout at a deficit.

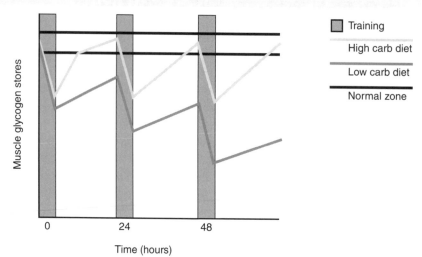

Figure 8.2 Muscle glycogen stores after repeated periods of exercise.

For breakfast, choose foods containing complex carbohydrate and some protein. Simple sugar (e.g., lots of fruit juice) will most likely leave you feeling empty as the ride progresses. Fatty foods take longer to digest and may not digest at all; they provide a poor energy source and can cause gastric distress. Large amounts of protein take very long to digest, and the energy derived will be used by your body only in dire situations. Items you may want to choose for breakfast include whole-grain breads and cereals, nuts and nut spreads, fat-free milk or yogurt, and fruit. Choose a variety of foods, and put the emphasis on carbohydrate.

Here are some tips for prerace or training meals:

- *Ensure that you are getting plenty of carbohydrate to fuel your daily rides.* Plain oatmeal is a good choice because it is high in complex carbohydrate and is also a moderate-protein, medium-fiber food.
- *Ensure that you are getting some protein.* Protein satiates your morning hunger and provides nutrition to rebuild your muscles.
- *Drink plenty of water.* You could even include small amounts of juice or sports drink because they contain calories, hydration, and electrolytes.
- *Try not to load up on fat.* Fat takes longer to digest and requires more water to help with absorption. Please note that restricting fat too much is also not a good idea, because fat is necessary for normal bodily function.

If you are training later in the day, a large breakfast will still be of benefit. You will tap into those breakfast calories later in the day. Make sure you fuel up with a few hundred calories before you ride later in the day, though. For example, you could have a snack after work, but you may want to cut out the fiber. Taking fiber later in the day may trigger a bowel movement in a colon full from digesting breakfast, snacks, and lunch.

Nutrition and Hydration During Training and Racing

Like bike handling or intervals, eating while training and racing is a skill that must be learned. It takes practice, not only in removing packaging while rolling along, but also in choosing foods that will be digestible during various levels of intensity. For lower-intensity rides, regular foods such as sandwiches may be easily digestible and may be a nice break from sports drinks, gels, or bars. When the pace picks up and more blood is shunted to working leg muscles, your digestive system may only be able to handle nutrition in liquid form. "Training your gut" is an essential cycling skill, because as you move up the ranks, the races and training will be longer.

Find what works for you. Try everything under various intensities and at various times during racing or training. For example, what might be easily palatable and tasty in the first 30 miles may be indigestible during the last 30 miles. Try various sports drinks, gels, bars, blocks, natural

The Feed Zone: Giving and Receiving Hand-Ups During Road Races

Staying fueled during a road race is essential. In many instances, you will be able to carry enough food in your pockets, along with two water bottles on your bike. Yet, in many road races, especially those over 50 miles (80.5 km), there will be a specific area called the feed zone where support staff can "hand up" bottles and food to racers. Executing proper hand-ups is essential to the success of the racer. If a racer misses or drops a hand-up, this may be the difference between winning and losing (or even finishing) the race. Hand-ups are easy, if practiced.

Practicing a drink hand-up.

How to Hand Up

When handing up a water bottle, hold the spout from above with your index finger and thumb. This allows the racer to grab the bottle around the neck. For handing up food contained in a *musette* (food bag), hold the musette by the tops of the strings, ensuring that it will not snag on you as the racer grabs it. If not using a musette, hold the food item from above by the wrapper, allowing the racer to grab it.

How to Receive a Hand-Up

Be sure to move to the side of the road where the hand-up will occur. You should do this well before you enter the feed zone. Slow your speed without impeding other riders. Putting your hand out to the side will let other riders know that you are grabbing a hand-up. Grab the bottle around the neck firmly. Be sure to leave some slack in your arm to absorb impact. Immediately put the bottle in the cage. The same technique is used for wrapped food. If grabbing a musette, grab it by the strings and sling it over a shoulder. Once you are clear of the feed zone, pull out the food and put it in your pockets. Drop the musette, alerting support staff beforehand to retrieve it along the course.

cookies, sandwiches, and healthy pastries. Try this strategy: Choose real foods such as sandwiches for slow, easy training or the start of a long race. Then move to bars, natural cookies, and gel blocks toward the middle of the race or training. Finally, finish with mainly liquid nutrition via sports drinks and gels. Sport foods made from natural ingredients are always best, as long as the fiber content is not too high.

Here are some tips to maintain energy levels while training and racing:

- *Consume 200 to 300 calories per hour.* Energy bars eaten with energy drinks will usually provide a complete nutrition profile—carbohydrate, protein, electrolytes, and even a little fat. Real food is always a better choice, though.
- *Eat real food.* Bring along sandwiches—for example, peanut butter and jelly or ham and cheese—and healthy, savory cookies, such as whole-grain fig bars (wheat- and dairy-free varieties are also available).
- *Eat a little at a time.* In addition, use water to help dissolve and digest the food. In this manner, the food is more palatable and leaves a person feeling less heavy.
- *Practice eating while training.* This teaches you to be comfortable while eating during a race, plus it reveals which foods are palatable and easy to digest on race day. Integrate some training to work on receiving *hand-ups* during races, which could mean the difference between finishing strong or not finishing at all. More information on hand-ups is provided later in this chapter.

Which Sports Drink Should I Choose?

Previously, it was thought that a sports drink needed to have a specific carbohydrate-to-protein ratio in order to more rapidly provide the necessary sugar to the blood and working muscles. For example, a 4:1 ratio of carbohydrate to protein was touted as the best combination for fuel during and after exercise. Although some evidence suggests that this ratio provides more complete availability of glucose to working muscles, other evidence exists showing that carbohydrates alone do the trick. When you are choosing a sports drink, the main goal is to find one that provides calories, tastes good, and does not induce gastric distress. One man's energizing potion is another man's poison, so it takes experimentation to find the sports drink that works for you.

Ensure that your sports drink provides some calories in the form of an easily digestible carbohydrate along with some electrolytes. For example, many drinks use maltodextrin, which is a long chain of glucose molecules that can be cleaved off by the digestive system as needed. This helps the athlete avoid a sugar spike and provides sustained energy. Avoid fruit juices because their sugar (fructose) is usually hard to digest under stress. Also avoid more complex sugar, such as disaccharide sucrose, for the same reason.

Nutrition and Hydration for Postrace or Training Recovery

Neil Shirley, professional cyclist from the Kelly Benefit Strategies professional cycling team, says, "You are not eating for today, but eating for tomorrow." After training or racing, many athletes are so hungry that they rapidly ingest calories with little care for what types or quantities they are eating. They have essentially already exhausted their energy stores, and their bodies are telling them to fill up immediately. The problem is that it is already too late—the body will not be able to process the large intake of fuel and store it efficiently for the next day's training or racing. This is a dangerous cycle to enter.

As you learned in the previous section, eating while you are riding is essential to maintaining your blood glucose so you can remain energized enough to train properly. You should never finish a ride feeling totally empty of fuel. You may finish a ride feeling fatigued in the legs, tired in the lungs, and exhausted mentally, but again, you should never finish in a state of extreme hunger. Train yourself to overcome finishing empty, and then tackle recovery refueling.

Recovery fueling does not have to start when the ride is finished; it should start *earlier*. For example, as stated earlier, a good cool-down after training or racing is essential, so why not use this time to start refueling as well? The cool-down should be slow and relaxing; therefore, you can pull out a few hundred calories and start working on them in the last half hour of the ride.

General Recovery Refueling

As you are discovering, strategies for replacing your muscle glycogen are important. Note that an entire diet of carbohydrate is not the answer, but a diet high in carbohydrate (approximately 60 percent of your daily caloric intake) is important to replenish your glycogen stores.

Follow these tips for refueling and regenerating after each ride:

- Immediately after completing a ride, or even during your cool-down, ingest approximately 300 calories of mainly carbohydrate.
- Shower, float in the pool, or sit in a warm tub. This will allow relaxation and digestion. Make sure you hydrate for the entire period.
- An hour after the ride, ingest an additional 300 calories of mainly carbohydrate.
- Lie down or sit down with your feet raised, and take a nap for 30 minutes to 1 hour if possible. This will allow relaxation and digestion.
- Ensure that you eat a complete, well-balanced meal (with an emphasis on carbohydrate) within 3 to 4 hours of ride completion.

- Ensure that you attain 9 to 10 hours of sleep at night by avoiding eating within 2 hours before sleeping.
- Eat a well-rounded breakfast, including foods that contain mainly complex carbohydrates and protein.

Immediate Postride Refuel

Immediately after a ride, you should consume a meal that contains approximately 300 calories. Again, some research has shown that a 4:1 ratio of carbohydrate to protein is the ideal composition of the calories ingested—meaning the carbohydrate is absorbed more readily in the protein matrix. However, the main function of the postride refuel is just plain calories, and a meal of all carbohydrate is acceptable. Ensuring that carbohydrate is the main source of those calories just makes sense. An energy bar is a good choice for this immediate postride snack; these bars usually provide the right amount of calories with healthful ingredients. Avoid processed sugar found in such items as candy bars. Avoid fat found in such items as potato chips. You want healthful fuels, which are found in fruit, nuts, whole grains, and low-fat milk.

Choosing a recovery fuel that is liquid may be beneficial. Healthful recovery drinks are available in a variety of endurance nutrition brands or in the form of a fruit-filled smoothie. A liquid may be absorbed more readily and may be easier on your stomach. In addition, a liquid is certainly the most convenient recovery fuel when you are exhausted after a long, hard training ride.

One-Hour Postride Refuel

Your one-hour postride refuel should contain approximately 300 calories. This meal should consist primarily of complex carbohydrates found in whole grains such as oats, bran, cereals, beans, pasta, and brown rice.

At this point, your muscles should have had time to absorb the less complex sugar consumed in the immediate postride refuel. Now you need slower absorbing fuels to top off your muscles' stores throughout the afternoon. Once again, the real focus is on healthful calories, so do not obsess about what exactly you are eating, as long as it is healthful. The foods mentioned are good suggestions.

Well-Balanced Meal

There is no specific guideline for the number of calories to be consumed in the meal that is eaten three to four hours after the ride. This meal is most likely one of the main meals during the day, so each person needs to eat to meet his personal caloric demands. Attaining a metabolic test to ascertain your BMR and using a calorie counter while riding, such as kilojoules from a power meter, may help you dial in your exact calorie needs based on exercise.

Eating Suggestions for a Three-Hour Training Day

Breakfast

- 1 bowl of whole-grain oatmeal
- 1 slice of whole-grain toast with peanut butter or honey
- 1 egg
- 1 banana
- 1 cup of strawberries

Three-Hour Training Ride

- 300-calorie light sandwich
- 300-calorie sports drink
- 300 calories in sport bars, natural cookies, or gels

Immediate Postride Recovery

- 300-calorie smoothie of fat-free milk and fruits such as mango, strawberries, and blueberries

One-Hour Postride Recovery

- 3 ounces (90 g) of whole-grain pasta with extra virgin olive oil or marinara sauce

Late Lunch

- 2 cups of spinach or broccoli
- 2 cups of berries
- 2 cups of couscous
- 2 handfuls of nuts

Dinner

- 3 ounces of baked salmon
- 2 cups of vegetables
- 8 ounces (250 g) of whole-grain pasta or whole-grain rice
- 2 slices of whole-grain bread
- 1 cup of vegetable juice

Throughout the Day

- 8 to 12 cups of water

For your three- to four-hour postride meal, choose a variety of foods to fill your plate. The advice to "eat a variety of fruits and vegetables" is never as poignant as when training at high levels. Again, the main focus of your meal should be carbohydrate. Your plate should also have some lean protein—lean beef, chicken, pork, fish, or beans. Finally, your plate should include an assortment of vegetables. There is an old adage that a person should "eat every color of the rainbow, every day." Take this advice to heart when sitting down to dinner. Have you had your greens? If no, then prepare some healthy green vegetables, such as broccoli or spinach. Have you had your orange? If no, then eat some carrots. These are not specifics, just guidelines—the key is eating a variety of foods.

Note that you should never leave dinner "stuffed." If you feel as though you need to eat until you are stuffed—because you are so hungry—this is a sign that your earlier eating during the day (i.e., while riding, immediately after riding, and one hour after riding) did not include enough of the right foods. You should leave dinner feeling sated, energized, and ready to tackle the next day's training—that is, after a good night's sleep.

Chapter 9

MAINTAINING YEAR-ROUND HEALTH AND CONDITIONING

Training is like Sisyphus pushing the boulder up the mountain only to have it roll back to the bottom. But if you do everything right, you get to balance the rock at the top one day a year.

—Dave Scott, six-time Ironman world champion

June races are won in January. Once the racing season comes to a close and you have taken a short break, the real training begins. Bicycle racing takes not only a large physical, mental, and social effort, but also a large effort in planning for the upcoming season. Even small amounts of careful preparation at the start of the off-season—and continued small follow-ups throughout the season—will largely improve your performance.

This chapter gives you guidance on how to periodize your training schedule based on the race calendar and how to recover from large seasonal efforts and short-term efforts. In addition, the chapter provides you with focused training workouts beyond on-the-road drills and efforts, and helps you work through common cycling ailments.

Race Calendar

As a bicycle racer, you train to race. To be in top physical condition for any given race, you must consult the local racing calendar so you can build your training around specific events. Slotting races into priority categories is the first step in setting up a periodization plan that will help you to be at your best when race day comes.

Race Priorities

The simpler the system for prioritizing races, the better. Break your races up throughout the year into high-priority races (meaning races in which you are aiming for a good result) and low-priority races (meaning races that you are treating as training). You may need to pull out the race calendar from the previous season and speculate on which races will occur again in the upcoming year.

High-Priority Races Designate no more than five races as high priority. The effort it takes to build up to and taper for these events will be the main focus of the cycling season. It is a good idea to pick high-priority races across two consecutive weeks; your fitness should carry through the events.

Many racers choose stage races as high-priority events, because the effort to have all systems—steady effort for time trials, climbing for road races, and skills for criteriums—peaking at once takes precise planning. Other athletes choose one-day races that suit their specific strengths, such as a popular climbing race or a 40K time trial. State or national championships are popular high-priority events because of the prestige that winning one of these races brings. Other racers choose events that their team has a vested interest in attending or a race that they know is in a fun location. I once chose a race in upstate New York as a high-priority event because it set the stage for a vacation through the Finger Lakes region for a few days after the event.

The best strategy is to choose events in which you have participated before, know the course, and have a good idea of who will be included in the competition. Always be a race detective by checking out courses, locations, and competition. Then, when it comes to setting up your periodization plan for the next year, you will have some clues about where you want to focus your efforts.

Low-Priority Races The rest of your yearly races will be low-priority races. For low-priority races, you are not concerned about a result. In addition, you will not be in top physical form for these races. You will most likely be training through the event. You should still take advantage of winning opportunities at low-priority events, but you shouldn't enter these races with winning as your focus. Think of a low-priority race as primarily a training race.

If it is your first time seeing a particular race course, or if you have done the race before and know that it does not suit your strengths, then make the race a low priority. You should never show up to a race without a plan though. Because your objective is not a great result—meaning a best personal effort—you should pick a specific skill or tactic to focus on for the race. For example, try a pack position drill where you try to stay in the top 10 riders for the entire race regardless of how tired you become. Try working on a different race-day nutrition strategy. Try to sit in for the entire race, not following any moves, and see if you save energy. Try to break away at every opportunity. Just try something different or work on improving a deficient race skill. According to Ned Overend, "Small races are the time to experiment with pace, equipment, and nutritional supplements. Too many people are so serious about races that they won't experiment." (Strickland 2001).

Periodization Planning

As covered in chapter 4, you need to periodize your training year so that you will be able to peak for particular events. A periodization plan also serves as a framework for building your specific training and workouts. By sitting down for a few hours at the start of the season to pick races, you will fare much better both in overall results and in sticking to your training plans once the season gets underway. See table 9.1 for examples of periodization plans for one- and two-peak seasons.

A good time to start setting up your periodization is after the last race of your season. Starting later may not give you enough time to transition and develop properly. Review your race results from the previous season; your results may be an indication of which races you excel or do not excel in. Then, comparing your results to the next year's race calendar, pick three to five races that are considered high-priority events. Grouping a couple of races on back-to-back weeks is a good idea—then be sure to space out at least six weeks to the next event. Now choose other races that will be low-priority races; these are races that you can train through. Low-priority races are important because they help you build race shape. In many cases, only racing itself can prepare you for the intensity and speed of competition.

Backtrack a minimum of four months (preferably six months) from your first high-priority event to mark the beginning of your transition period. This may be tricky the first season. Many first-year racers compete in races right up to the end of the season, and then they want to make the first race of the next season a high-priority event. If this is the case, you may need to treat the last race of the season as a low priority. Over the years, you will start to set up your season more wisely, perhaps starting much later or finishing much earlier than your compatriots in order to target specific races.

A blank worksheet to help you set up your annual plan is provided in the appendix.

What Goes Into Picking a Race?

Picking specific races that will be your season goals becomes more important the more years you race. At first, you should enter many different types of races—time trials, hilly road races, windy circuit races, fast criteriums, and weekly training races on the same course. As you develop

TABLE 9.1

Planning Out Your Race Year

ONE-PEAK SEASON

	Base	January
	Development	February, March
	Taper	April
	Race	May, June

ALTERNATE ONE-PEAK SEASON

	Base	March
	Development	April, May
	Taper	June
	Race	July, August

TWO-PEAK SEASON

	Base	November, December
	Development	January, February
	Taper	March
	Race	April
	Development	May
	Taper	June
	Race	July

ALTERNATE TWO-PEAK SEASON

	Base	November, December, January
	Development	February, March
	Taper	April
	Race	May
	Development	June, July
	Taper	August
	Race	September

more racing ability though, you will want to target races that suit your strengths. This does not mean you must avoid races that do not suit your strengths. In those races, you may surprise yourself, and your strengths may evolve and change.

The real question becomes not *what* but *when*. When during the season should you be targeting races? In addition to targeting races that suit your style, you should also target races based on the ebb and flow of competition. For example, by targeting early-season races and peaking for these races, you may get a jump on the competition as they are trying to "race themselves into shape." If your fitness peaks for late-season races, you may catch the competition worn down from a long season of racing.

Part of periodization is not only building toward your best fitness, but also peaking when others are not peaking. You should try to shoot for the common season goals that your competition is targeting as well. For example, a regional stage race is usually a season target for all regional race clubs. Yet, you should also identify which races your competition may not be targeting. This may be a chance for you to get a win by periodizing your training so you are in top fitness for one of these races. For example, a remote road race that is a longer drive away may not attract as many of the heavy hitters. As stated in chapter 7, bicycle racing rewards those who have the mental fortitude to continue racing and training despite poor race placings and training setbacks. You need to know when your competition is low in fitness, and you need to use this information to your advantage.

Rest and Recovery

In endurance sports, athletes become stronger during rest because this is when they consolidate their gains from training. As a beginning racer, you must understand that when you go hard, you need to go really, really hard—but when you go easy, you need to go really, really easy. This strategy can be applied on a small scale; for example, it can be applied to intervals, where you push beyond 93 percent of MHR, and then back down to well below 75 percent of MHR for recovery between intervals. You can also apply this strategy on a medium scale in racing, where you push enough power into the wind either solo or with a small group (at 27, 28, 29 mph) to force a breakaway, or you sit in barely pedaling as the race whips along chasing a different breakaway. But most important, this strategy can be applied on a large scale to a periodized program.

When your season ends, you need to take a complete break from the bicycle. This is a tough concept for the beginning racer to understand, both mentally and physically. The racer has experienced the excitement of finding a new sport, the pleasure of riding with comrades on a daily and weekly basis, and the rush of adrenaline and endorphins from heavy exercise. All these elements entice the beginning cyclist to not want to put the bike away for a couple of weeks. This can be a shortsighted viewpoint. When periodizing, think long term to next season.

Common sense dictates that continuing to ride straight through to the next season will only cause you to hit the "wall" or feel overtrained at some point in the future. You would not want to hit the wall right before your next season's biggest goal. Once you complete your last race of the season—and it is recommended that you actually pick a last race and stick

A Pro's Experience

Lea Davison (Team Maxxis/Rocky Mountain)

"One of the most important lessons I have learned as a professional athlete is that you need to rest and recover," says Lea Davison. She continues, "Driven, competitive athletes, generally approach training with the 'more is better' approach. Rest days are for the 'weak' and more workouts equal faster and better performances." Lea admits that this is a common mistake, even professional athletes, learn the hard way. She explains that it is very easy to train yourself into the ground, then hard to claw one's way out of complete fatigue. Lea says, "Recovery is equally important as quality training. Without proper recovery, your training is not as effective, you may be more injury prone, and you are less likely to enjoy the sport over time."

Lea explains that there are two different types of recovery: training recovery and season recovery. For training recovery, Lea always eats and drinks as soon as possibly after a training ride. For Lea, this includes a smoothie and a bowl of cereal within twenty minutes. When time permits, she also includes forty five-minute nap. Lea continues, "From day to day, I need nine to ten hours of sleep nightly." For further recovery, Lea steps into cold water. "I'm a strong believer in ten-minute ice baths and Vermont water is cold even in the summer time," she explains.

For season recovery, Lea takes two to four weeks completely off the bike. Lea explains, "I will completely rest for one week or more and then engage in other athletic activities, like hiking, Nordic skiing, and backcountry skiing. This time off can be tailored to whatever activity you enjoy, but it should leave you refreshed and excited to get back on the bike." She believes, proper recovery gives an athlete a more balanced approach and a greater chance for reaching their potential. Lea concludes, "Proper recovery is an art. It takes some time to fine-tune your personalized recovery approach."

What You Can Learn

As a amateur athlete, it is important to understand that recovery should not be put to the side in lieu of more training and racing or more intense training and racing. This mistake can easily be made as you see large early gains with increased volume and intensity. Lea has learned that a complete approach to training, which includes recovery as an integral and crucial segment, ensures that she reaches and maintains her athletic potential. In addition to focusing on intense physical exertion in racing and training, Lea also focuses on proper nutrition, sleep, and time away from the bike to maximize the fitness gains she makes in training.

to it, even if you feel as if you could race more—put the bike down and steer clear of exercise for at least a week, if not two weeks. Yes, your fitness will drop slightly, but the long-term recovery will far outweigh the short-term drop in fitness.

After a week has passed, start cross-training at very low intensity. After two weeks, it's time to pick up the bicycle again, but you should ride at perhaps half the volume (i.e., hours or miles) and at recovery intensity (i.e., less than 75 percent of MHR or less than 50 percent of your 20-minute threshold power). Mix a month of these easy rides in with your cross-training.

Concerning mesocycles such as base, you need to work in recovery weeks at least every sixth week, if not sooner (i.e., every fourth week). You do not need to put the bike down during the base or development mesocycles; you should just reduce the volume by 40 to 50 percent (i.e., hours or miles), while keeping the intensity relatively the same based on the mesocycle guidelines.

Event Tapering

You've followed your training plan, and you're in your best physical condition. You have practiced your skill drills, and you have a strategy for race day. You've also prepared yourself psychologically. What is sometimes missed is *tapering* for the upcoming event. Tapering is a reduction in volume—and possibly frequency—along with a limited reduction in intensity before race day. For a taper to be effective, it should start 7 to 21 days before the event; your workout duration should decrease by 30 percent every 4 or 5 days, but you should maintain the frequency of workouts within 20 percent and should maintain intensity.

To taper effectively, follow these tips:

- Discontinue weight work or on-the-bike force work up to 3 weeks before the event.
- Complete the last long endurance ride 7 to 10 days before the event.
- Perform exhaustive aerobic exercise only up to 3 days before the event.
- Maintain aerobic intervals up to 3 days before the event (but total workout duration will be significantly reduced based on the 30 percent decrease every 4 or 5 days from the start of the taper).
- Engage in rest or active recovery riding 2 days before the event.
- Perform a warm-up ride the day before the event to near event intensities.

Cross-Training

For endurance athletes, cross-training has increased in importance as better techniques have been developed and as increased benefits have been reaped on the bicycle. *Cross-training* is defined as engaging in various sports or exercises to achieve well-rounded health and muscular development. As a cyclist periodizing your training, you must keep in mind that your cross-training should be specific to developing your skills in cycling.

Cross-training begins as soon as you put the bike down and your season ends. At first, cross-training will be unorganized, and you will simply be doing things you enjoy. Examples include hiking, walking around town, kayaking, weightlifting, running, yard work, basketball, soccer, or any other physical activity. After a couple of weeks, your cross-training choices should be more specific to improving your cycling. When developing a cross-training plan, choose activities you enjoy that will also translate into cycling fitness. Here are some examples:

- Hiking uphill (improves quad strength for forceful pedal strokes)
- Yard work that forces you to push and pull (builds core muscles and arm strength to help you support yourself on the handlebars)
- Rowing (simulates the push and pull of a sprint)
- Weight training that targets specific leg muscles and upper body muscles (improves overall health and muscular endurance)
- Mountain biking (helps road riders improve their handling skills and keep their aerobic engine fit)
- Running (keeps the leg muscles strong and the aerobic engine fit; running should only be done if you are not easily prone to injury)

Periodized Weight Training for Cyclists

For cyclists, weight training is an important aspect of fitness, especially in the off-season. During taper and race periods, cyclists should not perform weight work for the lower body, and they should not perform exhaustive weight work for the upper body. During these periods, the weight work may detract from leg speed and may add an unnecessary stressor to overall performance. For overall functional health, athletes over 30 years of age should continue a weight regimen year-round, but this regimen should have less emphasis on leg work during taper and race periods.

Weight training can be periodized similar to your cycling training (i.e., transition, base, development, taper, and race). During transition, the athlete is becoming acquainted with weights and workout modalities; the workouts involve high repetitions and low resistance. During base, the athlete is training the body to handle the rigors of weightlifting; the athlete uses medium repetitions and medium resistance. During development, the athlete is working to strengthen the muscles specific to cycling, using low repetitions and medium to high resistance. During taper and race, the athlete is either not lifting weights or only continuing upper body resistance training at medium repetitions and low to medium resistance.

When lifting weights, the cyclist should keep a couple of points in mind: (1) Workouts should be efficient and minimally time consuming, and (2) weights should be chosen conservatively to avoid injury or strain.

A periodized weight training plan is provided in the appendix.

Training Logs

Without proper record keeping, a business would fail. This can also be said for bicycle race training. Without proper and detailed training logs, the racing athlete will fail. Keeping a training log is the most important aspect of any training program.

An athlete can record many aspects of training. At a minimum, the athlete should record the following for each ride: day, date, distance traveled, hours in the saddle, cycling route, and a postride comment. Other information that is useful to record includes energy consumed, average wattage, hours slept, nutrition, energy level before the ride, and energy after the ride. Not only should this information be recorded for daily rides, it should also be tallied or averaged monthly and yearly. Recording race entries and results is also important, because they will serve you in building a training plan for the next season.

Again, even the minimum is better than nothing, but the goal is to record reliable, repeatable, and accurate information. From these data, you should start to see trends in performance and training. For example, if you have never felt better and are putting out more watts than ever during interval sessions, you can consult your log to find out what you did leading up to this point. What series of workouts did you complete? How many miles? How many hours? How many days off on the bike or on? How much sleep? What did you eat? Ask yourself these questions as you review your data on a weekly, monthly, and yearly basis. Try to uncover trends. A blank cycling log that you can use is provided in the appendix.

Common Cycling Ailments

Like any sport, competitive cycling contains an element of injury. This section addresses common minor injuries. In most cases, these injuries can be treated at home or on the road. More extensive injuries—including injuries that involve large amounts of blood loss, fractures, or recurring pain—should be reviewed and treated by a physician.

Saddle Sores

Most cyclists experience saddle sores at some point. Saddle sores are the breakdown of the skin of the crotch. This condition is characterized by bumps and sores caused by the blockage of pores, which results from excessive sweating or pressure. Bacteria can infect the damaged skin to cause further irritation.

The best treatment for saddle sores is prevention. Here are some preventative tips:

- Dry your crotch thoroughly after showering in order to prevent moisture from being trapped; moisture creates a hospitable environment for bacteria.
- Always change out of your cycling clothes as soon as you complete training or racing.
  - At races, clean the crotch with wet naps, dry the crotch with a towel, and change into loose-fitting clothing before you travel home.
  - After training, shower immediately and dry the crotch thoroughly.
- Apply baby powder to your crotch before very humid or damp rides.
- When riding, take time to stand out of the saddle on climbs and even on long flats to relieve pressure on the crotch.
- If saddle sores are a persistent, yet manageable problem, apply chamois cream to reduce friction.
- Replace worn saddles because they can cause unfamiliar pressure points.
- Ensure that your saddle is fitted properly—angle, saddle width, and straightness.
- In some very rare scenarios, a leg length discrepancy may cause the cyclist to reach with one leg, causing more pressure and thus saddle sores on the reaching side. This can be alleviated with a proper bike fit.

You should see a doctor if saddle sores are persistent or growing, or if they show discharge. To treat saddle sores, take these steps:

- Thoroughly clean the crotch using an antibacterial soap or even an acne cleanser. Then dry thoroughly.
- Apply a medicated baby powder or a diaper rash ointment to heal the chafed skin and prevent further degradation.
- Soak in a clean, warm bath for 15 minutes. This will dissolve any material on your skin that could prevent healing, and it will open the pores to relieve any clogging.
- Wear loose-fitting, well-ventilated clothing (such as shorts) after showering. This will allow ventilation and drying.

Road Rash

All cyclists have crashed—or "gone down"—or will do so in the future. Road rash is an unfortunate result of riding at high speeds on paved roads. *Road rash* is essentially the removal of skin due to the friction of contact with the road surface.

Road rash can be classified the same way as burns: first, second, or third degree. First-degree road rash is just a reddening of the surface and does not require active treatment. Second-degree road rash is a removal of skin with the retention of a deeper layer of skin, which will regenerate surface skin. Third-degree road rash is the removal of skin and the exposure of the underlying fatty tissue and supporting tissue structures. Third-degree road rash requires treatment by a doctor and may require skin grafting. If subcutaneous fat layers can be seen, or if bleeding is persistent and not stopping, seek medical attention immediately; these cases may require stitching or skin grafts. If the crash involved other complications, such as hitting the head, seek medical attention immediately.

Second-degree road rash can usually be treated by completely cleaning the area of debris, including pebbles, road surface, and grease—this requires gentle scrubbing with warm water and soap and removal of debris from the wound. This will prevent future infection. If debris cannot be removed, go to the hospital. A triple antibiotic ointment should be applied. A nonaspirin pain reliever can be taken to relieve pain and reduce swelling around the wound area. A loose-fitting bandage should be applied.

Daily and sometimes twice daily cleaning of the wound is necessary. Rewash with soap and water, and reapply ointment. Keep the wound moist with ointment—reapplying liberally as necessary—to prevent scabbing. After a day or so (and before your next ride), rewash the area, but do not apply ointment. Instead, apply advanced healing coverings such as Tegaderm or Johnson & Johnson Advanced Healing. These products seal the wound from outside infection, and they provide a covering whereby the wound is protected, can breathe, and stays moist because of bodily healing processes. This technique will speed recovery and prevent scabbing, and it may reduce scarring.

Muscle Strains and Aches

Overuse injuries are often caused by training too hard too soon. Commonly, these injuries occur earlier in the season when the body is not yet prepared for intense efforts or increased volume. Prevention is the best measure, and here are some preventative tips:

- Ensure that you get a good bike fit by a professional. This will help reduce the likelihood of backaches, knee problems, ankle issues, or foot irritations.
- Do not increase intensity or volume too quickly. The 10 percent rule is a rough guide to start, meaning you should only increase volume or intensity (i.e., never both) 10 percent from week to week. In time, you will learn your limits above and below this rough guide.
- Work in periods of rest of at least a week long every four to six weeks of training.
- Take time off at the end of the season to properly recover physically.

If you do experience minor aches and pains, try to first diagnose possible causes of the problem by doing your own detective work or enlisting the help of peers or professionals. Ask yourself where the problem is located, what the possible causes could be, and when you notice it. From there, try to adjust to relieve the problem. For example, if it is a knee problem, possible sources could be a new saddle, new cleats, a slipped saddle, a broken or worn cleat, too much intensity, too much big gear work, too much high-cadence work, or too much volume. Fix a mechanical issue or adjust your training to accommodate.

The following are common muscle, ligament, and tendon strains, along with some tips for preventing them:

- Achilles tendon irritation due to too much climbing or big gear work too quickly. Always build volume and intensity conservatively. Wear high, looser-fitting socks to keep the area warm.
- Knee aches and pains due to improper saddle height or incorrect cleat orientation or float. Attain a professional fit.
- Sore hamstrings or hip flexors due to inefficient pedal stroke or too much high-cadence work too quickly. Adjust training to improve pedal stroke via isolated leg training or riding rollers. Adjust training to increase volume and intensity conservatively.
- Sore lower back due to too much climbing too soon, too much big gear work too soon, or handlebars that are too low and extended. Adjust volume and intensity conservatively. Attain a professional bike fit that provides maximum aerodynamics with maximum comfort.

The best remedy for muscle aches and strains is rest. An aspirin-free analgesic may make training bearable or may speed recovery by reducing inflammation.

Sunburn

Sunburn may not seem like a serious issue, but the repeated exposure of the cyclist's skin to ultraviolet radiation can lead to serious consequences down the road, including skin cancer. Therefore, the cyclist should apply sunscreen liberally on all exposed areas (including the lips). Choose nongreasy sunscreens that protect against both UVA and UVB radiation. The sunscreen should also be noncomedogenic and sweatproof, and it should provide some form of moisturizing lotion to prevent skin chapping or drying. Choose high-quality products, per recommendations from physicians, and apply the sunscreen liberally before and during rides. The best protection is coverage via clothing, but on warm days, sunscreen is a must.

Cold-Weather Riding

For many, training must be done during some months when riding outside is less than hospitable. The stationary trainer is a great alternative. Yet, if the roads are clear of ice and debris, and if you can handle bad weather, it behooves you to get outside for some endurance riding to keep your engine primed.

A good way to approach cold-weather riding is similar to how one would approach skiing. If you are not a skier, you can still relate. The key is the correct clothing. When temperatures dip below 32 degrees Fahrenheit (or 0 degrees Celsius), you need a layered system that stops biting winds on your front but allows your body to "breathe" out the back and in the armpits. Many companies make windstopper panels for the area of the chest and the front of the thighs; lighter material is used for the back and armpit areas to allow ventilation. You must try to stay dry—once you sweat and the perspiration is trapped on your body, you will become colder quicker.

Cycling Clothing When the Temperature Dips Below Freezing

- Winter base layer
- Fleece-lined long-sleeved jersey
- Bib shorts under fleece-lined bib tights
- Winter cycling jacket with high collar
- High ankle socks (wool blend)
- Sunglasses
- Helmet
- Neoprene booties
- Balaclava
- Base glove layer
- Thermal gloves

Here are some cold-weather riding tips:

- Apply baby powder on your feet, hands, chest, crotch, and armpits. This will help you stay drier and warmer.
- Place chemical warmers on your feet, hands, chest, and lower back. Make sure the chemical warmers are not directly on your skin, but on thin base layers. The warmers on your chest and lower back will warm your heart and kidneys, where much of your body's blood flows through to other parts of your body.
- Apply lotion liberally on the exposed parts of your face. This will prevent painful skin chapping.

- Carry an extra base layer to change into at a turnaround point. Peel off the sweaty one and put on the dry one. This will make your return journey warmer and more pleasant.
- Ride into the wind on the way out. On the way out, you are fresh and can handle more extreme environmental circumstances. Ride with the wind at your back on the way home; you will appreciate the perceived increase in temperature with reduced windchill.
- Put salt in your water bottles to prevent freezing.
- Start your ride later in the day when the sun is at its peak.
- Cover your mouth with a balaclava or bandana, because your trapped respiration will moisten and warm the incoming air.
- Choose hilly rides, but take it easy on the climbs so you do not overheat too much and are not wet for the descent.
- Get a band of other riders together, and choose a flat route, but set an endurance pace speed limit. Form a double paceline to provide wind protection, and take long, easy pulls.

Chapter 10

PURSUING LONG-TERM GOALS

Cycling takes so many hours to train and so many years to be really strong. Being good at cycling doesn't happen because you train hard one year.

—Rune Hoydahl, former professional mountain biker known for winning five World Cup races in a row and being the only mountain biker with World Cup victories in both cross-country and downhill

When athletes first take on bicycle racing and training, the initial feeling may be one of curiosity or excitement in trying something competitive, different, and new. After the initial surge, many racing cyclists find pleasure in honing their physical and mental skills. As with anything in life, the real pleasure starts once the athlete feels invested and is moving toward a defined target.

To achieve maximum satisfaction in cycling, you need to approach it as you would any other endeavor you wish to succeed in—think long term beyond initial pleasure or easily achieved goals. Because there can be only one winner per race, and because you will often have only a few chances per year to go for the win, you will get much more satisfaction in the sport if you have long-term goals beyond the excitement of racing. In fact, the cyclists who have long-term goals, even years in length, are usually the ones who achieve short-term success and have the best race performances.

This chapter covers proper goal setting, along with tools used for setting up goal time lines. You will learn to think beyond the next race or even the next season. Thinking five years down the road, which may seem like a long time from now, will help you to constantly build and improve in the sport of bicycle racing.

When you first start competing, winning a race may feel like a distant dream, but making smaller, attainable goals throughout your cycling career can eventually lead to great success if you stay focused and dedicated.

Goal Setting

Professional cyclists, just like amateur cyclists, invest tremendous amounts of time and energy into training for very short bouts of racing. Unlike other sports, where short-term achievements beyond wins are realized—for example, hits in baseball, catches in football, points scored in basketball—a cyclist may sit in numerous races before ever achieving a podium position, winning a mid-race sprint, or reaching the top of the mountain first. There are just too few opportunities in cycling—along with too many participants, myriad racing conditions, and teammates of differing specialties and abilities.

To overcome this lack of positive reinforcement, the athlete needs to set well-constructed goals that include both race-related goals and training-related goals. Achieving a race or training goal—outside of just "wanting to win"—will further develop the cyclist, which will enable the cyclist to have more opportunities for victory in the future. Avoid race-placing goals such as "I want to get first place at the local road race." Pick goals that relate to performance, such as "I want to put out more overall power in the sprint at the local road race."

The best goals are ones that are *challenging* and *attainable* (Daniels & Daniels 2006). This is a delicate balance. If a goal is too challenging, then it will never be reached and thus will be detrimental to your athletic performance and mental state. If the goal is too attainable, then it will be reached too quickly and thus will provide no boost to performance;

achieving this goal will be too boring to increase mental satisfaction. Setting goals takes practice.

To help, use the SMART technique to pick and set challenging and attainable goals. In this technique, you set goals that are specific, measurable, attainable, realistic, and timely (Drucker 1993).

Specific

Goals should never be general; they should always be specific. To develop specific goals, you should ask yourself the following questions: What do I want to accomplish? Where do I want to accomplish it? When do I want to accomplish it? How do I want to accomplish it?

For example, the following is a general goal: "I will improve my time trialing." A specific goal would be as follows: "I will improve my average power in the local, flat 40K time trial by May 15 by adding more lactate threshold intervals and $\dot{V}O_2$max intervals into my training during late March and early April."

Measurable

If you cannot specifically measure progress toward a goal in your training log, then the goal is most likely not an achievable goal. How can you get somewhere if you do not know the steps to take? Measuring progress keeps you on track, allows you to modify steps, and provides evidence for future building toward other goals. To determine if an athletic goal is measurable, ask the following questions: How much? How many? How will I know when it is accomplished?

For example, the following is an immeasurable goal: "I want to improve in the next race." A measurable goal would be as follows: "I want to improve my average power in the sprint during the next race."

Attainable

Goals can be (a) out of reach entirely, (b) within reach with the proper planning and effort, or (c) too easily reachable. The best goals are those that are within reach with proper planning and effort. Goals that are out of reach and goals that are too easily attainable are both ineffective and nonmotivating. Athletes should pick goals that require a bit of research for the proper planning of steps. The research will give the athlete ownership and investment in the outcome. It will also reveal if the goal is reasonable and will indicate the amount of effort that will be required to achieve it.

An easily attainable goal may be to ascend a local 1.5-mile climb 10 seconds faster after the first few attempts. You will most likely achieve this goal within a week or two. A more challenging yet attainable goal may be to pick a climb that you have challenged yourself on all season and to set the goal of beating your best time by 30 seconds to 1 minute during the following months. If you chose to increase the goal to 1 minute 30 seconds or even 2 minutes, the goal may be unattainable in the next few years.

Realistic

A realistic goal has an objective that you are both willing and able to work toward. A high goal is often easier to reach than a low one, because a low goal exerts low motivational force. Your goal is probably realistic if you truly believe that it can be accomplished through an investment of time and planned work. Additional ways to know if your goal is realistic is to determine if you have accomplished anything similar in the past or to ask yourself what conditions would have to exist to accomplish this goal. For example, an unrealistic goal for a beginner would be to get hired by a professional team during his first year of competition. A more realistic goal would be to be asked to join a local or regional team.

A Pro's Experience

Dez Wilder, Cannondale Professional Mountain Bike Racing, Professional 24-Hour Mountain Bike Racer

"Setting goals is an extremely important piece of my personal training," explains Dez. He finds the key is setting goals that are challenging but still achievable. For each racing cyclist, Dez believes, "As you achieve the goals you've set for yourself it's important to set new and more challenging ones for the future so that you continue to grow as a cyclist."

When Dez first started riding, his goal was to get fit and have fun. He initially had no long-term goals. But once he achieved racing fitness, he found himself trying to race and train as far as he could. As Dez explains, "One morning during a training ride when I was 18, I told myself that I was going to become a professional cyclist within the next 5 years. Based on my fitness and desire, the time frame I gave myself made the goal realistic." With this long-term goal in mind, Dez took his racing and training seriously from that moment forward. When training, he kept his original goal in mind so that if he fell short in a particular event, he would always have a reason to pick himself back up and continue training.

Dez's goal setting is not without strategy. He breaks season goals into smaller monthly or weekly pieces to avoid making them overwhelming. Dez picks a few high-profile or personally important target events each season at which he would like to perform well. He structures his monthly and weekly goals around those events. Dez adds, "If I have a small race coming up in the next few days, I make it my goal to take it a little easy on the bike and get plenty of rest. I remind myself that this race is only part of my preparation for a target event that might be weeks away. This doesn't mean that I don't try to do well in the smaller race, but I might not take as many chances in descents or I might try to keep the atmosphere light and fun so that I don't get too caught up in the results." Dez asserts targeting a few key events may be the difference between a handful of top finishes and a whole season's worth of midpack finishes.

Dez concludes, "Hard work and dedication have helped me achieve my first long-term cycling goal of becoming a professional. Without having set that goal, it would have been challenging to find continued motivation or focus when training and racing became difficult."

Timely

Goals need to be grounded within a time frame. Without a time frame, there is no sense of urgency, and the goal may never be accomplished. A time frame also provides a framework within which an athlete can build steps toward achievement. Be wary of goals that push you to reach them by a time frame that is detrimental to your personal or physical health. Also be wary of goals that cause ever shifting time frames. Set the target date and stick to it. If you do not reach the goal by the target date, *do not* change the time frame—instead, change the goal.

For example, trying to add 20 percent more average power to your flat, 40K time trial by the end of the season may be a substantial goal to achieve, but it seems realistic at the start. If the specific date to test your goal arrives and you fail to reach the goal, do not push the time frame back a month or two. It is better to review the progress you made over the period leading up to the test and how much you actually improved. If you improved 7 percent, then you should use the following strategy when setting the goal for the next season: Choose the same target date, but instead of shooting for a 20 percent improvement, shoot for 5 to 10 percent instead.

Distinguishing Between Goals and Workouts

To avoid confusion, you should note the difference between goals and workouts. A workout may dictate specific intervals, but a daily goal determines how you will conduct the intervals in comparison to either past or present performances (e.g., with more focus than last time, with more power than last time, or using a different buildup than last time). A weekly training plan may dictate a base period, but the goal indicates how you are going to achieve that base period in comparison to past or present base periods (e.g., better control of heart rate, different routes that do not distract from base mileage, and so on).

A solid example is the common simulation ride. It is a great idea, especially as race season approaches, to include a racelike group ride once a week in your training regimen. Attending the racelike ride is the workout. The goal should be something that follows the SMART principle: specific (staying in the top 10 throughout the ride), measurable (noting your pack position every 10 minutes), achievable (choosing a ride that includes riders around, slightly above, or slightly below your level), reasonable (choosing a group ride with a route that suits your abilities so that staying in the top 10 is not an impossibility), and timely (performing this goal near race season to hone your skills).

Daily Goals

The daily goal is structured based on the daily workout. The workout could be as unstructured as "an easy ride with friends to the coffee shop." Or the workout could be more structured, such as "a 30-minute warm-up followed by six $\dot{V}O_2$max intervals of 3 minutes each with 3 minutes rest in between followed by a 20-minute cool-down." Daily goals come from this daily structure.

A less structured daily goal for the first example might be to just enjoy a nice talking pace throughout the ride, avoiding the urge to attack your comrades or follow attacks by your comrades and also avoiding *half-wheeling*. Half-wheeling refers to cyclists riding next to each other, and both cyclists trying to keep their front wheel in front of the other person's front wheel, which in turn escalates the speed unnecessarily. A more structured daily goal for the first example might be keeping power under 150 watts at all times on the ride or keeping the heart rate below 75 percent of MHR. A daily goal for the $\dot{V}O_2$max interval example might be adding 10 percent more average power to each interval in comparison to your last session.

The important aspect of the daily goal is that you set it before you start the ride, agree to it with your riding partners (if necessary), and stick to it. Without the daily goal, all rides tend to fall to unstructured racelike training. As a competitive cyclist, you need to always have a purpose when you ride, and you must avoid hours on the road that do not move you closer to your goals.

Weekly Goals

While daily goals are connected with prewritten daily workouts, weekly goals take their cue from mesocycles, such as a development period. For example, if you are in the third week of a development period, workouts may include training that improves lactate threshold. Weekly goals would include building in longer intervals of LT training to total a 10 percent overall weekly increase in LT work time.

An important weekly goal may even be rest. Beginning competitive cyclists often find resting to be the most difficult part of training. Treat your rest weeks with the same diligence and particularity with which you treat your training. If the workout period has rest included on the schedule, then make the weekly goal to be as rested as possible by reducing life stressors, sitting instead of standing, napping, sleeping in, and avoiding high-intensity cycling.

Monthly Goals

Monthly goals are partly dictated by mesocycles, but more often they are dictated by numbers to be achieved. As stated in chapter 9, being a great record keeper goes hand in hand with being a great cyclist. Great record keeping is most important in achieving monthly goals.

A good monthly goal is to achieve a certain number of hours in the saddle or miles on the road or to complete as many workouts as possible without interference. Each mesocycle builds on the last—without a good base period, it will be impossible to achieve a good development period. Do not cheat yourself of the necessary hours. Make your monthly goal not only to perform the necessary workouts, but also to match the hours required to move seamlessly to the next mesocycle. Other monthly goals could include attempting to complete a certain number of races. To see if you reached your monthly goals, review your training log monthly.

Annual Goals

In cycling, physical development is essentially a bottom-up procedure—remember the analogy of the pyramid, where a big base means higher peaks. However, developing goals is a bottom-down procedure. As an athlete, you should ask yourself the following questions: What are my goals for the season? Do they involve a certain race? A specific power target? A specific skill? From these annual goals, you will develop monthly, weekly, and daily goals.

The annual goal will also dictate the annual plan. As discussed in chapter 9, the race calendar is used to develop a month-by-month structure to move through the mesocycles. These mesocycles will then dictate the weekly and daily workouts to ensure that an athlete's short-term goals support and contribute to the achievement of annual goals. Best performances at races on the race calendar are the goals (best performance is determined by a variety of factors beyond placing). Once these goals are chosen, it is up to the athlete to apply SMART principles to each of the goals. For example, simply wanting to win a certain race because it is hilly and you are a climber will not do. Instead, choose the goal of increasing your average power-to-weight climbing output for the race. With that goal, you can develop mesocycle goals of adding in more power development on climbs, all the way down to a specific power workout on climbs that are similar to the target race.

Five-Year Plan

Even when athletes are just starting out in cycling, if they are serious about developing to their potential in the sport, they should think beyond the current season, or even the next season. This may seem like a large step and commitment, especially if the athlete is just starting out in the sport; however, the five-year planning process is an invaluable tool to ensure that the athlete stays in the sport and reaches his or her potential. As stated earlier, bicycle racing rewards those who have the mental fortitude to continue racing and training despite poor race placings and training setbacks. Some cyclists will withdraw from the sport because of injury, burnout, or

Racing partners who share your enthusiasm but support you through setbacks can keep you focused as you develop long-term plans.

other life obligations. Many more cyclists will drop out because they lack clear direction. For athletes without clear direction, the sport of cycling can become overwhelming and lacking in gratification. As a result, many extremely talented athletes never realize their potential.

To avoid this unnecessary pitfall, you should begin to think of cycling in five-year cycles. This may seem like a long time, but the framework provided by five-year plans is manageable and applicable even to current daily workouts. As you improve and move up categories, you will begin to notice that—besides the occasional fluke who wins the race on the first go—the victors are usually those who have planned and prepared over many years.

After racing a season and experiencing races on a local and regional level, you should ask yourself the following questions:

- What races did I enjoy, and what races did I not enjoy?
- What races suit my talents, and what races do not?
- What races fit well into the other obligations in my life?
- What do I see as a deficiency or proficiency in my physical skills?
- What do I see as a deficiency or proficiency in my handling skills?
- What do I see as a deficiency or proficiency in my mental skills?

These questions are a good place to start, and they lead to the ultimate question: Where do I see myself in the sport in five years? Answering this question will provide you with a destination. From this destination, you can build a road map.

Sample Five-Year Plan

This planning skill is best explained through example. The following example is for an entry-level road racer with climbing proficiency. So much of cycling is time management and investment in improvement. Not to say that cycling needs to be considered work or a job (especially for those choosing it for recreational enjoyment), but applying a bit of thought to the overall process goes a long way. This sample five-year plan is not a cookie-cutter plan to be emulated; it is presented as a guide to show how you can approach cycling with a bit of a head start on the competition.

Road Racer: A five-Year Case Study

During the first year of racing as a road racer, Jack realizes that he can drop his teammates on any local climb over one mile in distance. Jack also notices that in all races with climbs of over one mile in distance, he made the lead group. Even though Jack is currently category 5, he knows that the State Road Championship is always held on a hilly course. Winning the category 5 state road title is a priority for him this season, as well as the category 4 state road title next season. But being wise, Jack's real long-term goal is to win the state road title as a category 2 racer sometime in the future.

Knowing that competition increases with each category increase, Jack realizes that a general goal such as "winning the state title as a category 2" will not help him attain the title. At that level, the competition will be more homogenous, and he may not even be considered a great climber in comparison. Jack sees his talent and knows he must hone it, so he embarks on a five-year plan to improve his climbing overall, along with other ancillary skills to make him a better overall competitor.

After year 1 of racing, Jack decides what makes for a great climber:

- Lean, light body
- Light equipment, especially rotating equipment such as wheels, tires, pedals, and cranks
- High sustained power-to-weight ratio
- Good rhythm in pedaling, timing, and breathing
- High cadence to limit leg fatigue and handle uphill accelerations
- Mental toughness to gut it out when you feel as if you are falling behind
- Mental toughness to not be afraid to push ahead and try to drop competitors even when you fear you could "blow up"
- Proper road nutrition consisting of easily digestible foods to maintain energy level, especially on climbs late in the race
- An efficiently shifting bicycle that enables you to avoid bad shifts when the moves go on the climb
- Tactical smarts to know when to surge on the climb, when to sit in, whom to follow, and what the course holds ahead

After thinking through what makes a great climber, Jack realizes that becoming a great climber is a very large task, but he considers himself fortunate to have the raw talent to develop. Jack realizes that with a five-year plan, he can individually target each component to the point of mastery, then move on to subsequent components. He divides the components into categories:

- Nutrition skills: when to eat, how to eat to stay lean
- Tactical skills: race strategy and tactics, equipment research
- Physical skills: pedaling, power
- Mental skills: gutting it out
- Mechanical skills: how to fix and maintain the bike

Targeting the Components

YEAR 2

Nutrition
- Jack does not worry about his body at this point because he is light and lean compared to his competitors, but he makes an effort to read up on general nutrition for endurance athletes.
- Jack reads about athletic nutrition so he can learn to pick foods that digest easily and provide proper fuel during training.

Tactical
- Jack starts a savings account to accrue money to spend toward purchasing lighter equipment.
- Jack's purchases will include a power meter for next season so he can begin monitoring his power-to-weight ratio.
- Jack reads books on race tactics to learn tactical smarts, such as when to surge on the climb, when to sit in, whom to follow, and how to take advantage of course profiles.

Physical
- Jack adds weekly pedaling drills, such as isolated leg training, to his program in order to develop good rhythm in pedaling.
- Jack adds weekly high-cadence pedaling drills so he can limit leg fatigue and handle uphill accelerations.

Mental
- Jack seeks out other riders and group rides where he may be outmatched on climbs. He does this in order to learn the mental toughness required to gut it out when he feels as if he is falling behind.
- Jack seeks out other riders and group rides where he may be the strongest rider. He does this in order to learn the mental toughness required to not be afraid to push ahead and try to drop competitors even when he fears he could "blow up."

Mechanical
- Jack decides to read up on simple bicycle maintenance so he will be able to tune his bicycle efficiently and avoid mechanical problems at key points in the race.

YEAR 3

Nutrition
- Jack experiments with various foods to see what works for him, especially when approaching climbs late in rides.
- Jack continues to read about nutrition; he also chooses to add in a few more weekly hours of endurance riding during the base period in order to help maintain or improve his leanness.

Tactical
- Jack invests in light pedals.
- Jack always applies and practices tactics, even on group rides.

Physical
- Jack attains a power meter and starts testing, charting, and monitoring his power-to-weight ratio on local one-mile climbs.
- Jack practices timing on one-mile climbs: when to push harder, how hard to start, how hard to finish, and how to handle grade changes.
- Jack continues high-cadence drills by increasing the highest sustained average cadence by 5 rpm.

Mental
- Jack rides weekly with a group of stronger riders and weaker riders in order to force himself to work on mental toughness in either dropping or not being dropped on climbs.

Mechanical
- Jack volunteers at a bicycle shop for a few hours each week to learn how to repair his own equipment and keep it in top race shape.

YEAR 4

Nutrition
- Jack develops specific race-day and training-day routines for eating in order to maximize energy.
- Jack adds cycling-specific weight training to his early-season routine in order to help develop more lean muscle.

Tactical
- Jack purchases an ultralight, but safe, race-day wheel set.
- Jack races in specific events to try tactics in race situations regardless of his results.

Physical
- Jack plans his training around specific power-to-weight ratios with incremental increases through weeks and months.
- Jack focuses on rate and intensity of breathing on every climb. He notes and responds to the rate and intensity of the competition's breathing on climbs.
- Jack continues to increase his highest average cadences and adds in seated or standing high-power bursts to his climbing routine.

Mental
- Jack reads more on the mental aspects of sport and applies techniques such as visualization and narrow internal focus.

Mechanical
- Jack mechanically tunes his own bicycle regularly.

YEAR 5

Nutrition
- Jack reads avidly and hones all nutrition skills learned for the past five years.

Tactical
- Jack reads avidly and hones all tactical skills learned for the past five years.

Physical
- Jack reads avidly and hones all physical skills learned for the past five years.

Mental
- Jack reads avidly and hones all mental skills learned for the past five years.

Mechanical
- Jack reads avidly and hones all mechanical skills learned for the past five years.

Assuming that Jack has acquired the necessary points to upgrade through the categories to category 2, he is ready to put his best effort forward at category 2 cycling. He spends the fifth year embedding all he has learned so that it becomes second nature. He can then focus on achieving a high placing, making the right moves, and enjoying a successful bid for the State Road Race Championships at the category 2 level.

This may seem like a long time to work on developing the specific aspects in order to achieve a long-term goal; however, many cyclists are balancing other life obligations. If Jack had gone full bore into each skill set in the first or second year, he may have experienced burnout, learned skills poorly, possibly injured himself, or been disappointed if he did not reach overly large goals quickly enough.

This time line is just an example and is not for every athlete. Use the questions and tools provided in this book to develop your five-year plan— and stick to it. This plan is your guidepost and your map, and it will be the only truly measurable way to monitor, track, and achieve improvement.

Appendix

Cycling Log

Date	Scheduled ride	Actual ride	Distance (mi)	Time (h)	Climb (ft)	Perceived effort (scale of 1-10)	Comments
Weekly total							
Weekly total							
Weekly total							
Weekly total							
Weekly total							
Monthly total							

Annual Plan Worksheet

Week #	Races or events	Priority	Mesocycle	Hours
1				
2				
3				
4				
5				
6				
7				
8				
9				
10				
11				
12				
13				
14				
15				
16				
17				
18				
19				
20				
21				
22				
23				
24				
25				
26				
27				
28				
29				
30				
31				
32				
33				
34				
35				
36				
37				
38				
39				
40				
41				
42				
43				
44				

Week #	Races or events	Priority	Mesocycle	Hours
45				
46				
47				
48				
49				
50				
51				
52				
Total hours				

From R. Panzera, 2010, *Cycling Fast* (Champaign, IL: Human Kinetics).

SAMPLE MONTH				
Week #	Races or events	Priority	Mesocycle	Hours
24	None	N/A	Development	18.00
25	None	N/A	Development	18.00
26	Red Trolley Criterium	Low	Development	18.00

Periodized Weight Training Plan

TRANSITION (4 WEEKS STARTING IN TRANSITION AND MOVING INTO BASE)

Exercises to build overall body strength. Do all of these exercises extremely comfortably and with excellent form. Choose a weight at which the 20th rep is almost impossible to finish with excellent form. Once the 20th rep becomes easy, increase weight. Take a 1-minute rest between sets.

Exercise	Sets/reps	Weight
Leg sled	1 × 20	
Machine squat	1 × 20	
Assisted pull-up	1 × 20	
Assisted dip	1 × 20	
Leg curl	1 × 20	
Leg raise	1 × 20	
Crunch	>20	N/A
Back extension	>20	N/A

PREPARATION (4 WEEKS DURING BASE)

Exercises to increase strength to prepare the body for strength phase. Similar exercises to transition phase, but fewer reps. Do all of these exercises extremely comfortably and with excellent form. Choose a weight at which the 12th rep is almost impossible to finish with excellent form. Once the 12th rep becomes easy, increase weight. Take a 1-minute rest between sets.

Exercise	Sets/reps	Weight
Machine squat	1 × 12	
Deadlift	1 × 12	
Hanging knee lift	1 × 12	N/A
Machine row	1 × 12	
Push-up	2 × 10	
Leg curl	1 × 12	
Leg raise	1 × 12	
Crunch	>25	N/A
Back extension	>20	N/A

STRENGTH (6 WEEKS DURING THE END OF BASE OR DEVELOPMENT)

Exercises to build maximum strength. Do all of these exercises extremely comfortably and with excellent form. Choose a weight at which the 6th rep is almost impossible to finish with excellent form. Once the 6th rep becomes easy, increase weight. Take a 1-minute rest between sets.

Exercise	Sets/reps	Weight
Machine squat	2 × 6	
Leg sled	2 × 6	
One-leg machine leg sled	2 × 6	
Hanging leg lift	2 × 6	N/A
Machine row	2 × 6	
Push-up	>20	
Deadlift	2 × 6	
Crunch	>30	N/A
Back extension	>20	N/A

MAINTENANCE (8 WEEKS AND THROUGHOUT SEASON DURING DEVELOPMENT AND TAPER)

Exercises to maintain strength during racing season. Do all of these exercises extremely comfortably and with excellent form. This workout should not last more than 30 minutes at a moderate pace. Choose a weight where the 6th rep feels as though you could go to 10 reps. No need to increase weight. 1 minute rest between sets.

Exercise	Sets/reps	Weight
Leg sled	1 × 6	
One-leg machine leg sled	1 × 6	
Hanging leg lift	1 × 6	N/A
Machine row	1 × 6	
Push-up	>25	
Crunch	>40	N/A
Back extension	>20	N/A

The exercises will require a fitness center membership, and it is recommended that you speak with a certified personal trainer who can fully explain and demonstrate each of the exercises.

Glossary

accordion effect—Occurs when the peloton slows on entering a hill or corner, and then accelerates as the hill starts or as the peloton exits the corner. The cyclists in the back of the peloton slow—and lose momentum—as the front of the peloton bunches up, and they need to accelerate quickly as the front of the peloton speeds up.

active recovery—A period in which the cyclist performs shorter, less intense riding to allow the body to recuperate.

aerobars—Handlebars for time-trial bicycles the place the body in an extended position by allowing the athlete to rest elbows on pads and place hands on extensions. This provides an aerodynamic position with flat back, further forward position over the front of the bicycle, and reduced frontal body area.

anaerobic threshold—The point at which you begin working your muscles almost exclusively without oxygen.

attack—When a competitor tries to break away from the peloton.

basal metabolic rate—The approximate amount of energy (in calories) that an individual burns each day at rest.

belly breathing—A breathing technique in which a person breathes from very low in the abdomen, resisting the urge to breathe high in the chest. Cyclists may use this technique as part of the centering procedures intended to reduce distracting thoughts.

bike throw—Pushing the bike forward for a last-second surge to the finishing line. To execute a bike throw, sprint to within a few meters of the line, and in one swift motion (pushing forward on the handlebars), drop your body low and flatten your back.

blocking—An advanced process by which an individual slows the pack to allow other riders to attain a gap. When blocking, a rider should never cause other racers to slam their brakes or maneuver dangerously.

blowing up—Overexerting yourself to the point where you can no longer ride hard. Also called *cracking*.

bottom bracket—The intersection of the seat tube and the downtube; the connection point for the crank.

breakaway—Or *break*. A group of competitors in a race who have created a gap on the peloton.

breaking the chain—Attacking and dropping the peloton so they put up little or no chase.

bridging the gap—A term used to describe closing a gap of time or distance between riders in a race or a group ride.

bumping—The skill of leaning into contact made with other cyclists while riding.

bunch sprint—A sprint for the finish line involving a large body of the competitors in the race.

centering—Procedures used to reduce distracting thoughts before and during competition. Centering emphasizes muscle relaxation, belly breathing, and thought control through self-statements.

center to center—Method of measuring bicycle components in which the measurement is taken from the center of the handlebar or tube on one side to the center of the handlebar or tube on the other measured side.

chainstays—Tubes on bicycle frame connecting the bottom bracket to rear dropouts.

chief judge—The individual assigned by the race's governing body to oversee all matters regarding individual placement in the race and to handle all disputes.

chief referee—The individual assigned by the race's governing body to oversee all matters of conduct of the racers before, during, and after the race.

circuit races—Races that cover multiple laps of five miles or less in succession. Lower categories (4 and 5) usually cover less laps than upper categories (1 and 2).

classics (and semiclassics)—*See* one-day classics.

club—Association of cyclists with a common objective, such as gathering riders of varying ability levels for group rides. Clubs usually have an educational component for beginning cyclists. Many racing teams are born from clubs.

coach—A person who provides guidance to a racer, whether per monetary agreement or for payment in kind.

coachee—A person who solicits the services of a coach.

components—Parts of a bicycle other than the frame and wheels (i.e., brakes, handlebars, shifters, crankset, and so on).

countersteering—A cornering technique where the rider leans the bike more than the body, putting positive forward pressure on the inside hand as it is extended. Increasing the lean of the bike with more inside hand pressure tightens the cornering, while decreasing the lean of the bike with less inside hand pressure widens the cornering.

cracking—Overexerting yourself to the point where you can no longer ride hard. Also called *blowing up*.

criterium—A race that is held on a flat, fast course in which the distance per lap is less than 1 mile (1.6 km). The course also includes tight, fast corners.

cross-training—Engaging in various sports or exercises to achieve well-rounded health and muscular development.

cyclocross—Form of bicycle racing that consists of laps around a 3 to 4 kilometer (2-2.5 mi.) course featuring pavement, trails, grass, hills and barriers requiring athletes to dismount, carry the bike, and remount.

downtube—Tube on a bicycle frame that runs from the headtube to the bottom of the seat tube.

draft—A position behind or to the side of a rider that enables another rider to stay out of the wind.

drag—Force acting on a cyclist moving through air parallel and opposite to the direction of motion. Assuming constant drag, drag will vary as the square of velocity. Resultant power needed to overcome this drag will vary as the cube of velocity.

drive a breakaway—A term used to describe being the protagonist in the breakaway—increasing or maintaining a hard pace, setting up the paceline, and encouraging other competitors to assist the breakaway.

dropout—Slot where the axle of the wheel attaches to the bicycle frame.

drops—Lower, deeper part of the bicycle handlebar.

dropped—When a rider is gapped from the group or peloton during a race and is unable to regain contact.

ego orientation—A goal orientation in which perceived ability is measured as a function of outperforming others.

feed zone—The location specified (by race promoters and the chief referee) for on-the-course hand-ups of food and drinks to racing cyclists.

finishing straight—The last few hundred meters in a race.

fixed gear—A single-gear bike that does not freewheel. The crank rotates forward with forward motion and backward with rearward motion. Fixed gears are used in track races on velodromes.

flow—Mental state in which the athlete is fully immersed in the racing or training experience by a feeling of focus, involvement, and success. A sense of control and mastery arises effortlessly.

fork—Portion of a bicycle that connects the front wheel to the bicycle frame, stem, and handlebars via the steerer tube. Allows the rider to steer and balance the bicycle.

form—A term used to describe a racer's general race fitness. Form is a subjective term, but good form usually indicates that a racer is peaking.

forward imagery—Envisioning future outcomes based on real-time training.

freewheel—Design of a bicycle rear wheel in which a clutch allows the wheel to spin freely when the pedals are stationary.

frequency—The number of times a cyclist participates in a training or racing effort. Usually measured in days per week.

gap—A separation of time and distance in a race or training ride from one group to another group on the road.

gatekeeping—A blocking process of letting others coming off either a paceline or lead-out train slip back into the paceline or lead-out train in front of you, thereby allowing you to maintain draft without actually moving up and doing any work in the wind. Also used to keep a sprinting competitor off your team's lead-out train.

half-wheeling—Refers to two cyclists riding next to each other, and both cyclists trying to keep their front wheel in front of the other person's front wheel, which in turn escalates the speed unnecessarily.

hammer—Jargon for pedaling as hard as you can for extended periods.

hand-up—The technique for handing up water bottles and food to a moving racer in the feed zone.

headtube angle—The angle (measured to the rear of the headtube) between the headtube and an imaginary line running parallel to the ground.

headtube height—The length of the headtube.

heart rate monitor—Mobile telemetry device that measures and records pulse rate. A monitor usually consists of a transmitting chest strap and receiving unit, which displays heart rate as beats per minute. The receiving unit is usually attached to the wrist like a watch or attached to the bicycle handlebar.

hole—An empty space in a pack in front of you that you are entering or that is closing because of rider movement.

hoods—Rubber or plastic areas at the top of the brake levers that provide holding surfaces on the handlebars.

hook—When one racer's handlebar hits another racer's handlebar, causing both racers to swerve or crash.

imagery—Rehearsing a competitive scenario and outcome in your mind before or after the actual event.

increasing-radius turn—A turn that starts sharper and finishes straighter.

intensity—The level of effort put forth during a workout.

intermediate sprints—Mid-race sprints along a road course, usually in flat sections. The first person is awarded the most points, and subsequent placings are awarded points on a sliding scale. These points do not affect the outcome of the overall racing, but they accrue toward the goal of a sprint champion, which in many races indicates the quickest racer of the event. Intermediate sprint points are usually tallied along with sprint finish points to determine an overall sprint leader.

intervals—A type of training in which the cyclist divides hard efforts into manageable chunks of approximately 1- to 4-minute intervals (with rest periods in between) in order to perform more total work in a training period. Intervals can also be as short as 8 seconds and as long as 20 minutes, depending on the system trained and the objective of the workout session.

jumping—Short bursts of high-revolution pedaling in easy or moderate gears.

king (or queen) of the mountains—Mid-race finishes at the top of the significant climbs; the first person is awarded the most points, and subsequent placings are awarded points on a sliding scale. These points do not affect the outcome of the overall racing, but they accrue toward the goal of a king of the mountains, which in many races indicates the best climber of the event.

lactate threshold—The point at which blood lactate begins to accumulate beyond lactate clearance. When lactic acid builds up in muscles, it causes feelings of fatigue.

lead-out or lead-out train—A team performing a high-speed paceline in the closing kilometers of a race to prevent attacks from other teams and to ensure that their sprinter is near the front before the dash for the finish line.

leaning—A cornering technique in which both the bike and the cyclist are angled in the same direction. The handlebars are not turned, just angled with the bike and body. (Not to be confused with leaning skills drills.)

license—A number and card provided by a sanctioning body that give a cyclist eligibility to race (and in some instances, medical insurance in case of an accident during racing).

losing a wheel—Becoming gapped or blocked in by slower riders in the run-up to a sprint, hill climb, or other race-defining moment.

macrocycle—The largest cycle in a workout program. A macrocycle is usually one year or one season in length.

mesocycle—Cycles within a workout program that are weeks or months in length. The macrocycle is divided into mesocycles.

microcycle—Cycles within a workout program that are weeks in length. The mesocycles are divided into microcycles, and you develop your weekly workouts from these microcycles.

monuments—One-day cycling classics, each which has a long history and awards prestigious palmarès for overall victory. The five monuments are: Milan-San Remo, Tour of Flanders (Ronde van Vlaanderen), Paris-Roubaix, and Giro di Lombardia. *See* one-day classics.

multitool—Portable hand tool that combines several individual tool functions (allen wrenches, screwdrivers, tire levers, and so on) in a single grip.

musette—A shoulder bag used for food and drink given to racers in a feed zone during a bicycle race. This bag can be easily grabbed by a moving racer. The shoulder strap is placed over the neck and shoulder, the contents are removed and placed into jersey pockets or bottle cages, and the bag is then discarded.

one-day license—A one-off pay-per-use license that allows a racer to race in the lowest available category. Medical insurance is usually provided for the one event.

one-day classics—The most prestigious one-day professional yearly cycling road races. Most of the events have been on the professional calendar for decades. The oldest classics date back to the nineteenth century. Semi-classics are usually on the calendar between a string of classics to provide training, preparation, and additional spectacle for fans during the height of the classics season (mainly spring). *See* monuments.

outside to outside—Method of measuring bicycle components in which the measurement is taken from the outside of the end of the bar (or tube) to the outside of the bar (or tube) on the other measured side.

palmarès—Record of achievements and placings; prize list.

pacing—Maintaining lower power or heart rate levels earlier in an effort so you can continue to do the same effort or more effort later in a training session. Pacing applies to entire training rides or races, segments of training rides or races, and intervals.

pacelining—A practice in which a group of cyclists are organized to efficiently take turns riding in the wind and sitting in protected from the wind.

peaking—Achieving the best mental and physical shape that the racer can attain. Racers attempt to peak for certain sections of the season in preparation for specific events.

pedal and cleat systems—Interface in which the cleats on a cyclist's shoes to lock into the pedals. Pedal and cleat systems are highly adjustable. A rider can usually set the release tension (the force needed to cause the cleat to disengage from the pedal), the release angle (how many lateral degrees a cleat must be twisted to disengage), and the float (how many lateral degrees the cleat will move while engaged).

peloton—The main racing group in a race.

periodization—A training strategy in which the workout program is divided into cycles, or periods. Each period builds on the past period to provide ample and constructive development of physical elements.

points race—A mass-start race (held on a track) where points for first, second, and third place are given on set laps, such as laps 5, 10, 15, 20, and so on. The winner is the racer who accumulates the most points.

power—Work divided by time, where work equals force multiplied by distance. To increase on-the-bike power, one must either increase force (the numerator) or decrease the amount of time (the denominator) it takes the pedal to complete a revolution (i.e., increase cadence).

power meter—A tool that provides an absolute measurement (in watts) of the power generated by the cyclist. Power meters measure, record, and display power as wattage in real time. Some meters use the bottom bracket of the bike as the source for extrapolating power, while others use the rear wheel hub, and still others use wind velocity and rider drag for power.

prime hunting—The act of entering a race with the sole purpose of acquiring as many mid-race prizes as possible, having little regard for overall individual placing at the end of the race. Many racers find this strategy more lucrative than actually racing for a placing at the finish.

primes—Prizes given within a race, usually a criterium, to liven up the racing. Primes (pronounced preem-z) are usually announced during the race on the lap before the award, and they are awarded to the first person across the finish line on the subsequent lap. Primes and prizes do not normally affect the overall standings of a race; these are one-time offers.

promoter—Any individual or group of individuals who receive local permits and governing body licensure to hold a race under the auspices of all permitting jurisdictions. Promoters put on races for a variety of reasons. The main reason may often be economic gain, but many races are put on solely for the social growth of the sport.

protected racer—A teammate for whom all other teammates work.

pull—The time spent on the paceline or the front of the pack.

pull through—To move into a vacated lead position from second in a paceline or pack.

pull off—To move off the lead position after taking a pull for a paceline or pack.

race—A cycling event put in place by a promoter (who receives licensure from a governing body) in which individuals can participate in events of competition against other individuals. Races come in a variety of forms, including road, mountain, time trial, cyclocross, criterium, and track.

recovery (rest)—A break taken from cycling either consisting of *active recovery* while on the bike or full recovery when off the bike.

reel in (the break or the competition)—Jargon for the peloton picking up the pace to capture an individual or a breakaway.

reverse imagery—Envisioning future outcomes based on previous training.

riding unattached—Competing in a race with no club or team affiliation. The person's racing license reads "unattached" in the Club/Team field.

road rash—The removal of skin due to the friction of contact with the road surface.

rollers—Bicycle trainer that does not attach to the bicycle, instead the cyclist balances on the rollers. Rollers consist of three cylinders (called "drums" or "rollers")—two for the rear wheel and one for the front—on top of which the bicycle rolls. A belt connects the rear rollers to the front roller, causing the front wheel of the bicycle to spin when the bicycle is pedaled. Riding rollers takes practice, because balance is required. They are noted for improving bike handling, balancing, and pedal spin.

rotating paceline—A paceline in which each rider comes to the front in an ascending line and then moves back in a descending line. Also called a double paceline.

saddle sores—The breakdown of the skin of the crotch. This condition is characterized by bumps and sores caused by the blockage of pores, which results from excessive sweating or pressure.

sandbagging—The act of willfully not upgrading to a higher racing category in order to continue to win or do well without an effort for improvement. This practice is looked down on within cycling. It is not good for the racer (because the racer does not advance to competition levels that he has achieved), nor good for racing in general (because it leaves little room for advancement in certain categories and prevents other racers from having a level playing field on which to learn the craft of racing).

scratch races—Mass-start races (held on a track) of a set amount of laps where the winner is determined by who makes it to the finish line first.

seat stays—Tubes on a bicycle frame connecting the seat tube to the rear dropout.

seat tube angle—The angle (measured to the rear of the seat tube) between the seat tube and an imaginary line running parallel to the ground and through the bottom bracket.

seat tube length—The distance from the center of the bottom bracket to the top of the seat tube.

sit in (sit on)—Staying in the draft of an individual or a group of racers without contributing by riding in the wind and providing a draft.

snap the rubber band—To break clear of a peloton or group.

specificity—Training specific elements at specific times to achieve a specific state of fitness.

splits—Breaks between riders in a peloton.

stage race—A multiple-day event that has a variety of one-day races, or stages.

steering—A cornering technique in which the rider turns the handlebars to change the direction of the bicycle. Riders are constantly steering their bicycles by shifting their weight to the right or left of the saddle and putting pressure on the left or right side of the handlebar.

steerer tube—Part of the bicycle fork that goes through the headtube and connects with the stem.

stem—Component on a bicycle that connects the handlebars to the steerer tube of the bicycle fork.

strategy—A plan for achieving a specific goal during a race or event.

systems training model—A training paradigm by which you train all of your physical cycling systems to improve your overall physical fitness.

tactic—A method that allows a strategy to be employed.

tapering—A reduction in volume—and possibly frequency—along with a limited reduction in intensity before race day.

task orientation—A goal orientation in which perceived ability is measured as a function of mastering a specific skill.

team—Association of cyclists working toward common training and racing goals. Many teams are born from clubs but are usually smaller and contain riders belonging to similar racing categories. Teams are affiliated with a national racing body (e.g., USA Cycling) and usually have the added responsibility of promoting one race per year.

tempo—Refers to riding in heart rate zone 3 or at 75 to 85 percent of your 20-minute sustained power.

time trial—An individual event where racers are awarded places based on time. The lowest time decides the winner. This is not a mass-start event. Riders are generally started at intervals of 30 seconds, 1 minute, or 2 minutes. Drafting is not allowed. Riders are allowed to use aerodynamic equipment, such as aerobars and disc wheels.

tops—Part of the handlebar closest to the stem. The tops are a common spot to place the hands when rolling at easy, steady paces or when climbing hills, as they afford a more upright position on the bike, which allows the cyclist to open up her hip angle.

top tube length—The distance between the top of the headtube and the top of the seat tube.

track racing—*See* velodrome.

training races—Short races that are usually part of a race series held on the same course. These races allow riders to practice race skills and to test themselves against local competition. This race format is how many racers start out either in their first years of racing or after a winter break. Training races allow racers to test their form.

Union Cycliste Internationale (UCI)—The worldwide governing body for bicycle racing. All national sanctioning bodies defer to the rules and regulations set forth by the UCI for the conduct of bicycle racing within their respective countries.

unweight—Taking the weight off your hands on the handlebars; you still have your hands on the bars, but you do not need them to prop up your upper body. This is useful when hitting unexpected rough road, and it will allow you to relax your upper body.

velodrome—An indoor or outdoor oval track designed specifically for bicycle racing. A velodrome contains banked turns, stands, and an infield where racers prepare to race. For safety reasons, fixed-gear bicycles are used on these tracks.

virtual seat tube length—Normally measured as the distance from the center of the bottom bracket to an imaginary point extending from the end of the seat tube to where the top tube would cross if it ran parallel to the ground.

virtual top tube length—The distance between the top of the headtube and the top of the seat tube if it was as tall as the headtube. Most bike manufacturers provide this measurement in frame specifications.

volume—The amount of time spent performing any effort.

$\dot{V}O_2$max—The maximum amount of oxygen that an athlete can use during maximal exercise (measured as milliliters of oxygen per minute per kilogram of body weight). A $\dot{V}O_2$max test requires progressive exercise to a maximum effort. This test is performed in a sport science lab. Collection and measurement of the volume and oxygen concentration of inhaled and exhaled air determine how much oxygen the athlete is using.

warm-up—The process of slowly activating all physiological systems by slowly increasing intensity in preparation for intense exercise.

wheel base—The distance between the dropout (i.e., where the axle of the wheel attaches) of the front wheel measured in a straight line to the dropout of the rear wheel.

wheel touching—One cyclist's front wheel contacting another cyclist's rear wheel.

Bibliography

Abt, S. 2002. *Off to the races: 25 years of cycling journalism*. Boulder, CO: VeloPress.

All about bicycle racing. *Bike World Magazine* editors. World Publications: Mountainview, CA: 1975.

Armstrong, L. and C. Carmichael with P.J. Nye. 2000. *Lance Armstrong performance program*. New York: Rodale.

Armstrong, L., and S. Jenkins. *It's not about the bike: My journey back to life*. Putnam Adult; 1 ed. 2000.

Armstrong, L., and S. Jenkins. 2004. *Every second counts*. New York: Broadway Books.

Baechle, T., and R.W. Earle. (Eds.) 2008. *Essentials of strength training and conditioning*. 3rd Ed. Champaign, IL: Human Kinetics.

Baker, A. 1997. *Smart cycling*. New York: Simon & Schuster.

Baker, A. 1998. *Bicycling medicine: Cycling nutrition, physiology, injury prevention and treatment for riders of all levels*. New York: Simon & Schuster.

Baker, A. 2005. Tapering for events. San Diego: Argo.

Baker, A. 2006. *Altitude climbing endurance: ACE training for cyclists*. San Diego: Argo.

Baker, A. 2006. *Bike fit*. San Diego: Argo.

Baker, A. 2006. *Progressive training systems: High-intensity training for cyclists*. San Diego: Argo.

Baker, A. 2006. *Strategy and tactics for cyclists*. San Diego: Argo.

Bernard, W. 1978. *The three Ms: Merckx, Maertens, Moser*. Yorkshire: Kennedy Brothers.

Brown, S. 1997. Bicycle tires and tubes. British Cycling. http://new.britishcycling.org.uk.

Burke, E.R. (Ed.) 1986. *Science of cycling*. Champaign, IL: Human Kinetics.

Burke, E.R. 2003. *Optimal muscle performance and recovery*. New York: Avery.

Burke, L.M., B. Kiens, and J.L. Ivy. 2004. Carbohydrates and fat for training and recovery. *Journal of Sport Sciences* 22 (1): 15-30.

Burke, E.R. 2002. *Serious cycling*. 2nd ed. Champaign, IL: Human Kinetics.

Carmichael, D.K., Gardner, A. 2007. "Overuse" training can produce painful side effects. www.healthday.com.

Chu, D.A. 1998. *Jumping into plyometrics*. 2nd ed. Champaign, IL: Human Kinetics.

Complete bicycle time trialing book. 1977. *Bike World* magazine editors. Mountainview, CA: World Publications.

Cox, R.H. 2007. *Sport psychology: Concepts and applications*. 6th Ed. New York: McGraw Hill.

Cordain, L., and J. Friel. 2005. *The paleo diet for athletes: A nutritional formula for peak athletic performance*. New York: Rodale.

Coyle, E.F., A.R. Coggan, M.K. Hemmert, and J.L. Ivy. 1986. Muscle glycogen utilization during prolonged strenuous exercise when fed carbohydrate. *Journal of Applied Physiology* 61 (1): 165-172.

Cycling Australia. 2008. Rules and Policies. www.cycling.org.au/default.asp?Page = 8350& MenuID = Membership/20013/0.

Cycling Australia. Constitution. 1991. www.cycling.org.au/site/cycling/national/downloads/Attachments/CONSTITUTION_as_at_010108.pdf.

Cycling Australia. 2009. Technical regulations. www.cycling.org.au/site/cycling/national/downloads/website2008/Content/NavigationMenu/AboutUs/Regulations/TechnicalRegulations/2009%20Technical%20Regulations.pdf.

Daniels, A.C., and J.E. Daniels. 2004. *Performance management: Changing behavior that drives organizational effectiveness*. 4th ed. Performance Management.

Decaluwé, B., and B. Haake. March 26, 2008. Chavanel strongest on debut in cold Flanders. www.cyclingnews.com/road.php?id = road/2008/mar08/dwars08.

Decaluwé, B. March 30, 2008. In repeat mode, Chavanel captures win: Freire's streak ends. www.cyclingnews.com/road/2008/mar08/brabantsepijl08/?id = results.

Donohue, G. 2009. Top Achievement. www.topachievement.com/smart.html.

Drucker, P.F. 1993. *The practice of management*. England: Collins.

Eberle, S.G. 2000. Endurance sports nutrition: Eating plans for optimal training, racing, and recovery. Champaign, IL: Human Kinetics.

Faria, I.E. 1978. *Cycling physiology for the serious cyclist*. Springfield, IL: Thomas.

Fotheringham, W. 2003. *A century of cycling: The classic races and legendary champions*. St. Paul: MBI.

Friel, J. October 2006. *The cyclist's training bible: A complete training guide for the competitive road cyclist*. 2nd ed. Boulder, CO: VeloPress.

Israel, D. Nutrition. 2001. In *ACSM's resource manual for guidelines for exercise testing and prescription*. 4th ed. Jeffrey L. Roitman, ed. Philadelphia: Lippincott Williams & Wilkins.

Johnson, R.K., L.J. Appel, M. Brands, B.V. Howard, M. Lefevre, R.H. Lustig, F. Sacks., L.M. Steffen, and J. Wylie-Rosett. August 2009. Dietary sugar intake and cardiovascular health. A scientific statement from the American Heart Association. *Circulation*.

Kugler, F. 1972-1974. Bicycle racing is an art: A year-round training program. Reprints from *Velo-news*, Volumes 1-3.

Lucas, S.E. *The art of public speaking*. 3rd ed. 1989. New York: Random House.

Magill, R.A. 2004. *Motor learning and control: Concepts and applications*. 7th Edition. Boston: McGraw-Hill.

Martin, G.L., and J.A. Lumsden. 1987. *Coaching: A behavioral approach*. St. Louis: Times Mirror/Mosby.

Mayo Foundation for Medical Education and Research. 2009. Omega-3 fatty acids, fish oil, alpha-linolenic acid. www.mayoclinic.com/health/fish-oil/NS_patient-fishoil.

McArdle, W.D., F.I. Katch, and V.L. Katch. 2006. *Exercise physiology: Energy, nutrition, and human performance*. 6th ed. Philadelphia: Lippincott Williams & Wilkins.

McElmury A., and M. Levonas. 1977. *Basic training: Monthly schedules and advice for the racing cyclist*. Boulder, CO: Velonews.

Mikler, K. Paris-Roubaix: Museeuw outfoxes 'em all. April 14, 2002. VeloNews. www.velonews.com/article/2056/paris-roubaix-museeuw-outfoxes--em-all.

Nicholls, J.G. 1984. Conception of ability and achievement motivation. In R. Ames and C. Ames, *Research on motivation in education: Student motivation*. Vol 1. New York: Academic Press.

Pruitt, A. 2006. *Andy Pruitt's complete medical guide for cyclists*. Boulder, CO: VeloPress.

Radcliffe, J. 2005. High-powered plyometrics. Champaign, IL: Human Kinetics.

Schmidt, R.A., and T.D. Lee. 2005. *Motor control and learning: A behavioral emphasis.* 4th Ed. Champaign, IL: Human Kinetics.

Santoni, J. (Director). *Le course en tête (The Eddy Merckx Story).* 1974. World Cycling Productions.

The soul of Johan Museeuw. March 9, 2004. Daily Peloton. www.dailypeloton.com/displayarticle.asp?pk = 5788.

St. Pierre, R. *Cycle racing tactics.* 1978. Yorkshire: Kennedy Brothers.

Straw, J., and A.B. Cerier. 2002. *The 4 dimensional manager: DiSC strategies for managing different people in the best ways.* San Francisco: Berrett-Koehler.

Strickland, B. 1997. *The quotable cyclist: Great moments of bicycling wisdom, inspiration, and humor.* Halcottsville, NY: Breakaway Books.

Tsatsouline, P. 2001. *Relax into stretch: Instant flexibility through mastering muscle tension.* St. Paul: Dragon Door.

USA Cycling. 2005. *USA Cycling club coach manual, Version 2005.1.* Colorado Springs: Author.

USA Cycling. 2008. *USA Cycling level 2 coach manual, Version 2008.1.* Colorado Springs: Author.

USDA. 2005. Dietary guidelines: Carbohydrates. www.health.gov/dietaryguidelines/dga2005/document/html/chapter7.htm.

Ward, P. 1970. *King of sports: Cycle road racing.* Yorkshire: Kennedy Brothers.

Whitmore, J. 2009. *Coaching for performance: Growing human potential and purpose.* 4th ed. London: Brealey.

Whittle, J. 2003. *Le Tour: A century of the Tour de France.* St. Paul: MBI.

Who are the Best 20 Classics Riders in History? April 1, 2004. Daily Peloton. www.dailypeloton.com/displayarticle.asp?pk = 5914.

Widmaier, E.P., H. Raff, and K.T. Strang. 2006. *Vander's human physiology: The mechanisms of body function.* 10th ed. Boston: McGraw Hill.

Woodland, L. 1976. *Cycle racing: Training to win.* Albuquerque: Transatlantic Arts.

Web Sites

USA Cycling: www.usacycling.org

Mexican Cycling Federation: www.fmc.com.mx

Italian Cycling Federation: www.federciclismo.it

French Cycling Federation: www.ffc.fr

Union Cycliste Internationale (International Cycling Union): www.uci.ch

Index

Note: An *f* following a page number refers to a figure, a *t* refers to a table.

About the Author

Robert Panzera, MA, is a USA Cycling-certified coach and NSCA-certified strength and conditioning specialist. In 2009 he received his master's degree in kinesiology with a specialization in biomechanics. Panzera is a competitive cyclist in road, track, and cyclocross events. He is the owner and operator of Cycling Camp San Diego (CCSD), which specializes in week-long training for serious road cyclists. The camp is particularly popular with performance cyclists who want to make the leap to racing. During the camps, participants typically ride more than 60 miles per day with total elevation gains of 4,000 to 8,000 feet. Panzera and CCSD take pride not only in physically training cyclists but also in preparing them to race via instruction in bike handling, nutrition, and cycling psychology.